REVEALING JESUS

evangelism raw and real

By

VALERIE HOPMAN

FOR THE ONE Publishing

FOR THE ONE Publishing, Alberta, Canada
For inquiries, permission requests, and more, go to: fortheone.val@gmail.com

Cover Photo: Wanphen Chawarung

Cover: Special thanks to Kelly Mulner and Melinda Prichard for all your help

Author photograph by kmulner@mulner-photography.com
Editing: Audrey Harder, Terry Hopman

ISBN: 978-1-7777015-0-5 Paperback edition

ISBN: 978-1-7777015-1-2 eBook edition

Revealing Jesus Evangelism Raw and Real / Valerie Hopman —1st ed.

I dedicate this book to my Family:

My husband, Terry

and children - Seth , Sterling, Sarah,

Silas & Morgan

I am incredibly grateful for how all of you, in various ways, have supported and enabled me to reveal Jesus in many endeavors over the years. My prayer is that you will love the Lord your God with all your heart, soul, mind, and strength, and love others as yourself.

Contents

THE GYM

I put my headphones in my ears, turn on my worship music and begin my workout at the gym. I love this time, it is a distraction-free, evangelize-free zone. I don't have much time and need to be done in half an hour so that I can continue on in my busy schedule. I don't wear make-up. I don't talk to anyone. I simply struggle my way through the machines and weights; sweaty, tired, until it hurts. I focus on my worship music and know that I am turned "off" from people. Week after week, month after month, I stick to my noble mindset and have "me time". Then one day, out of the corner of my eye, I see a gentleman limping as he goes from machine to machine, exercising other parts of his body. I am working really hard on the elliptical and although I try to focus on worshipping my Lord, I can clearly see this man is suffering physically. For the next fifteen minutes I keep singing in my head the songs playing from my iPhone, "Lord I love you," and my spirit starts to argue, "*What about him? Do you love that man too?*" "*Lord! This is my 'off' time. Besides it would be so weird and there's nowhere to go to not be noticed . . . Argh!*" I get off and start working on my arms. I can see him better from there. I'm huffing and puffing, sweat is dripping down my forehead and the Holy Spirit clearly says, "*There is no 'off' time for evangelism. You carry my Presence. You are to be ready in season and out of season.*" I look at the man and my heart comes into alignment with the tenderness that God has toward him. I take a deep breath and go to meet him at the paper towel station. "Hello sir, I noticed you are limping and I was wondering what happened to your leg?" He too was soaked with sweat and was surprised to be asked. He shared with me he had a terrible accident two years ago. He was still struggling to improve mobility and be free of pain. The recovery process had been very slow. So I popped the question, "I believe in a God that heals, can I pray for your leg?" He looked at me seriously and said, "Yes, you can." I prayed over this man's leg for complete healing, trying to ignore my awareness of all the people around me. When I was done, he asked, "What church do you go to?" I told him and he said, "I go to a church here in town. I believe in a God that heals too!" "Ahhh, you are my brother in Christ!" I say. He smiles at me, "Thank you for praying for me, that means so much to me." We have a bit of small talk and part ways. I forget to ask him how his leg feels, I am just so excited to bless a brother in Christ. My box of "me time" got blown apart, and I saw the gym with a new perspective. I have one third of the Trinity living inside of me (Don't worry, I know that's not technically the proper theological way to say the Holy Spirit lives in me); there are no off limits as to where or when He will flow through me. Who am I to make the rules? So I tell the Lord I'm sorry and my answer is always a "yes" to Him.

A few days later, a lady I've seen coming for two years starts a conversation with me in the locker room. For an hour I decipher her story between the cuss words; her anger, her hurts, her family situation. I tell her who God is to me and we begin a relationship of discussing life spontaneously during workouts . . . at the gym.

This morning I went to the gym and there is a woman with a physical disability. I don't really know her but I often respect how she works so hard to use the equipment when it is clearly a struggle for her. After probably a year of seeing her around, today she struck up a conversation with me and we ended up talking about all sorts of things. She has an autistic daughter and I too, have a special needs daughter. At one point she was talking about when she was in a difficult situation and made the comment, "I don't know what happened in that situation and I don't believe in God but someone, something intervened." I smiled, listened and thought, "What do you want me to say to this woman Lord, just give me an opportunity." Soon the lady asked me what I did for a job. I told her I was a stay-at-home mom, homeschooled my daughter part time and volunteered in various ways, such as going out on the streets of downtown and hanging out with street people; encouraging and loving them. This piqued her interest and she asked a few questions. I shared about their addictions but that I had no judgement; they had wounds they were trying to numb but needed healing instead. She asked me if I was associated with any addiction recovery programs. I told her I wasn't at all. She asked what organization I went and did this with. I explained it was not with an organization but with a team from many churches. She then changed the subject. I asked her what happened to her that she had a physical disability. As she described it and how it affected her she suddenly told me she actually struggled with alcohol. She lowered her voice and looked around to make sure no one was around too close and shared with me she does these drinking binges, not all the time, but she does and she is thinking of going to Alcoholics Anonymous but just can't bring herself to do it because of the God component of the program. She then asked me if God was, like, a big part of my life or something. Ha ha, so we spent forty five minutes chatting all about Christianity in comparison to other religions, what sin actually was, what happens when you die, why a "good" person doesn't measure up to God's standards, what Hell was, and what Jesus actually did when He died on the cross. A blessing for me is that she talked a lot, so while she talked, I asked the Lord what He saw about her. When I had been there for almost an hour talking with her, I had to get going so I said, "Joanne, God sometimes shows me things about people through pictures. While we were talking He showed me a basic, strong leather belt around your waist. It was strong and sturdy, which is the type of person you are but it also represents the truth and foundation the Lord wants you to build your life upon. God also showed me a blue diamond that He has deposited inside of you. A diamond is formed through pressure and the outcome is beautiful to look at. You have had to deal with many pressures but the things inside of you that have formed have been given to you from God and are beautiful for people to look at." She stopped me there and said, "That is so weird you said that. Just last week this other guy told me very similar things. He was saying I'm like this solid woman and the things that have happened to me have developed a lot of character in me that others see!" I continued, "Well, I guess God is confirming that message to you. The last picture I got for you is of a crown on your head, a kingly one, that represents authority. The Lord wants to set you apart for His purposes to impact many people. I would encourage you to first be submitted to His authority because through Him, He will give you authority that is the right kind, one that will protect and help others, not control them." She again responded, "That is so funny, people do say I am a leader and that others often are impacted by me! Whoa, like how did you do that?" Before I could answer, Joanne said, "There's another woman around here who reads those cards for people, and like the palms of their hands. She also sees spirits and stuff . . ." I quickly and carefully chose my words, "Different source! When someone is doing that kind of stuff they are receiving from a dark source. I love Jesus, I go to Him because He knows all things. He made you, He loves you. I have a relationship with Him. And because of that I have spent much time praying and learning to hear His voice. He wants to show you that He knows you." She listened intently and understanding came across her face, "Oh, I see!" After a bit more explanation I said, "I have to get going but I want to encourage you to think about all that we talked about." She said, "Well, I know something has to change in my life. I can't keep doing what I'm doing." We parted and I'm looking forward to seeing if another conversation occurs with her.

REAL INTRO

Sooo I'm going to write a book. The Lord has made it clear to me and now I must obey. I bought a laptop this week as a step to being able to begin this. I hope to use these stories I've been recording.

A couple of things to be aware of before beginning. I purposefully did not capitalize the word satan. I do not want to give credit, acknowledgement or value him anywhere he is involved.

Next, I use the term "pressed in" many times to describe when I listen up to the Holy Spirit about others or a situation. I know this may not be a familiar term and I'm not even sure when I started using it. When I "press in" it's as if I am pressing my spiritual ear to the heart of God, to know His thoughts, feelings and perspectives in a situation. I am blocking out other distractions, laying aside my first impressions of my natural mind, not wanting to rely on my own logic and rationale but rather, wanting to be led by the Spirit of God. I am pressing in closer to hear His voice and not my own or other's.

I wonder about the way to convey what a precious and unimaginable worth a person has been attributed with. They haven't been given this worth by what they do or the success they've achieved. Worth has been placed upon each person by God, the Creator. The One Who fashioned each human being, and before the world was created, decided that this one person . . . and this one person . . . and this one person . . . will live, breathe and be engaged in this world, at this point in history, for the reasons He decides.

RAW INTRO

Have you read a lot about evangelism and taken many courses on how to be an effective witness? If yes, me too. I have loved being equipped with tools. I have not enjoyed methods or formulas that neatly promise a specific outcome. Although they may be instructive, many turn the people we are trying to love into projects and leave us speechless when the method doesn't fit into a situation. It leaves me feeling like a failure when this happens.

Maybe you have not learned much about evangelism or taken any courses. However, if you have a heart for God and for people, you are reading the right book. Do you love hearing stories of evangelists reaching the lost, people getting saved, healed, and delivered? So many of us have admired these heroes and think, "Wow, that's amazing, I love what they are doing . . . but, I could never do that." We love to see and hear the shiny, successful stories of evangelism but when we go out and "try" evangelism, we often face other realities and go home thinking, "That's just not my gift". This book is raw and it is real. Read it. It will change you, and you will be equipped to obey Jesus by sharing the gospel.

I love researching the Greek and Hebrew meanings to the words in Scripture. I love good, solid theology. This is not a book on theology and, although I will touch on a number of aspects, there are certainly many other books to read if you are wanting to research the theology of every word and action. We may disagree on various subjects but we can agree on the core: Jesus Christ is the Way, the Truth and the Life, nobody comes to the Father except through Him. (John 14:6) You may read the stories in this book and decide the situations should have been handled a different way, or I should have said something more or less or different. I may even agree with you.

Nevertheless, this is what happened. Names and details have been changed, of course, to protect the identity and confidentiality of those involved. I believe in the entirety of the Holy Bible, the complete biblical gospel of Jesus Christ and the work He did on the cross, and will recite the Apostles' Creed wholeheartedly. I am not here to debate the "what ifs" and the "you should haves". I don't feel the need to convince the skeptics or defend how God chooses to work. I love Jesus and am passionate about the people He made. I am writing to stir *you*, the church, into a blazing fire of people who are willing to step into their identity as royal sons and daughters of the King, who have been given authority to carry the Presence of God into the world. I call you, my brothers and sisters, into an amazing adventure of obedience and unquenchable love by intentionally Revealing Jesus.

CHAPTER 1

MY JOURNEY

"This is our time on the history line of God. This is it. What will we do with the one deep exhale of God on this earth? For we are but a vapor and we have to make it count. We're on. Direct us, Lord, and get us on our feet."
- Beth Moore

Aug 30/2010

"I went to the church and was so nervous. The team met, probably about ten people, worshipped and prayed. But this time was different from other groups I have been a part of. They were serious, focused on God and . . . unashamed. They laid hands on the person that was going to speak from the back of a truck on the streets. It was inspiring to see believers operate this way. Down on the street I was so nervous that I was shaking. I just wanted to observe. I stood on the curb and watched as about 100 'street people' gathered around. Immediately I became self conscious of my cute top and fresh look. I pulled on my sweater and zipped it up. One guy came up to me and began chatting. He knew so much about the Bible and Christianity that I wondered if he was actually part of our team. I thought to myself it would be really embarrassing if I witnessed to one of our own team members. Then I watched as our leader began preaching, just standing on the back of a truck. I couldn't believe how blunt he was about Jesus, yet loving, and then gave the salvation message. He asked if anyone wanted to give their life to Jesus and about 6-8 people actually put up their hands!! I couldn't believe it. I realized I actually didn't know what to do if I went to talk to

anyone that put their hand up. I didn't know what I should say or how to evangelize so I didn't. I mostly listened. I was so nervous I just was glad some people made small talk with me. At the end we gathered in a circle when all the street people were gone, right there in the middle of the cul-de-sac and everyone shared what had happened. Then we prayed. Right there on the street. I was so amazed and completely confirmed in my spirit that this was the ministry I was to be involved with."

Sept 10/2010
"Lord, show me how, when and what to say. Lord, when I read in Acts about Philip and how You used him to cast out demons, heal people and then the crowds gave their lives to You, it just makes me desire that You would raise someone up to have that ministry here in this city, on the streets downtown, anywhere You choose to work. Lord, I want to have faith and to be so close to You. I want to have Your power working through me in that way. Oh Lord, You are stirring something inside me and I surrender to Your Spirit. I am Yours."

Ha ha, doesn't God have a great sense of humour?! I dug these gems up from my prayer journal. I actually don't remember praying it and had to smile when I recently read it. The Lord has raised many people up in our city and it's fascinating to see. Little did I know, however, that one of those *someones* was going to be me. After two and a half years involved with the evangelism street ministry, under two different leaders, I suddenly found myself presented with the opportunity to lead the ministry called Monday Night Evangelism. I prayed, fasted and was terrified. The Lord confirmed very clearly that I was to go forward in it.

Oh and by the way, two weeks later after my first time out, I nervously made small talk with a gentleman. Throughout the conversation I kept wondering how I would ever get to talking about Jesus with him. After fifteen minutes I mustered up the courage to ask him if he had ever gone to church. He looked at me and laughed, "Yes, of course, I go to your church, I'm on your team!"

You cannot get involved with evangelism and not grow. Evangelism has grown me incredibly in so many ways. It has been Amazing. Heart-wrenching. Uncomfortable. Eye opening. Difficult. Exciting. Painful. Full of Spiritual Attack. Full of Wonder, Revelation, Misunderstandings. Intense. Funny. Evangelism has brought me into a deeper intimacy with Jesus than when I didn't evangelize. When I don't evangelize, that's what I miss, the intimacy it creates with my Lord as I watch Him work and follow His lead. Perhaps that is why Jesus commanded us to. He knew.

CHAPTER 2

DO YOU HAVE TO USE THAT WORD?

"Give me one hundred preachers who fear nothing but sin and desire nothing but God, and I care not whether they be clergymen or laymen, they alone will shake the gates of Hell and set up the kingdom of Heaven upon Earth."

-John Wesley

"Can you change the word from 'evangelism' to 'ministry'? It won't be so intimidating for people in the church to join."

I have been asked that question a few times. My answer: If we are scared of the word "evangelism" as believers, then we have a much bigger problem.

Evangelism. Scary word? Is it only for those with the "gift" of evangelism? What do you think of when you hear the word? It doesn't matter what Christian crowd I ask, young or old, I get the same answers. "It's scary." "What if I don't know the answers?" "What if I do damage?" "It's awkward." "They might think I'm crazy." "They might get offended." "What if I ruin the relationship?" "I don't know how to turn the conversation spiritual." "They might get angry." "They might mock me."

And the answer is: Yes. Evangelism can involve all those things. Does it change anything? We all know as Christians we are commanded to evangelize, or do we? We should settle this now because if we think it is a gift then we can opt out and say it isn't our calling, nor our gift. If it is a command, well, now we may squirm and wonder when we can fit it into our schedule. So is it a gift? Is it a command? The answer again is: Yes.

Ephesians 4:11 & 12 says, *"And He gave the apostles, the prophets, the evangelists, shepherds and teachers, to equip the saints for the work of ministry, for building up the body of Christ."* Here evangelism is presented as a calling or a gift given. In other scriptures, such as, Matthew 10:7 (these are Jesus' instructions to the 72 He sent out), He was demonstrating and giving the same instructions to us as believers, *"As you go, proclaim this message: 'The kingdom of heaven has come near.' Heal the sick, raise the dead, cleanse those who have leprosy, drive out demons. Freely you have received; freely give."* If you need a more general command, here it is in Mark 16:15: He said to them, *"Go into all the world and preach the gospel to all creation."*

The word evangelism comes from a Greek word, *euangelion,* meaning "to proclaim the good news". Evangelism is <u>telling</u> others the gospel. It is not a "nonverbal" witness. The word proclaim or preach in the above verses is the Greek word: *kerysso* - to be a herald, to publish, to proclaim publicly. Just to be clear. The idea of these words is to intentionally announce something publicly.

The word preach comes from the Latin *prae,* "before," and *dicare,* "declare." When you preach, you're not just talking - you're declaring something with conviction.

Matthew 28:19 - 20a says, "Therefore go and make disciples of all nations, baptizing them in the name of the Father and of the Son and of the Holy Spirit and teaching them to obey everything I have commanded you." So here evangelism is commanded. There are many other verses that support the command of evangelism without actually using the word *evangelism* .

After a small amount of research you will find that evangelism is both a gift and a command. Some are anointed in evangelism and it is evident to others the Lord's gifting upon them. However, all believers have been commanded to evangelize. In fact, all spiritual gifts and calling are given to believers to build, edify and strengthen the church *and* to go seek and save the lost. You tell me your gift, I'll tell you how you can use it in evangelism.

Perhaps because scripture does not use the actual word *evangelism* very much is the reason the word is so threatening. If we were commanded to *minister* to the world, we can swallow this easier. To minister is: "to care for or take care of someone or something". Actually, we often think evangelism is to minister. We make sandwiches for the homeless and happily check off our evangelism duty for the week. We go pick up garbage for our community or do yard work and claim we have evangelized. These are fantastic things to do and all can be used to display love and kindness . . . the world is also doing these things. They are actually *good deeds* and because we are Christians we believe we can label them evangelism. Good deeds are . . . good. Good deeds can be used in evangelism as tools and a pathway to show love but it is not evangelism. Good deeds are being done by many: People of other religions, Hollywood actors, politicians, atheists and many others. All are doing it for different reasons. A comment often made to me is, "This is really great you're doing this. It must make you feel really good." My flesh wants to throw up on them. I can think of a lot of different ways to feel good other than forcing myself out of my comfort zone, being in the freezing cold, handling responses I don't know how to handle, or having my heart break from encountering broken, lost people who reject the only One who can save, heal and deliver them. Don't get me wrong, I love so many things about evangelism but it is not something that we use to feel good, define our value or determine how much merit we earn. These are some of the reasons why people do good deeds. In Christ, we do good deeds out of love for the Lord and love for others. But good deeds are not evangelism.

How are we teaching Evangelism?

We as leaders and pastors tell people to be a blessing to others and by doing so we will draw people to Christ. This may be true and good, but what can happen is we define the word *blessing* as doing a good deed, service, or an act of kindness to people outside of the church, to unbelievers. So how it may work, for example, is when we see someone is going through a crisis, we get together, make casseroles and then deliver them, in the Name of Jesus. This is really great and it IS a blessing, however, we may pat ourselves on the back, check off our list and say we just evangelized. The problem is we didn't evangelize. We didn't proclaim the good news. We did a good deed. Again, good deeds are, well, good and we do them out of love for Jesus and others but we did not reveal Jesus, nor ***re***present Jesus, nor bring an encounter with Jesus. Most importantly to recognize is we did not equip believers to evangelize. We left them with the idea that to evangelize believers will need to add one more duty to our busy lives and that this somehow will fulfill the great commission to go and make disciples. But it doesn't. Instead, all we did was just redefine evangelism. Why do we do this? I have observed that it is often because evangelism conjures up a resistance in us in response to the negative images we have of it. We don't like the idea of having to stand on the street and shout through a megaphone, or hand out tracts on a bus station platform. We don't want to carry the burden of the responsibility or pressure to get somebody saved within a conversation by presenting the formula of the four Spiritual laws or some other technique. Rightly so, the focus is on the *doing* and not the *being* . These stereotypes of evangelistic methods are at times effective but certainly not all that evangelism is. I will repeat myself once more: works, deeds, evangelistic methods can be very, very good but they are only tools to be used as the Holy Spirit leads and they may compliment evangelism but they are not to be confused as evangelism. The question is, are we going to equip believers to reveal Jesus? Or do good deeds? It is not wrong to have people do good deeds and to serve but we should not call it evangelizing. Good deeds can be used in evangelism to open up an opportunity to share the good news. Good deeds are done by other religions and by nice, moral, humanitarian people of the world. We are not called to join them, we are called to bring the Kingdom of Light to the darkness; the message of salvation through Christ to a lost and hurting world. This is done by proclaiming, declaring, preaching, sharing, and speaking the message.

So what is evangelism? It is presenting the gospel. Well, what is the gospel? We would probably take anywhere from five minutes to an hour to explain it as Jesus coming to earth, fully human and fully God. Dying on a cross for the penalty of our sins and rising to life, conquering death and making a way for us to have forgiveness of sins and relationship with God. This is all true and it is the gospel, however, let's go a little deeper and look at the actual definition.

The Gospel according to the Oxford English Dictionary is this: The Revelation of Jesus Christ.

I love this definition! It's the **revealing** of Jesus, The Christ, and what He did.

WDJD? (What Did Jesus Do?) He had an encounter with people and they were never the same.
We want others to have an encounter with Jesus. We want to Reveal Jesus to people. We want to uncover and unveil Who Jesus Christ is and what He did.

We carry the Presence of God. The Kingdom of Heaven is within us. We bring the Kingdom of Heaven to the darkness of this world and we take territory from the enemy. Territory physically but also spiritually in people's lives, where the enemy is occupying. We leave the fragrance of Christ.

Jesus said He only would do what He saw the Father doing. (John 5:19) We have to spend time with God so that we learn to hear and see what the Father is doing. Then we can do what we see He's doing, whether that is speaking His words, taking action through serving, giving a hug or handshake, financially blessing someone . . . the ways He will show us are endless.

Jesus said He came to <u>glorify</u> the Father. (John 17:5, John 12:28) The word glorify means to not only praise and worship, but to describe or represent, to reveal the majesty and splendour of God, to cause to appear. You are to also describe and ***re***present the Father, to reveal the majesty and splendour of God, to magnify, bringing Him into view which causes God to appear in their line of sight!

Could we truthfully turn this into an "I" statement in describing our identity and role in Christ?
I describe the Father. I ***re***present the Father. I reveal the majesty and splendour of God. When I come in contact with people, I cause God to appear through His Spirit in me. I reveal Jesus. (Acts 1:8, Romans 8:14, Matthew 10:20)We have to get out of our heads that evangelism is only mastering certain techniques, or purely presenting theological information, or handing out tracts or Bibles. It can include the use of these methods, BUT ONLY when we are aware of what we are really doing. In evangelism, what are we really doing? We are to Reveal Jesus, Reveal the Father, Reveal the Holy Spirit. We bless, we serve, we minister, we love and we must be intentional to pair these beautiful actions with the good news of Jesus Christ so that He will be glorified and revealed.

The world is hungry for an encounter with the One, True God.

CHAPTER 3

ORDINARY

"Light yourself on fire with passion and people will come from miles to watch you burn." - attributed to John Wesley

I am a mom of four kids and married at 19 years of age. I worked outside the home for the first three years of our marriage and then started having babies. I have loved being a stay-at-home mom and raising our children. I take the responsibility of pouring into four souls, nurturing, and discipling them, which will impact their future here on earth as well as into eternity, very seriously. I certainly have not had the time to earn theological degrees or get letters behind my name. I don't have any worldly, valuable description or accreditations when introducing myself. I have, however, resolved to love the Lord my God with all my heart, soul, mind, and strength. Sometimes successfully and many times not. I have chosen to discipline myself with reading, memorizing and studying scripture, time in prayer, and hungering after the things of the Kingdom of Heaven.

I certainly don't have anything that would cause the world or the church to take notice on paper. Credibility and qualification being measured on intellect and knowledge has crept into the church as our culture worships the god of understanding. Don't get me wrong, I think knowledge, study, accreditations and such are fantastic. I know caution needs to be exercised in who influences us when many are running around with fictitious religious beliefs and twisted scripture. However, too often it rolls off our lips to tout the fact that the disciples were not educated and very unlikely choices of Jesus. We parade this around our circles to validate the layman's involvement in *volunteering* . But quietly we all *know* that the "ordinary" person, even if totally dependent upon the Holy Spirit, is not able to compete with the educated, those brimming with knowledge, with letters behind their names, those who can win religious debates, when being considered qualified to lead, teach and "win souls" for Jesus . . . hmmm, that statement doesn't sit right, does it? And it shouldn't. We know this is not the way it should be and yet sadly it infiltrates our systems, our churches, and our judgements of others. Please do not miss my point. I, of course, think that education, knowledge, and accreditations represent many things that can be very, very good. My point however, is that our judgement of ourselves and what we can or cannot do may be skewed and dismissed by measuring ourselves by the value system of our world and not by God's standards, which brings me to my next point. Since we've already established that evangelism is something we are all called to, let's take a moment to really check our thinking. You may feel similar to how I felt when I described my experience in this book's Raw Intro. Ordinary, scared, and not spiritual enough. You may hear of, or may have seen, evangelists or the "qualified" reaching the lost, helping people getting saved, healed, and delivered through their stories, videos, and ministries. You admire them but you immediately place them in a different category of perhaps being of a higher spiritual level or gifting than yourself.

Let's get our identity mindset as children of God in alignment with His kingdom.

1 Cor 1:18-2:16

For the message of the cross is foolishness to those who are perishing, but to us who are being saved it is the power of God. For it is written:

"I will destroy the wisdom of the wise; the intelligence of the intelligent I will frustrate." Where is the wise person? Where is the teacher of the law? Where is the philosopher of this age? Has not God made foolish the wisdom of the world? For since in the wisdom of God the world through its wisdom did not know him, God was pleased through the foolishness of what was preached to save those who believe. Jews demand signs and Greeks look for wisdom, but we

preach Christ crucified: a stumbling block to Jews and foolishness to Gentiles, but to those whom God has called, both Jews and Greeks, Christ the power of God and the wisdom of God. For the foolishness of God is wiser than human wisdom, and the weakness of God is stronger than human strength.

Brothers and sisters, think of what you were when you were called. Not many of you were wise by human standards; not many were influential; not many were of noble birth. But God chose the foolish things of the world to shame the wise; God chose the weak things of the world to shame the strong. God chose the lowly things of this world and the despised things—and the things that are not—to nullify the things that are, so that no one may boast before him. It is because of him that you are in Christ Jesus, who has become for us wisdom from God—that is, our righteousness, holiness and redemption. Therefore, as it is written: "Let the one who boasts boast in the Lord."

And so it was with me, brothers and sisters. When I came to you, I did not come with eloquence or human wisdom as I proclaimed to you the testimony about God. For I resolved to know nothing while I was with you except Jesus Christ and him crucified. I came to you in weakness with great fear and trembling. My message and my preaching were not with wise and persuasive words, but with a demonstration of the Spirit's power, so that your faith might not rest on human wisdom, but on God's power. We do, however, speak a message of wisdom among the mature, but not the wisdom of this age or of the rulers of this age, who are coming to nothing. No, we declare God's wisdom, a mystery that has been hidden and that God destined for our glory before time began. None of the rulers of this age understood it, for if they had, they would not have crucified the Lord of glory. However, as it is written:

"What no eye has seen,
what no ear has heard,
and what no human mind has conceived"—
the things God has prepared for those who love him— these
are the things God has revealed to us by his Spirit."

The Spirit searches all things, even the deep things of God. For who knows a person's thoughts except their own spirit within them? In the same way no one knows the thoughts of God except the Spirit of God. What we have received is not the spirit of the world, but the Spirit who is from God, so that we may understand what God has freely given us. This is what we speak, not in words taught us by human wisdom but in words taught by the Spirit, explaining spiritual realities with Spirit-taught words. The person without the Spirit does not accept the things that come from the Spirit of God but considers them foolishness, and cannot understand them because they are discerned only through the Spirit. The person with the Spirit makes judgments about all things, but such a person is not subject to merely human judgments, for,

"Who has known the mind of the Lord
so as to instruct him?"
But we have the mind of Christ.

I am the ordinary. I am the unqualified. You are the ordinary. You are the unqualified, no matter how many letters are behind your name. I am the Church. You are the Church. We are only qualified by Jesus. He has called us to be filled with the Holy Spirit, power, and love. We are to be lovers of Jesus and lovers of people. It is through our "yes" and "let it be done" that God moves in our obedience, trust and love for Him. Praise God for the ordinary. Get excited, for the God Who has conquered all things has chosen us!

I was grocery shopping at the same store I always do every week. I was focused on my list and as I reached for the lettuce I heard a voice, "How are you today?" I looked up and saw a lady who was an employee, restocking the produce. I quickly answered, "Good, how are you?" She paused and said, "Uh, not so good." I stuffed my lettuce into a bag, smiled and said, "Oh, that's too bad, hopefully your day will get better." Then I grabbed my grocery cart and strolled away. Suddenly I felt the conviction of the Holy Spirit, "Val! What an invitation to conversation. Why didn't you engage her spiritually?". I wrestled with this as I got the rest of my groceries. I made it to the till and reasoned I would see her another time and engage then." Once at home, I dropped my head and realized I should've gone back and talked with that woman. But, well, I was too embarrassed and I wasn't in "evangelism" mode. I chalked it up to another "fail" and asked the Lord to forgive me. When I got into bed that night her face kept coming to me. In fact, all week I wrestled. I prayed for her and could not get her out of my mind. Two weeks went by and I was once again at the grocery store. Same time, same place. I had a lot on my mind with tasks and at that moment, wasn't at all thinking about her. I was literally reaching for some lettuce and again heard a voice, "Hello, how are you today?" Immediately, I froze with deja vu. Yep, it was her. She didn't seem to recognize me at all. She was just being friendly. My heart was beating and I said, "Good, how are you?" She said, "Oh it's been pretty rough. I am just finishing the night shift so I'm pretty tired." Suddenly another customer came over and said, "Excuse me, can you tell me where the chives are?" The employee turned and tended to the lady and I wheeled my cart away. I went to the cleaning aisle and stopped. "Lord, should I just wait until next week? I don't know what to say. Now it'll be really weird to go back to her, I feel so ridiculous. . . . Ok, well what would you want me to say?" I closed my eyes and waited. "She's in pain", came the Holy Spirit's voice very clearly. I took a deep breath, "Well, should I just go pray for her physical healing? I can do that . . . but Lord, I need You to show up and well, actually heal her. Ooooo, this is so awkward. I think I'll wait until next week." Then the Holy Spirit came loud and clear, "I told you Val, don't ask me to speak to you if you aren't going to obey." I never want to quench the Holy Spirit's voice, so out of Holy fear and obedience I immediately turned my cart around and went straight back to the produce section. I went up to her, "Uh, hello, I just talked to you a few minutes ago . . ." She looked up and said, "Oh, hi, can I help you with anything?" Out of breath from nervousness I began, "Actually, I saw you two weeks ago here restocking groceries. I'm sure you don't remember but ever since, well . . . (just say it Val!), God has been putting you on my mind. Just now, when I saw you again, God revealed to me that you have pain and I was wondering if I can pray for you?" The woman looked stunned and then burst into tears. She held her arms out to me, "Can I give you a hug?" Totally surprised I said, "Yes, of course!" I glanced around to see if there were any managers or supervisors that would see her. She began to explain to me her husband of thirty years had just left her a month ago. It was a total shock. She's been wrestling with panic attacks, shock, and depression. It had been affecting her job and she was financially having a difficult time. I grabbed a tissue from my purse and handed it to her. I realized it wasn't physical healing she needed. It was her heart! She had emotional pain! When she was done sharing with me I said, "That is so tough! I am so sorry you're going through that. Obviously God wants you to know He sees you, He sees what you're going through and He sees your pain, so much so that He got me to come to you to let you know. Can I pray for you?" She nodded and I put my hand on her shoulder and prayed over her. She thanked me, I encouraged her and then left. I walked out of the store thinking, "Wow Lord, I was so close to missing out on watching You work, just because of my own fear." But the story doesn't end there. A week later I am back grocery shopping and there she is. She rushes over to me and says, "Hey, I have a question for you. Did someone tell you about my situation last week? Did someone send you over to me?" I was taken back and assured her I had not been told by anyone and I knew nothing about her but that it was indeed the Lord who had compelled me to talk to her. She shook her head in amazement, "Well, I went home and I phoned my daughter and told her about what happened. She is not religious at all and she said, 'Mom, if that happened to me, I would know there's a God.' I then got to thinking, was it God or did someone set you up to come to me?" I smiled and again assured her I had not been told by anyone. I asked her if she had any spiritual beliefs. She then shared with me that her grandma was actually an evangelist preacher who spoke to hundreds back in the day. She had impacted her a lot when she was a little girl. "I used to follow Jesus, go to church and read my Bible but for the last twenty years I just sort of stopped . . ." Her voice trailed off. Sadness and regret were in her eyes. I encouraged her, "Well, the Lord is waiting for you and wants to renew His relationship with you!" We chatted a bit more about the Lord and then a customer needed her. She quit her job shortly after and I didn't get to follow up with her to see whatever happened in her life. I know that the Lord was pursuing her and I trust the Holy Spirit will continue His work He began in her. What I learned is that the Holy Spirit was beckoning me to participate with Him in my ordinary, every day.

Let me remind you of who you are in Christ:

You are sons and daughters of the Most High God. (2 Corinthians 6:18, 1 John 3:2, John 1:12)

You are royalty. (1 Peter 2:9)

You are heirs of God and coheirs with Christ. (Romans 8:16- 17)

You have been given authority to trample on snakes and scorpions and to overcome all the power of the enemy. (Luke 10:19)

CHAPTER 4

INADEQUATE? ME TOO!

"In a culture of evangelism, there is an understanding that everyone is engaged. Have you ever heard someone say, "Evangelism is not my gift," as if that excused him from sharing his faith? That's a kindergarten understanding of evangelism. All Christians are called to share their faith as a point of faithfulness, not gifting. (Matt. 28:19)" - Mack Stiles

Journal entry after the third time doing street evangelism:

"Lord forgive me for not knowing what to say to those that oppose You. I feel so unsettled in my soul that I did not know what to say. Forgive me, Lord. I understand now more than ever the dark spiritual aspect and how we are not fighting against flesh and blood. Lord, show me how to fight spiritually, show me how to discern, teach me what to say. Lord I just feel so inadequate of what I saw and my lack of knowing how to handle it or what to say. Oh Lord I need to be taught. I don't want to walk in the flesh but in Your Spirit. I need Your leading, Your guidance, Your Spirit, granting me discernment, knowledge, Your words, and enabling me to have faith. I give You the street ministry and my involvement, may You be glorified, I am Your servant."

I have gone and evangelized with the most amazing men and women who are mature believers and it was great. I've also gone out with new born Christians, who have only taken their steps of faith weeks before. You know what I noticed? BOTH were extremely effective. What the new believers didn't know in regards to theology, they made up for in their passion and zeal of being set free from sin. They are so in love with Jesus you just can't help but want to know more.

I went out with two gentlemen who were just new to the faith. They were covered in evil tattoos and when I gave one the mic to share his testimony with their former crowd I had to bite my lip when the "f" word accidently came out to describe his new found freedom in Christ. I shrugged at the other believers with me as we exchanged looks. I saw this really grabbed the crowd's attention, causing them to be silent. He sheepishly looked at me and said in the mic, "Oops, I guess Jesus has a lot to work on me." Afterwards so many came to talk with the two men and in their raw, novice way they prayed over those who were seeking. After everyone had gone they asked if they could keep going, telling others about Jesus. So they took me into some darker areas of the city's downtown. We ran into a drug dealer they knew. They did their special handshake/greeting and the dealer looked at me confused as I clearly didn't look like I belonged. Then he asked, "Do you need some stuff?" To which the new believer said, "No, no I don't. But I have found Jesus." He paused and continued, "You need f#*ing Jesus!" There was this moment of silence as my eyes were wide open as to what would happen next. The dealer looked shocked, then serious and he replied, "I do need f#*ing Jesus!" The new believer said, "Can I pray for you, man?" To my surprise the dealer said yes and there on the sidewalk we prayed over this man. After a couple of encounters like that I had to chuckle and thought, "Wow, this is the craziest evangelism I've ever seen." What I learned from this experience is that I need to get some tattoos and start swearing! Just kidding. Seriously though, these believers were never taught evangelism, denominations, theologies nor even had read much of the Bible. However, they were freshly in love with Jesus and so thankful for what He had forgiven them for. They just had to tell people their testimony and what Jesus had given them access to, which was forgiveness, healing and relationship with the God who loves them.

I've had to lay down my judgement and repent over and over as I have heard different people preach, speak and pray, because to be honest, I have thought some of them were not very good. Then to my surprise people get saved, healed and delivered! I myself have said the gospel beautifully and had no impact. I've also fumbled my words, been flustered and shared the gospel all disjointed then watched people burst into tears and surrender to Jesus.

Right now, let's lift off the burden of requirements that you are carrying of being inadequate to do evangelism. Do we need to be diligent in prayer and learning the scriptures in order to defend our faith? For sure! Can we grow and learn in how we do evangelism? Absolutely! In fact, you can't do evangelism and NOT grow. Evangelism always grows you in some way. The truth is, whether you were demon possessed one minute and then delivered the next, you are ready to evangelize.

Mark 5:18-20 As Jesus was getting into the boat, the man who had been demon possessed begged to go with him. But Jesus said, "No, go home to your family, and tell them everything the Lord has done for you and how merciful he has been." So the man started off to visit the Ten Towns of that region and began to proclaim the great things Jesus had done for him; and everyone was amazed at what he told them.

It was Easter Monday and a night we want to make very special. We had a lady make hot cross buns. We also had tea that had been donated, that those on the street really enjoy, along with hot chocolate and pizza. I had felt that I should preach. All week thoughts crossed over me of maybe asking one of the 'big guns' to preach since it was Easter. As I sat in the Good Friday service and enjoyed the fantastic job our church did, I suddenly felt very ill-equipped to preach on that Monday. I can't present it as well as these people. I can't present the amazing good news of Jesus on the cross and rising to life again. I don't have the heart-wrenching stories that relate to the Easter message or those on the streets. I squirmed and felt stressed all weekend as I kept praying and asking the Lord what to preach, how to preach, and what to say. I know the Easter story and message inside and out as I have heard it all my life and presented many different ways. The weight of the importance of the message was heavy on me. I tried to logically think through why I shouldn't feel this way. I've preached a ton on the streets, this night is no different. The Holy Spirit always shows up. I will get inspired on the last day and should not feel stressed about it. So as the Easter festivities occurred, I enjoyed them and in the back of my mind was always looking for direction from God that would give me insight on what to say. When Monday came, I found myself with lots of time and no kids around. So for three hours I sat, prayed and wrote out what to preach. Honestly, it was a struggle. However, it did finally come together. I went through it a couple of times and then had to get going. As I drove, I prayed. I battled the thoughts and feelings of fear, inadequacy, and worry that came. I declared who I was in Christ. I chose to think of the excitement of the cross and the meaning. I reminded myself of the passion I had for the Lord and this truth. Through worship with the team, I engaged with my Lord and focused on Him. As I grabbed the mic and began, I found I had great focus and spoke for twenty minutes. I had such clarity and amazed myself to hear how clear I was able to explain the meaning of the cross, the resurrection and relationship with God. Completely, the Holy Spirit gets all the credit! When I was finished I had a team member come up to me and tell me how amazing I presented the message. I really appreciated it because I had wrestled and fought hard on this one. A different team member came and grabbed me. She had a man she had been speaking to the last two Mondays. He had decided to give his life to the Lord. He had listened to my preaching and understood fully what he was doing. She led him through a prayer to accept Jesus as Lord and Saviour. We explained what exchange was happening spiritually in him. We offered support, material, discipleship and baptism. We hugged him and welcomed him as our brother. It was one of the most genuine, well thought out conversions I had seen in a long time. It was thrilling to be a part of it.

I often hear people say they are going through a rough time, struggling with questions, aren't feeling close to God, etc and so they feel like it would be hypocrisy to do evangelism. To them I say, it may actually be hypocrisy to not do evangelism. If you acknowledge that Jesus is still Lord and believe in your heart that God raised Him from the dead, then it doesn't matter your circumstances. What matters is to be authentic and be able to testify to people, "Yes, I'm struggling but I know that my God has not left me, nor forsaken me. I may not understand it but I don't have to. I know Who He is and I will trust Him." The world is tired of 'perfect' Christians who are proclaiming Christ only when they are on top of the mountain. It's when you're in the valley proclaiming Christ that the weight of your testimony becomes powerful. There is something that happens to the struggling believer who in obedience is evangelizing regardless of what they feel. When we proclaim our faith in the midst of difficulties we take our eyes off of ourselves; it strengthens our spirit and renews our minds as we speak truths of what we believe and who our God is. It is a sure way to realign with the Lord's perspectives. You will walk away after evangelism with a different heart posture even though your situation has not changed. The Lord knows this is what happens and perhaps, in part, this is why He commands we be obedient by being ready in season and out of season. (2 Timothy 4:2)

CHAPTER 5

I'M AFRAID I WON'T KNOW ALL THE ANSWERS

I pray that you may be active in sharing your faith, so that you will have a full understanding of every good thing we have in Christ.
Philemon 1:6 NIV 1984 edition

I hear this similar phrase from honest Christians all the time when talking about their fear of evangelism, "I'm afraid I won't know all the answers." You won't. Plain and simple. So let's not fear it.

Tonight our team discussed an apologetics conference many of us had attended. It was full of fantastic information. I shared with the team that near the end of the conference I had texted my husband and half jokingly said, "I don't think I can evangelize anymore. I'm not qualified." I found out many of us went away feeling intimidated with our lack of expertise on subjects. As I looked at the people on our team sharing feelings of inadequacy, I saw the depth of their faith and the love each possess. I knew their life stories, how they are living in obedience, and their strength in the Lord. I commented on these things to them and said, "I'd rather be out ministering with you where I see the power of God flowing through you and your deep love for Him, than with someone who has loads of knowledge, can answer every question but has no fruit of the Spirit."

This is what all believers need to grapple with and decide. Do we wait until we have all the answers, or do we go in full dependency of the Holy Spirit? I have learned from a fresh, one week old believer, full of passionate joy in their new freedom, boldly going out and telling everyone they can about Jesus, and I have learned from someone who has been evangelizing for ten years. Knowledge and equipping is good but it cannot take the place of the overflow of the Spirit from deep intimacy with the Lord, that flows out of believers to powerfully touch people at their core.

One time our team had been invited to a festival in our city. It was a Christian festival that was being held at a public park by some local churches. There were only a few of us that showed up. As soon as I got there, I saw that the public who were in the park were of Sikh and Hindu background. At the time I had no knowledge or understanding of these religions. I realized I was very ill-equipped. I had some choices. I could stand for the next two hours and observe, hoping someone would see me, approach me and ask spiritual questions. I could smile and hand out tracts. I could ask the church organizers if there were any tasks that needed to be done, like picking up garbage or directing the crowd. Or I could engage with people, one on one, even though I knew I would not know much about their spiritual views. Even though it was very uncomfortable and felt scary, I decided to approach people. I saw a couple sitting watching the singing on the stage. I greeted them and asked where they were from. We had a pleasant conversation about their country. They were Hindu and we had a short but respectful conversation about our differences of faith.

I then saw two gentlemen who had just come from playing tennis, standing way at the back listening to someone preaching. I went and approached them. I greeted them, looked at the preacher and asked, "What do you think about what that person is saying?" They said they had seen something like this on TV but did not understand why exactly there was this festival. I was able to explain to them that local churches were wanting to share what their faith was about. I asked them if they had a religion that they followed. They shared that they were of the Sikh religion. I honestly responded, "I actually have no idea about the Sikh religion. Please tell me about it." For the next hour they shared with me about their faith, I asked questions and then shared my faith. We compared the two different belief systems. I asked them who Jesus was to them and they honestly did not know if they knew anything about Him. They thought he was mentioned in one of their books but weren't sure what was said about Him. I said, "Well, since we both are seeking spiritual truth, it would be good for you to read what is in our book, the Bible, about Jesus and what He said about Himself. Then you can take it and compare it to what your book says about Him. Would you be willing to do that?" They looked at each other, and agreed that would be a wise thing to do. So I ran and got a new testament Bible for them in Punjabi, which was their native language. I folded the page where the book of John began. I asked them if I could pray for them. They let me and we shook hands. It was a fantastic conversation. I certainly did not know all about their belief system but I was able to hear and understand their hearts, perspectives and sense their spiritual hunger. I left them with truths, the Word of God and a good experience with a Christian.

At another time, out on a downtown street, there was a very tall, approximately 6'5", strong, young man who had come for a slice of pizza. His eyes were dark and angry. He had a huge scar across his face. Definitely not someone you'd ever be drawn to, yet . . . I was. My 5'3" self approached him and I quickly picked up on his arrogance. He acted proud and was disgusted at me but I could also see he was concerned with what others were thinking as they saw him talking to me, the known Christian. I pulled him a little ways from the crowd so that our conversation was private but close enough I wouldn't get killed without someone at least witnessing it. I began to ask him questions, "Where are you from?" He answered, "Why? I'm not telling you." I shrugged, "That's fine. How are you doing?" As we chatted I could see in the background one of my team members staying close but innocently far enough away, just praying and interceding for me. He told me to call him Joe, obvious to both of us that was not his real name. As I continued to be kind and chat he slowly began to engage. He bragged that he was actually running right now from the law. He had a warrant out for his arrest. There was a guy who had hit on his girlfriend and Joe went after him, messed him up real bad, broke his face up, put him in a wheelchair. Joe chuckled, "Let's just say he'll be messed up for life." This had happened a few provinces away and Joe was running. I really didn't know what to say and so I said, "Well, what made you so angry? Was the guy really deserving that?" Joe went on to tell me how the guy certainly did but eventually admitted he, himself, did have an anger problem. I asked him if he had ever heard about God or had any spiritual beliefs. Joe got really angry about that. Through seething words he spat out, "How could I ever believe in a God who doesn't do anything?!" I asked him, "What have you asked of God that He didn't do anything about?" Joe told me of how for years as a very young boy he was sexually abused by his step-dad. How he prayed that it would stop. He shared he had grown up on a reserve and at ten years old was sent to a counsellor to deal with the trauma of the past abuse. On his first session the counsellor began to repeat the sexual abuse and each time he was in that office for the next three years he was forced to perform terrible sexual acts with him until he ran away. I am retelling Joe's story in a much more delicate, appropriate way than how he described it to me. Tears streamed down on his face that showed the terrible pain that was inside him. He angrily wiped them quickly, over and over, making sure no one was looking. He gasped, "How can a God let that happen to a little boy?!" I had no idea what to say. He choked on his tears and fought to regain composure. Every proper Christian answer that came to my head seemed cheesy and empty in that moment. Finally, I honestly said, "I don't know why that happened to you. I do know that those men have the freedom to choose evil and they did. I know that God is a God of love but He is also a God of Justice." My passion for justice in me rose, "I can guarantee you Joe, God will not let those men get away with what they did to you. They will give an account for their evil, they will pay, whether on this earth or in eternity in hell, there will be justice for what happened to you, because God hates what happened to you. They will get what they deserve." For a split moment Joe looked at me with a glimmer of softness toward a God that would do that for him. I asked him if I could pray for him and surprisingly he said yes. I prayed over Joe the best I knew how and told him there was a God who loved him. It was all he could take and he said he had to get going.

I thought to myself after that conversation, if that same situation had happened to me as it did to Joe and there was no Jesus in my life, well, I'd be full of anger too. I'd want to beat anyone who crossed me. I'd also probably drink and do drugs, anything that would numb the pain and memories. I'd be convinced that if there was a God, He allowed the abuse and I'd probably hate Him. I'm sure there were so many other ways to handle that conversation. I could've pursued him further or presented the gospel more, but in that moment, I didn't have all the answers, and any that came to mind seemed insincere, so all I could do is tell him one of the character traits of God and pray that the Holy Spirit revealed something that night to Joe. I am so glad that the Holy Spirit helps me in conversations like that, giving me the words that I don't have. I think of Joe once in a while and I pray he seeks Jesus, the One who redeems, restores and makes all things new. I hope to see Joe in heaven one day and we will excitedly talk about *the rest of the story.*

CHAPTER 6

OH . . . HE/SHE WON'T BE OPEN

"Compassion costs. It is easy enough to argue, criticize, and condemn, but redemption is costly, and comfort draws from the deep. Brains can argue, but it takes heart to comfort."

- Samuel Chadwick

Have you ever judged people based on their appearance? Ha ha, if you answered "no", I don't believe you. Of course we all have, even if we don't like to admit it. I desire to be non-judgemental but it is an area I am always growing in. Just when I think I have overcome it, I catch myself in it again even though I don't want to be that way. I find being judgemental happens in evangelism. I see someone and think they will never be open to the gospel or conversation. I have to override my intense impulse to walk away from them. Who would be the people that we judge? I suppose it would be different for everyone. I have been guilty of looking at others of different religions and cultures not wanting to hear the gospel because I assume they are established in their own belief system. When I see someone dressed really edgy, with piercings and tattoos all over their body I may think they are going to be angry or be mocking if I bring it up. If I see others of high social status, I feel intimidated that they may have all sorts of disdain for the beliefs I hold, maybe even belittle me. There are many other ways we judge when it comes to deciding to whom we will evangelize. I've had to take a look at the reality that I may be correct in these scenarios but I also may be drastically wrong. We all have to overcome judgements and choose to walk in obedience instead of what is really at the root of the judgements - and that is fear. I mean, why do we care so much if all the above scenarios come true? We are fearing the rejection of man again. So let's put it to death. Let's not walk in the ways of the flesh but let us walk in the ways of the Spirit. (Galatians 5:16-26, Romans 8:5-9)

At the mall, I saw a man, probably in his late twenties. He was clearly from another country and I knew it was most likely that he was of another spiritual belief system than Christianity. I was drawn to him but cringed that he may have very strong opinions or be rude to me in some way. I waited a minute or two but kept getting drawn to him amid my judgements. I shared it with some of the ladies I was with and we began to pray and follow him as he walked. He sat down at a table and looked engrossed with his phone. The ladies and I stopped a few meters away from him. I asked them to ask God what He wanted us to say? One lady received from the Lord the word - "plans". I took that to the Lord and quickly got the message that God knows the decisions the man had to make and God would direct him. God had plans for him, for the future of his life, and wanted to be there with him. We went over to him and introduced ourselves. I explained that it may seem weird but that God had drawn my attention to him. I gave him the message and he was very receptive. He did not know what plans this would refer to, but thanked us. I asked him if he had any spiritual beliefs about God and he told me he was a Muslim. I asked him questions about who he believed Jesus to be. He said he believed Jesus to be a very good prophet and that our faith and his were the same. We asked how he would know when he got to go to heaven. As he spoke, I realized he did not know the Muslim faith well, and had a weak understanding of the Quran. Most of the knowledge of his faith was likely just inherited as an identity and told to him from tradition and oral teaching. I shared with him that I happened to have a little book about Jesus that recorded what Jesus did and the things He said. I asked him if he would read it to compare the Quran's account to this man, John's account, who happened to be Jesus' best friend. He said yes and took it but that he preferred to watch and listen to things rather than read. I was thinking, "Ya, who cares, just read it." But then he continued saying he had discovered someone online that he really liked listening to and told me his name, it was a very well-known Christian Speaker... my eyes opened wide, as did my teammates. "Yes, he speaks about truth, keep listening to him!" we encouraged him excitedly. I wrote down the name of Nabeel Qureshi for him to also listen to. We asked him if we could pray for him and he eagerly accepted. So I prayed and ended "In Jesus' Name". We left him and I discussed with the ladies how amazing it was that God was already pursuing this man, had him listening to truth from Christian speaker and then drew us to him so that we could put a gospel of John in his hand. My judgements of the man were partially right, in that he did have a different spiritual belief system and partially wrong, in that he was very open to discussion and not rude at all. How thrilling it was to be part of the spiritual seed and chain link of his spiritual journey!

At the transit platform a woman with purple hair and piercings all over her face stood beside me. I pressed into the Holy Spirit and brought her before Jesus. I saw a light in her and a light in Jesus. The words - *She's searching,* came to me. Here's where I made a mistake. I jumped to the conclusion she was searching for Jesus, and it was because, well . . . of the way she physically looked. I greeted her and she was very friendly and I shared with her that God had highlighted her to me and she was happy to hear that. As I went on I told her God had given me a picture of her standing before Jesus and there was a light within her and a light within Jesus. She clapped her hands and was thrilled to hear that. I told her I felt like she was searching and to be careful not to settle for any counterfeit light. She looked at me puzzled and said, "Hmmm, I know I don't look like it but I actually go to church with my sister every week." Her train came and she began to get on it. Before I could say anything she called, "Thank you!" As the door of the train closed I instantly knew I had misinterpreted the picture. The light within her was probably the same light that was in Jesus and I was being shown she was a believer. I should have asked her if she was searching for anything spiritually instead of telling her my assumptions. I shook my head at myself. I, above all people, because of my experiences, should know not to judge by outer appearances. I quickly apologized to the Lord for filtering my flesh into it. I asked Him to do damage control with that lady and still speak to her in it. I sighed and prayed for her.

There was a group of homeless people under an overpass, some sleeping and some hanging out. Another team member and I went over with some food to make contact. When we are armed with food we become the "friendlies" and accepted among the street crowd. The people that hang out under this overpass are usually the most destitute of the street crowd that we come in contact with. Most are usually banned from all the local shelters, commonly known for being addicts and/or dealers. Local shelters have requested that our team not set up near this area in order to prevent the shelter's clients who visit us from mingling with the more troublesome crowd. Safety is also a concern as statistically there is a stabbing once a week in this area. That can be alarming, intimidating, scary and not a safe place to be. However, I figure there are six days that there are no stabbings, so the odds are in our favor. As we engaged and gave food, I saw a couple in a makeshift bed on the sidewalk. Their eyes were closed but I was drawn to them so I gently said, "Hey, would you like some banana bread?" The man opened his eyes and lit up, accepting the offer. He thanked me and went to go back under the covers. I always have a decision to make in evangelism: do I take the encounter to a spiritual level or am I just to be kind, hoping my actions will be enough to display Christ? I've learned to make the decision quickly and to take it to the next level as I've missed too many opportunities in times past. It was a little awkward but I broke the silence, "Can I pray for you for anything?" The man popped his head back out of the blankets and was very open. He said he'd like prayer for wisdom and then said, "Solomon asked for wisdom and it was considered very good by God, so I will too." I raised my eyebrows and said, "Oh, are you familiar with the Bible a little? Were you raised with some sort of spiritual belief?" He explained he was actually raised in a very atheistic home but at fifteen years of age God got a hold of him. He was invited to a youth group and through attending he accepted the Lord. He admitted he wasn't a very good Christian and not doing well but he still loved God. I prayed for him for wisdom. His girlfriend beside him was mentally incoherent. It was obvious she was on some sort of drug, and that he was caring for her. She wasn't happy that we were there. His name was Jack. We chatted a bit and I asked, "Is there anything we can do for you, Jack? Can I get you some hot chocolate and pizza?" I was hoping to create more conversation. He replied yes so my teammate and I left to get some and quickly discussed what we observed. Both of us noticed that we could see a difference in his eyes, like the Holy Spirit was there. When we returned I asked, "So Jack, tell me why you are not a very 'good' Christian?" He shared with us that he was on fentanyl and I asked why. He said it was for two reasons. The first reason he gave was that he was a framer for fifteen years and had hurt his shoulder and his back quite badly. He could not get rid of the pain, even with medical solutions. Secondly, he had internal emotional pain, trying to deal with his past. He was desperate to escape it and to feel differently. This is a common answer I hear. I responded, "Well Jack, you know your Bible and there's that verse that says, 'don't get drunk on wine . . . but be filled with the Holy Spirit.' I think those two things were put together in a verse to show us that alcohol, drugs, or other vices, are something that makes us feel different, but as you know, it's temporary and leads to things that damage us. The Holy Spirit is the only One that can actually heal and change the way we feel permanently. You believe in a God who heals, don't you? Can I pray for healing for you, physically and emotionally?" He agreed completely and wanted prayer. So I put my hand on his shoulder, hesitating at first, being careful to keep my body distant so that his girlfriend would not feel territorial or threatened. I felt very strongly that I should touch his shoulder. I prayed for healing, both physically and emotionally. When I was done I said, "Jack, I see the Holy Spirit in you. He has not left you. He has so much for you and longs for deeper connection with you. Seek his face. This is just a season." Jack said he really appreciated us talking and praying with him. We walked away broken-hearted for our wayward brother in Christ. We took a couple moments to pray for him, his future and his freedom. My heart still aches for him as I know he is missing out on so much the Lord wants him to have in Jesus.

Another time I was simply walking and I came across two women and a man. One of the women was elderly and had been drinking. She was being supported by the other two. She had a huge black eye. A trio like this I typically would avoid and try not to make contact with lest I stir them up to make me feel uncomfortable. However, I decided to rush over to them and asked if I could pray for the woman's eye. They were surprised and quickly responded yes. I cupped the woman's face in my hands and began to pray over her. As I prayed, her tears ran over my hands. I hugged her when I was done and the other two thanked me. Yes, the woman had a strong smell of alcohol on her breath but the Holy Spirit ministers Spirit to spirit. I walked away with my hands covered with her tears, it powerfully convicted me to not hesitate to pray for people. It was a reminder how all of us just have to stop judging others by their appearance and stereotypes and *see* them the way God sees them.

One evening a man came to our gathering outside on the sidewalk. I hadn't seen him before. He appeared to be in his fifties, had a long beard, tattoos, and facial piercings. He looked hardened and intimidating. He engaged someone from our team and said he needed to talk to someone in charge. They brought him to me. I quickly grabbed a young, new team member to join me, greeted him and asked him what was going on. He held up his left wrist and there was a huge stitched line that was all bruised and swollen. Twenty-seven stitches, to be exact. He shared that he had tried to commit suicide three days before. He cut his artery deeply. When medics arrived they put a tourniquet on his now bruised upper arm, told him he had four minutes to live, and asked, "Do you have anything you want to say or talk about?" Tears welled up in his eyes as he told me he lost seven litres of blood and was passing out as the medic was yelling at him to stay with him. I asked him why he tried to kill himself. He told me he hated his life, he was done, he was so tired and worn out by life that he just felt like he couldn't take it anymore. Through my questions and our conversations the following is a sanitized (swearing removed) summary of what he shared with me. He had been part of a biker gang for years. He wouldn't tell me which one, but he was their tattoo artist. He sincerely told us it was a scary gang where he had seen and sometimes participated in horrible violence. He had been with a woman for years who he said was a real tough lady (again my terms to explain). She had emotionally beaten him up and completely destroyed him. He wanted out of the gang after being part of it for years and it had taken him three years to finally get out. He said that one of the gang leaders supported him by telling the others he was mentally messed up in the head and it was in their best interest not to have him around any more. He muttered under his breath, "Maybe I am, I don't even know." He told us that in his past he had been shot. He also had kids and mentioned that he was not allowed to see them anymore, which really bothered him. Pulling off his shoes and socks he proceeded to show us his toes which had no toe nails. He shared that he owed the gang money and because he couldn't pay they pulled out his toe nails. Next he opened his mouth and pulled his lip back, showing me that the right side of his top mouth had no teeth. The gang had knocked out all his teeth there. He had never in his life been homeless, and it seemed that for much of his life he had been quite well off. He had never hung around with the homeless crowd or the junkies, and now that he was, he hated it. He spent a lot of time in fast food restaurants just sitting there putting in time. Since leaving the gang he lost his tattooing business, his woman, his kids, his money and pretty much everything. I asked him for his name and he answered, "Lucifer". Unimpressed, I asked again, "No, really, what's your name?" He sincerely insisted, "That is what they call me. That is the name everyone calls me." "Well," I said, "I am not calling you that so what's your real name?" He shook his head, "I can't tell you my real name." I understood and said, "Ok, that's fine, what would you like me to call you?" He thought for a moment and answered, "DL, call me DL." I continued, "DL, you know that we follow God and I have a question for you. If you could ask God for anything, what would you ask him?" He paused for a second and then got really intense, "I'd ask him, Where the #%*& has He been? What has He done for me? Why did He abandon me?" His answer showed me he had been exposed to something about God somewhere along life's journey and that he obviously felt abandoned. I asked him, "What was your experience with God?" I found out he was raised a Jehovah Witness, then he switched and got involved with Mormonism, then switched again into Catholicism. Even though I tried to phrase the question in many ways I couldn't quite pinpoint when and how he had felt abandoned by God. He said that he and God were done. God had forsaken him. That he and God have completely separated and that there was nothing between them. He shared he had tattoos on his body, that I couldn't see which were very satanic. He covered his mouth on one side so that only I could see him speaking and then quietly mouthed what the tattoos were to me. He also signalled with his hand what they were because he didn't want my young team member who was sitting there silent to know or to be exposed to them. To be honest, I had no idea what the signals meant or what he was talking about, as my satanic knowledge was not that extensive at the time, I guess, ha ha. He seemed to think they were really bad and was awaiting my acknowledgement. I nodded my head and in sincerity said, “Oh wow!” He went on and on about how him and God had “broke up” and that God had abandoned him. From a spiritual deliverance perspective I was thinking, “This guy is in so much bondage, what a mess. What a long road it would be for him to get free.” I was praying for help from the Holy Spirit to show me what to do with this man. From a warrior perspective I thought, “Whatever. God can free him in a second.” From an evangelist perspective I felt like I was done being the listener and needed to speak. I also sensed that if I approached the conversation with theological information, it would not impact him as he was too angry about God to receive it and too much in despair to think it through. I knew he needed an encounter with Jesus and to hear straight from God in order for his heart to be touched. I began, (in my biggest, firmest, biker tone) “DL, you seem like a pretty tough guy. I’m not going to sugar coat anything with you, I’m going to be blunt and straight with you because I think you can handle that.” DL nodded, “Yes I can. I don’t want anything sugar coated, tell it to me straight!” I said, “Well, you were given another chance at life. You tried to kill yourself and you should have died but Jesus has conquered death and He decided, no. He has more plans for you on this earth and He’s giving you more time to change things. You have been given the gift of time and of life for a reason. You think this is hell on earth right now? Well, when you die, you are going to the real hell which is 100 times worse!” DL interjected, “No it’s not, hell is what I’m living now and nothing can be worse!” I raised my eyebrows, “Oh yes, it will be worse. You have no idea! As it is right now, you will never stop hating your life and nothing is going to get better for you. You can do all sorts of things to try to help you right now, and some even may work for a short time, but the way you're feeling now is not going to change. The only thing, the only Person, that can help you is Jesus Christ. And I’ll tell you why - He conquered death on the cross, and He conquered everything you are dealing with and have done. He has not abandoned you. You have decided that you are a ‘god’. It is you who have decided the true God will not have anything to do with you. But the opposite is true. He is pursuing you, and that is why you are here. He wants to have a relationship with you again but He will not force it on you. He is waiting for you to say, ‘yes, I want that’. God has given you the gift of time, the gift of breath to give you another chance to turn to Him for your healing, your freedom, and to help you." He thought about it for a moment and then said, "God has forsaken me and He won't speak to me." I asked him if he heard voices. He seemed quite upset that I would think that, as if he was crazy. "No, I don't hear voices, I'm not crazy. I just keep having the thought - 'It's time to die'." Internally I thought, "same thing" and it confirmed my suspicion of demonic involvement with suicide. I asked him, "DL, if you could hear from God a message tonight, would you want to?" DL insisted, "God will not talk to me." I smiled at the challenge, "Well, some of my friends and I have pursued a relationship with Jesus and have learned to hear His voice. We could ask God and see what He has to say to you."

He thought for a moment and then said slowly, "Okay, let's do it. Yes, I want that. . . . but I don't think He'll talk to me. .. .Is it going to be weird or anything?" I laughed, "Oh no!", but I was thinking, "What could be weird about asking God to speak to DL, aka lucifer?" We specialize in weird . . . and awkward . . . and uncomfortable.

I looked for someone on our team that knew how to listen clearly to the Holy Spirit. I needed someone I could really trust to come in cold turkey and just hear from God. As I quickly walked around I saw my trusted friend Melinda, who was also deep in conversation. I didn't want to interrupt but I went over to her, looked her in the eyes and said, "I am so sorry to interrupt, but I <u>really</u> need you for five - ten minutes." She told me later that it was actually perfect timing. She joined me and I explained to DL that we just needed a few minutes of quiet, to close our eyes and listen to God. DL closed his eyes with us and we sat in silence. I had Melinda begin because I did not want to influence her or have DL discredit her if I explained anything. She asked him if he had any injury or pain in his left leg. At first he said no, but then paused and said, "Actually, I have a pin in my left knee. It makes me limp sometimes from the pain." She explained that she felt it was not only a physical ailment that God wanted to heal but also that it symbolized his walk with the Lord. She was hesitating because she did not know if he had a relationship with the Lord or not. I told her to just say it straight because the details were too complicated to get into at this time. Melinda went on to say some other things but I had stopped listening and was really pressing into the Holy Spirit because I did not understand all I was receiving from

Him. Melinda finished, I began to speak. I told him I saw a vision of him with a black belt on and then he took it off. He began using it violently, out of rage and anger, but the cause of that anger was actually hurt and wounds. He whipped the belt and it had wrapped around a man's leg. But when I looked closer it was his own left leg that it wrapped around. It yanked him off his feet and caused him to crash to the ground. But it was himself that was doing it. DL stopped me then and said, "You got it partially right, I did have a black belt that I took off, wrapped around my neck and hung myself in the bathroom, but I was unsuccessful in killing myself." It took me a moment to stop being stunned and then I told him I did not think the belt was representing his suicide attempt but had to do with his walk with the Lord as well and that he was constantly causing himself to fall because of deep wounds from his past. I did find it interesting that there was a parallel between the black belt and the suicide. I kept going. The next picture I saw of him was as a young boy around ten years old with a wound on his face. He was taking water and trying to wash his face, because he really wanted to be good and do right, but the wound had made it so hard and he did not know how to get the wound off his face. Then I saw him as he was now, and Jesus stood before him and put His hand on his stomach (not his chest) and power went from His hand into DL, into the deep places. It was like a double edged sword stabbing him deep. It was painful, yet it also was healing deep areas. Jesus then said to me, "I will do this, but only if he asks me to and is willing to let me." So I explained all this to DL and helped him understand the meaning behind it. When we were done I asked him if he had any response or thoughts. He sat for a moment processing all that I had said. His tone had changed and he said, "I think I'm going to come to your church. Go ahead, give me your literature and I'll read it." I laughed and because of his JW and Mormon background I wanted to make sure he understood that membership or joining our church was not what we were about. I explained he did not have to come to our church, but our desire was for him to have a relationship with Jesus. I asked him if we could pray for him. He said yes. We put our hands on him and he thought that was a bit weird but I laughed and told him we were a touchy bunch and wanted to give him some love. As Melinda prayed, tears were welling up in his eyes and spilling out. While she prayed I felt the Holy Spirit telling me to put my hand on the back of his neck. I kept seeing an image of me doing that to him but I wasn't sure why. I sensed it was something to do with a negative spiritual authority that had access to his mind and was able to direct and manipulate him like a puppet to make him go in certain directions. I also felt I was to put my hand on the wrist where the wound from his attempted suicide was and to pray to redeem it. So when it came time for me to pray, I did. I prayed in the many ways I sensed the Holy Spirit led me to. I did put my hand on the back of his neck and rebuked the spirit of death, suicide, murder, control and I commanded the ungodly authority to let go. I put my hand gently on his twenty-seven stitches and prayed off the trauma and the suicide. I prayed for quick healing and then it rose up in me to proclaim that the scar would be a reminder to him for the rest of his life that Jesus had conquered death. On that day, Jesus had decided no! Death could not have DL but that Jesus had plans for him and more days had been ordained for him. I proclaimed that not one day would be stolen from him, that he would live out what God had decided he would live out, and that the scar would be a testimony of God's love for him. A testimony that God took DL's mess and gave him good things that glorified God and gave DL real peace and joy.

When we were done he took a deep breath. His demeanour and attitude had totally changed. He said, "Ok, I'm coming to your church! I'll sit in the back so that I don't scare anyone because I know church folk won't feel comfortable with me." I laughed and assured him he would be welcome (I would have to pray and trust God to ensure that the people in the church would not avoid him). I told him we would even meet him there and sit with him if he wanted. He told me to give him the info, so I gave him one of our contact cards as well as my first name and a Pastor's name in case he contacted or showed up at the church. That way the church would know where to send him and why, once seeing our names. He accepted the gospel of John and told us he would read it but would need someone to talk with him about it and help him understand it. I told him he could come any Monday and we would be happy to do that with him. We gave him big hugs and then had to wrap up as the evening was over.

I marvel at God's incredible love for DL. Even though he attempted to take his own life God chose to extend it and arranged to bring him to our team and have us expose him to truth and love. It amazes me how sometimes intellectual conversation can go round and round without accepting reason, yet hearing from God breaks deep into someone's heart and spirit, where mere words just cannot penetrate.

On another night as a team member got into a discussion with a group of people, I saw a man looking for money. Looking disheveled, dirty and wearing a backpack, I guessed he was probably someone living at homeless shelters or in low income housing. I smiled at him as he could tell I was watching him. He looked warily at me and didn't look too friendly. I greeted him and asked him how he was doing. He said okay and I told him I was praying for people and wondered if I could pray for him. He made a lot of eye contact with me during our conversation and seemed to really be taking in what I was saying. I prayed for him and had said something in my prayer about Jesus having plans for him. When I was done he said, "Jesus has bad plans for me." Surprised, I said, "No He doesn't, why would you say that?" He told me the last year had been horrible for him and he felt Jesus was causing these things. I asked him what his spiritual beliefs were and he told me he really didn't have any. I asked him if he was raised with any spiritual perspectives. He said he was raised in a Catholic church but he had turned away. I told him that God does not make "bad plans" for people. He created us and loves us. However there are a few possible reasons things were difficult. I said, "There is the devil. He is an enemy of God and wants to destroy us because . . ." He interrupted me and his eyes got big, "I know there's a devil, I've seen him. You're right. I've experienced him." I asked, "How so?" He told me he had played with a ouija board when he was younger and the devil showed up. I asked him to tell me about that experience. He told me candles blew out and lit again, things moved, there was a dark presence there and it freaked him out. He never touched one again. So I asked him, "Have you ever talked to God about that experience? Have you ever repented and said sorry for going and playing a game with the devil when you knew he was an enemy of God?" He stopped and very soberly said, "No, I never have." I began to explain, "It is something very important to do. The devil can have access to you because you gave it to him long ago. When you go to God and repent, He will free you. You are doing exactly what the devil wants. He wants to cause you to turn away from God and be separated from Him, blaming God for bad things in your life. Don't turn from God, run to Him! Don't allow the devil to destroy you. God wants you to have life in Him!" He was really listening and I asked him if he read much. He said, "No, not really." I asked him if he would consider reading the Bible. I told him there was so much truth in it that would help him. The man went from being very engaged to being done with the conversation, "I better go now, you have a good night." He reached over, gave me a hug and we parted.

I was sitting in the dentist chair getting a routine cleaning. The dental hygienist chatted a bit but then busily focused on the task at hand. While I sat there, I prayed, "Well, Lord, since I'm just sitting here, is there anything you want me to say to this lady when she's done?" I prayed for the next twenty minutes for her and asked the Lord what He saw in her. When we were done, I wondered how open she would be to what I had to say. Perhaps I would make her really uncomfortable or she would roll her eyes when I walked away. After she finished giving me her assessment and instructions I said, "Before I go can I quickly share something with you? I love Jesus and while you were cleaning my teeth I was praying for you. He showed me some things about you that He loves." I proceeded to share it with her. To my surprise tears welled up in her eyes and she said, "Thank you so much! I have met born again Christians. One man a few years ago actually told me that God had a calling on my life. This . . . this was a bit different . . . gosh, I'm tearing up!" She waved her hand in front of her face as she tried to gain composure. I smiled and said, "It sounds like God is trying to get your attention. You may want to pursue who Jesus truly is." She nodded and contemplated that for a moment. We had to go as she was on a time schedule and I did not want to affect her job. I had no idea she would be so open to hear what I had to say. I'm thankful I didn't shrink back.

We may never know what people have gone through or what they are presently going through. For us to make a judgement that someone will not be open to hearing the gospel or to a spiritual conversation enables us to give in to the feelings of our own fear of rejection. It is much wiser for us to follow the Holy Spirit, to take risks and to not worry about who will be closed or opposed to what we desire to share. We never know what state each person's heart is in until we open up ourselves to the Holy Spirit and then engage in a spiritual conversation with others.

We have to get over ourselves and our insecurities. We need to be willing to engage with those around us, to love Jesus enough, to love them enough that we let go of our own fear of rejection, awkwardness, and self focused agendas. Only then will we experience God working through us to glorify Him to others.

CHAPTER 7

EAGER BEAVERS: Getting Them To Say The Prayer

"Jesus told us to make disciples, not decisions."
- John Pereira

How many times do we measure the success and value of a ministry by how many people get "saved". I'm asked questions all the time, "How many people get saved when you go out?", "How many people get saved in a month during your ministry? A year?"

Oh, to just get someone saved and into heaven for eternity! If it were only that easy to measure. We could wipe our brow and say, "Phew, fulfilled the great commission".

When we think about how people get saved, scripture is clear Who is doing the saving. John 6:44 says, *"Noone can come to me unless the Father who sent me draws them."*

John 15:26 says *"But when the Helper comes, whom I will send to you from the Father, the Spirit of truth, who proceeds from the Father, he will bear witness about me."*

Of course, we know salvation is the work of our Triune God but somewhere along the way Christians thought we could just put a few sentences together and if someone would say them then they would be eternally saved. It's a fine balance, isn't it? Saying "the prayer" of salvation is good IF the person truly means it from their heart. Ah, but then there's the theological discussion of once saved always saved.

Verses are used to support the viewpoint that one can lose salvation and others are used to present the viewpoint that one cannot lose their salvation. Debates include the question: was the person even saved in the first place? As evangelists, we have such a passion for the lost it is tempting to push people to cross that line, to just repeat after us and say magic words that will give them “fire insurance”. It is also very tempting for the lost to say those prayers and relieve any fears they have of life after death. However, when we get so eager and the explanation hasn't been fully given as to what they are actually saying yes to AND saying no to, we later run into those who have divorced their commitment or vow, sometimes a week later or perhaps years later. So many times I’ve heard it said, "I tried religion, it didn't work." or "I tried Jesus, it didn't do nothin’ for me." “It”, didn't do anything because that's what it was, an “it”, a religious script, no different than leaving food at a shrine, hoping to appease the deity and win favour. So we have to be careful to listen to the Holy Spirit and have discernment. We do not want someone to make a flippant, momentary decision in response to pressure or appeasement.

During one of our regular outreaches, a gentleman who had come to see what we were doing began talking to one of our male team members while I was engaged in another conversation. After five minutes the two of them approached me and the team member said, “Val, this man, Harold, would like to give his life to the Lord.” I didn’t know the street gentleman but he had stood beside me listening to my street preaching earlier and had joined in singing with the worship team all that night. I didn’t know anything about their conversation. I stood with the two of them and asked the team member to go ahead and pray with him. He led him in a traditional salvation prayer. As he was praying something just wasn’t sitting right with me. When they were done I asked, “Harold, have you ever prayed something like that before?” Harold replied, “All the time, I pray it over and over, just to make sure.” My team member was surprised. I asked Harold if he understood what Jesus actually did for him. He said yes and explained it to me quite beautifully. I realized he had already made a decision to follow Christ and hadn’t needed to say the salvation prayer yet again that evening. What he needed was discipleship and mentoring. Harold started sharing with me about his life. His mom died when he was four and his grandma took him in. Then his grandma died when he was eight years old. Harold then found himself in an environment where he was sexually abused for many years by a male and turned to drugs to cope with the abuse. He shared he was now free from all addictions except did a little pot occasionally but he really just wanted to serve Jesus. As I listened, the Holy Spirit showed me spirits that were attacking him. "Harold, can I pray for you?" He nodded and my team member and I laid hands on him. I prayed and rebuked the spirits I was sensing. Then I said, "Harold, I want you to know, you are a son of the living God. He has adopted you and nothing can separate you from him, not even death. You are a man who has integrity, who has depth, and I sense the Lord is wanting you to know He sees your heart. He wants to heal you deep down. Earlier you showed me songs you wanted to be sung. They were very powerful songs that showed me what touches your heart. I want you to know something, Harold, you never have to pray a salvation type prayer again. You don't have to fear not being saved because you are saved." Harold broke down and cried and then began to pray to the Lord from his heart, telling him how much he needed Him and thanked Him. We encouraged him further before leaving for the evening. My heart's desire was to see him engage in discipleship with a team member in the weeks to come.

This is a good example of why we must be careful to listen to where people are at and not just rush to get them to say the "salvation prayer".

During an evangelism training session I was teaching, I asked the following question to a group of believers: "What is our goal of evangelism?" Same question, different group, but still yet another person answered that our main goal was to get people to say the prayer of repentance in every conversation. Again, I spoke, "No, actually it is not. Our goal is to proclaim the gospel - which is the revelation of Jesus Christ. We are to reveal Jesus and to make the Father known. We are to bring an encounter with Jesus to a person by carrying His presence, His Holy Spirit within us and speaking truth. If people declare they will give their life to the Lord, that is great - but only if it is the Holy Spirit who has brought them to repentance. If a person is feeling pressure from us, or we have manipulated them in some way, or we threaten them with hell, then their declarations are merely just words. Their hearts have not been changed. We may walk away and pat ourselves on the back but we likely have not revealed Jesus to them." I later talked with this gentleman and explained my perspective further. He agreed with me and said he was trying to make the point that we should not be fearful to invite a person to pray for salvation. I agreed with him but said we must be careful not to make it our goal to get a person to say the repentance prayer in every evangelistic conversation. In evangelism we must always ask and listen to the Holy Spirit for what He wants for every person we engage. He alone knows their hearts, what they need to hear, and how they can best be ministered to. There are no formulas or rules. Jesus presented the way of His Kingdom to people, in love, in truth, with all the fruits of His Spirit, and gave each person a choice and an experience with Him. Jesus revealed Himself to all of creation in the physical form of a man. One way He reveals himself now is through us. *We* are to reveal Jesus to all of creation. We can only do this because we have His Spirit in us, not by getting someone to say "the magic words" of salvation.

There was a lady who was waiting for the train on the transit platform. She stood in one spot and then moved to another. As I watched her, I prayed and received an image in my spirit of a large flower within her. It was big and beautiful. I approached her and said, "Hello, my name is Val and as I was standing there I, . . . well, I love Jesus and He drew my attention to you. He gave me this picture of you with this large flower inside of you. It was big and beautiful. I asked Him what that meant. He showed me it was beauty that has grown inside of you. It was also what people see about you, beauty inside and it's beautiful to look at. God loves that about you." The woman's face lit up into a huge smile. She thanked me very warmly. I asked her if she had any spiritual beliefs and she said no she did not but that she considered herself spiritual. Her tone and body language showed me she was ending the conversation. I reopened it by asking her if I could pray to Jesus for her. She was very open to that. I prayed out loud asking God to reveal Himself to her and acknowledged that He was the way for her to have true peace, true joy and to know true love. When I was done she thanked me, I gave her a hug as her train came. I didn't have the time to go through the gospel; I knew my time with her would be short. She did not need to be argued into the Kingdom. She needed to experience the true God, the Jesus who wanted to get her attention. I would've loved for her to give her life to the Lord in the three and a half minutes before her train came. Nothing is impossible with the Lord, however, I needed to put away my agenda and follow the Lord's; He is the only one who knows the heart and the timing.

CHAPTER 8

BLOOPERS AND JUST PLAIN AWKWARD

"Let eloquence be flung to the dogs rather than souls be lost. What we want is to win souls. They are not won by flowery speeches." - Charles Spurgeon

I give you complete permission to laugh and to groan at the things in this next chapter. I have giggled with the Lord over these situations and ask Him to somehow have me *bear fruit in every good work* (Colossians 1:10) and to *work all things together for good because I love Him* (Romans 8:28). I apologize ahead of time. It's going to get really raw.

I was sitting on the curb with a gentleman from the homeless shelter. We had a very good conversation about Christ. I asked him if I could pray for him. He was not a believer but said yes. He was a very respectful man. Without explanation or direction I put my hand on his shoulder and began praying. In hindsight, I realize he didn't know if he was supposed to do something in order to join me in praying. He was not able to put his hand on my shoulder the way I had done to him because of the way we were sitting. He did not want to put his hand on my leg because that could seem inappropriate. So as my eyes were closed, I suddenly felt his hand clasp my leg just above my ankle in an action to signify he was joining me in prayer. That is amusing. However, to add to the weirdness, I hardly ever wear shorts when I'm out in that area of town, partly because the evenings are cool and partly out of modesty for this specific activity. That night I was wearing capris as it was a hot summer evening. I didn't skip a beat as I was praying for this man but I was groaning inwardly as I had not taken time to shave my legs that night. Well, there we were with his hand on my hairy leg above my ankle and me trying to stay focused on praying for him. It was a bit of a strange situation for sure and one I giggled about later as I drove home.

Too raw and awkward? Ha ha, I'm just getting started. There are so many stories to draw from that I just couldn't bring myself to print, but I giggle as I tell them to my husband. After hearing countless stories, he usually rolls his eyes and says he's not surprised. We often get fearful that evangelism may get a bit awkward or that things will not go quite the way we had hoped. At first "awkward" just started to happen and I would squirm through it but as I pressed on I just decided that I would "do" awkward. I wonder how awkward it was when Jesus stood in front of the crowd and didn't say anything about the woman caught in adultery. He just bent down and started writing something in the dirt. (John 8:1-11) We've heard the story so many times it just seems normal now but I wonder how weird that would be if it happened today. Or how about when the woman ran in and started pouring perfume on Jesus' feet? Okay, not too strange, but then to wipe them with her hair, cry and then kiss them?! (Luke 7:36-40) Jesus often answered the religious leaders in very strange ways that would have caused awkward silences and puzzled looks. It happened even when the disciples came and found Him with the Samaritan woman. First, it was really strange culturally for Him to be talking to a Samaritan, let alone a woman, and a wayward one at that. Second, how confusing would it be for the disciples to go get Jesus food and then to have Him say He has food they know nothing about. (John 4:5-33) Imagine the difficult situation when facing the owners of the pig herd that just ran off the cliff in a crazy fit. (Mark 5:1-17) Let's face it, if things don't go smoothly for us in evangelism, we don't want to do it. If we take a risk to bless, pray, or talk to someone about Jesus, we want everyone to be saved, healed and delivered and there to be joy and appreciation. We love to hear those shiny, polished stories that turn out well. But what happens if we don't experience those things?

I started a conversation with a lady on a sidewalk, asking her how she was doing. She was very bitter and angry, telling me all her woes. As I listened to her, I asked the Lord what He wanted to show me about her. God gave me a picture of her heart with holes in it. I was thinking this represented her condition spiritually and that she must have had much trauma in her life or something. When it came time for me to speak, I changed the direction of the conversation, "So while we have been chatting, God has shown me that you have holes in your heart . . . " before I could go on, the woman's eyes got big and she said in an irritated voice, "Oh really! Well, isn't that just great. Maybe you could ask Him 'why' then, too?! I was born with six holes in my heart. I've had multiple surgeries and problems my whole life. Maybe He could explain that to me!" I was so shocked! She literally had holes in her heart! I continued talking to the lady, explaining God's love for her and his desire to have a relationship. I even prayed for her. She didn't stop being irritated with me and left indignant. Inside, however, I was blown away by the Holy Spirit's accuracy in the image He showed me. My faith had grown and I was actually very excited, even though it had created an unplanned, unpolished and uncomfortable situation.

As believers we often have a line in the sand that we draw and say, "I'll talk about Jesus if . . . if they understand, if they are nice, if they receive it, if they will still be my friend, if they don't think I'm weird, if I'm not rejected, if I don't say the wrong thing, if they get healed, if I'm comfortable, if it works in my schedule, if I know the answers, if I've had a relationship with them after a certain period of time, if I'm feeling close to God, if God shows up in a clear way, if, if, if, if . . ." What's your 'if'? I, myself, have had all of those if's. I didn't want to be perceived as weird, or to be rejected. I found it embarrassing if people didn't get healed after I prayed. I've also been way too busy at times to take time to engage with people about spiritual things.

Jesus told us to go, proclaim the good news, heal the sick, raise the dead, cleanse the lepers, raise the dead . . . there were no 'ifs'. Really think about this. What is your if? No, seriously, stop reading this book for a moment. Ask yourself this question: I will talk about Jesus to people if . . .

While I was shopping at the grocery store I noticed I continually passed the same man in each aisle. After passing for the fourth time I decided to ask the Lord if there was something He wanted me to say to this man. As we continued to cross paths again and again I pressed into the Holy Spirit. I was not sensing anything from the Lord. Finally, I went to get into the cashier line and as the groceries were being scanned, the same man came into my line behind me. As we both were bagging our groceries I would take glimpses of him to see if the Holy Spirit would highlight anything to me about him or if I could engage him in a conversation somehow. I just wasn't getting anything and the man seemed oblivious to my presence. My heart was pounding as I knew the Lord was bringing this man to me but I just didn't know what to say. Since he only had a few items he turned and left. I kept bagging my groceries and watched him walk away. I was at such a loss to know what to say. It took me another five minutes to finish and as I pushed my cart to the car and unloaded my groceries, I was conversing with the Lord, "Why did You bring this man to my attention and not reveal to me anything? Why did you keep bringing him to me? Should I have simply started a conversation with him?" Then the Holy Spirit brought this thought into my head, " *He's got pain in deep places and it's old pain* ." I sighed as the man was gone and I prayed, "Well Lord, if I see him somehow, I will talk to him." The wind was blowing like crazy and I closed my trunk and as I looked up I saw that man walking on the other side of the parking lot towards his vehicle. He had stopped at the convenience shop outside the store and was now leaving. I had that deciding moment of whether to obey or not. I let out a groan, "Lord, this is going to look so weird!" I ran across the large parking lot and jumped in front of him. He was startled and I was out of breath. "Hello sir! I am so glad I caught up with you. I noticed you in the grocery store and God kept drawing my attention to you. I was wondering if I could share with you what He showed me?" The wind was whipping around us and he said, "Uh, I guess so. I'm not a religious man." I waved my hand indicating it didn't matter and said, "The Lord showed me you have deep pain and it is from the past." He raised his eyebrows and said, "No, nope, sorry, I don't. I'm actually a really positive person. Everything's going good in my life." His response was not what I was expecting. I was so puzzled and confused. The Lord wouldn't have me run across the whole parking lot just to have heard wrong. As we both stood there I could see the man was uncomfortable yet polite. I asked, "Do you have a spiritual belief? Do you believe in God?" He shared with me he believed there was a God but beyond that, not really. As I was trying to ask the Lord where to take the conversation, trying to think fast of what to say next and having my hair blow wildly all around me, the man said, "That's really nice of you to stop me though. I just really am great." As I floundered in conversation, out of the corner of my eye I saw a friend of mine. She had seen me and come to say hi, but overhearing the conversation, knew what I was doing and was standing, listening to this man reject me. I felt a bit embarrassed. I mean, it would've been really great if she would have been watching this man get saved through my super duper evangelism techniques. The man noticed her as well and I could see in his eyes wondering what in the world was going on. I had claimed that I had randomly come to talk to him but now there was another woman standing there listening who, he observed, knew me. "Can I pray for you?" I asked. He kindly declined and told me again, "That's really nice of you but no thanks, I'm good." So feeling like I had nothing else to say in the situation, I decided to wrap it up and close the conversation. "I just want you to know that God loves you so much, He sees you deep down, He wants to bring healing to some area of your life. You could ask Him sometime, it couldn't hurt?" I shook his hand and as he walked away he said, "Yeah, I mean I got divorced years ago but now life is just great." As soon as he said those words it was like the Holy Spirit just went BAM to me. That was his deep pain that had been revealed to me. I knew he had pain but he was totally not ready to tell me about it. The man walked away and I turned to go greet my friend and sheepishly tell her why I was doing what I was doing. I, of course, learned huge lessons from it all. I approached this man very abruptly and did not deliver my message well. This was not a street guy who knows he's a mess and broken. This was a man in his own community, at his local grocery store. For me to abruptly inquire of a deep, inner, personal truth, likely made him feel vulnerable and defensive. I did not engage with much tact. Why did this happen? I don't know. I just knew that I had to be obedient. I came home and told my husband my failure story and he encouraged me saying, "Val, you don't know what is going on inside that man right now and how the Holy Spirit is working. It's not a failure. You were obedient and you don't know the impact of the words you said." He's right. But if I were to base the success of the incident on my feelings, I would have probably decided to never do that again. If I were to base it on the man's reactions, I definitely wouldn't feel the conversation had any value. Unfortunately, I can't even share some sort of glorious ending to the story. What a better story it would've made if the man would've fallen to his knees weeping and given his life to the Lord. However, I've never seen him again. So why tell the story? Because we are not to be obedient only if we see the outcome and only if we do everything perfect. We must be obedient even if it's awkward and we never know the end of the person's story here on earth.

One time I had a pastor's wife come to evangelize on the streets with me. I was very excited and wanted to show her what we did. I also wanted her to experience watching God work and have her get excited about evangelism. We were on a well-known bar strip and began talking to a man. He was very intelligent and had many questions for me about the Christian faith. I tried to answer them the best I could. After about fifteen minutes he said, "Well, before I talked to you, I wasn't sure if I believed in Christianity and God, but now after talking to you, I definitely don't!" I winced, smacked my forehead and groaned. I tried to recover the conversation but, yeah, it just went all downhill from there as I groveled to re-convince him. So after a few more rejections, I decided to take her to a more seedy part of the city to expose her to that area. We came across three people: two women and a man. They were drinking and the one woman was completely drunk and incoherent. The other two accepted prayer but then they asked us to pray for the woman who was now lying on the grass, seemingly unconscious. They told us they were worried she would choke so we suggested getting her onto her side. As we helped them do this, the woman ended up on the sidewalk. She laid on the cement and began throwing up. All I can say is . . . it was a lot of noodles. To make matters worse, she started to expel diarrhea out the other end as well. As the liquids poured out onto the sidewalk from both ends I started to dry heave. I just couldn't help it. My dry heaving was mixed with the sounds of this woman puking. The pastor's wife happened to be a nurse and had someone call 911. The responder on the phone told her to put her fingers in her mouth and make sure the airway was clear. We paused as we watched the woman puking more noodles up mixed with alcohol. I kept dry heaving. My friend shook her head, nope, not without gloves, the woman was breathing just fine. The ambulance arrived and took over. I got myself together and as we walked away the pastor's wife took a deep breath and said, "You know, I think I'm done for tonight." Yeah, it wasn't exactly the impression of evangelism I was hoping to leave with her. Years later we've had a good laugh and I hope she will join me again someday.

On another occasion, near a popular bar strip, I approached a woman standing on the sidewalk. I was with two other new team members. She was simply waiting to cross the street and I asked her if she had any spiritual beliefs and if she was a good person. She told me she believed in a higher power, that she was a good person and because of that it would all work out in the end. I began to put my tool of "The Way of the Master" by Ray Comfort and Kirk Cameron to work. As I went through the Ten Commandments, one of the new team members started to get upset. He did not like that I was having her admit to the sins of lying, stealing and blaspheming. Although she was not upset at all, he interrupted quite angrily and said, "God loves her and those things don't matter if she comes to Christ." I turned and began to explain to him that I was showing her how the Ten Commandments were a mirror. At the time, I was pretty new at using this tool so I have no doubt that my presentation was not smooth. I turned back to her and continued. As I was telling her she would not be going to heaven based on God's "goodness" test and I was beginning to drive the point home that we all need a Saviour, he again interrupted me and said, "I don't agree with how you're doing this, you need to stop." I held my hand up to stop him as I didn't want to address his concern right then. She looked from him then to me in a confused way but I continued. I could hear the third team member saying in the background, "Just let her finish, just wait til the end." By the time I did finish, we all felt a little awkward. I encouraged her to read a Bible and she went on her way. I spent the next half hour explaining to the team member why I had approached her that way. He was more comfortable presenting an all love based gospel rather than focusing on people's sin. It was pretty uncomfortable having disunity with a fellow Christian while witnessing to an unbeliever.

Even though I am married and have four kids, near the beginning of getting involved with street ministry my dad was not too thrilled about me being exposed and vulnerable to the unknown events and the culture of the downtown streets. I grew up on a farm and he was concerned about the lack of safety and the exposure to the rough city life. One day I decided to take my dad for a drive and show him the area where I often went to evangelize, just so he could picture it and perhaps take away some of the concerning stereotypes he had. As we drove through, there were a lot of homeless individuals standing on the sidewalk. The traffic light where we were at turned red and right beside us two men began to push each other around. The light seemed to just stay red forever and we watched the two men start punching one another. Then one man got the other one down onto the ground and throughout the entanglement one man's pants and underwear came right down to his knees. It sure seemed to be a long red light. I grimaced as we drove away and said, "Uh, I've never seen that happen before." "Mm hmm," was all he said. Ha ha, I don't think my dad gained any comfort or reassurance from that drive.

Another time I went to the mall and was ready to have fun evangelizing. As I began to engage people, it was anything but fun. I faced rejection after rejection. I couldn't get anyone to engage in any of my questions and many would not respond after I shared what I felt the Lord was showing me about them. Finally, one lady, we will call Ann, began to engage with me. She was reading a book. So I asked her about it. I listened to her explain all about this book as she was very chatty. Then eventually she asked me what type of books I liked. It was a perfect opportunity. I started with sharing that I liked biographies and true stories. She jumped in and spent ten minutes telling me of all sorts of biographies I should read. When she took a breath, I managed to say I read the Bible, found it to have so much depth and was always discovering new things in it. I asked her if she had read the Bible. She told me how she had attended a Catholic school with very negative experiences. Ann told me she had taken some sort of degree in religious studies in University and went on about the discrepancies of the Bible. I listened very politely and gracefully defended. I posed questions to gently challenge her opinions. She had a very strong personality and eventually did not like me continuing to question her opinions that she believed, which were not based on any facts. I asked, "Well, who is God? When you think of God, what comes to your mind?" Ann thought for a second and said, "God is the accumulation of all the good intentions of everyone in the world. That's what I believe in." I responded, "So God is not a Being?" She said, "Well, yes. I do believe He is a Being. You know what, I'm happy for you and your faith. Just remember this, Jesus was not a Christian, He was a Jew! That's all I'm going to say." Ann began taking steps away. At that very moment three young adult women came out of the store we were beside and as it was closing time they began locking up the store. They were blocked from walking away as the woman I was talking to was on one side of them and I was on the other. I was trying to make sense out of Ann's statement and so as she walked away, in the most friendly way possible I said, "Well, a Christian is a follower of Christ, so of course He was not a Christian. That was the name that came after for people who followed His life and teachings." Ann swung around and called back, "Yes, but Jesus was just a Jew. He was a good teacher and I believe in the good things He said but even He didn't come up with the Christian religion! There is more than one way to go to God!" I was aware of my audience of young women and called back to her, "Ah yes, but what did Jesus say? 'I am the Way, the Truth and the Life, No one comes to the God except through Me.'" Ann was determined to have the last word and called, "Jesus never said He was God." The statement was so false and yet Ann had spun around and walked away ending the conversation. I looked at the young women who were standing in nervous tension. One exclaimed, "What was that about?" I smiled weakly and said, "That was about who Jesus is." Another one exclaimed, "How does that even happen? Like, that was so crazy? We just came out and we were like, 'What is going on?'!" Then suddenly, their attention was drawn to a nearby baby and they rushed over to him. Engaging and ogling over him, I had no opportunity to explain more to them. I didn't know how to recover the conversation, nor did it seem like I needed to. That whole evening was brutal. That night and the whole next day I had such a heaviness and disappointment over the whole thing. I wondered what the point was in any of that conversation or the ones before. It certainly felt like one failure after another and maybe it was. It was one of those times where I truly needed to wipe the 'mud' of my face, straighten my spiritual crown and go out again.

I imagine you are shaking your head thinking I need to get better training or perhaps you're feeling a little sorry for me. As I think about these experiences and many more, I smile. I smile because they have developed a resilience in me. I share them because you too will experience bloopers and very awkward moments when it comes to sharing your faith. That does not mean we stop. It means we *get* to learn, we stay humble, we *get* the opportunity to push back our fear of man's disapproval and we develop resilience and perseverance.

Good Awkward, Bad Awkward

IMAGINE you are at a doctor's office, meeting a new doctor. You are nervous because you have personal things you need to share that are not just physical but affects your overall health. After introductions, you observe your new doctor is very genuine, kind, wise and you decide to trust him/her, telling your deepest secrets. Finally you build up the courage to tell everything going on in your life. You actually burst into tears at one point, conveying how things have affected you. Suddenly, two people burst into the room that the doctor knows but you've never seen before. The doctor turns to them and tells them everything. They talk about your situation like you aren't even there. They use medical terms you don't understand and offer you their advice. How would you feel? Your confidentiality has been betrayed and makes you feel vulnerable. Furthermore, you feel lost in their medical knowledge. It's very unprofessional and you wonder if you ever should've been so open. This is similar to what can happen when those outside the church culture engage with those inside the church culture.

Once I was talking with a man on the sidewalk during a time of an evangelistic outreach and the conversation had gone really deep. He had become very emotional when sharing about his past with me. Right at the height of emotion an eager believer just came and stood beside me. It was a little awkward as this man was feeling vulnerable and immediately choked back the emotion. So I introduced the team member to him and tried to make it as natural as possible. I began to explain about Jesus and what He did for us. All of a sudden another new team member popped up beside me on the other side. The man sort of looked puzzled with the addition of another random person joining a conversation uninvited. The man didn't know if this was a stranger or a friend of mine. I recognized this would normally be very weird to come listen to a conversation midway through when it was clear it was very personal. I didn't really know these new team members since I had just met them earlier that night, but I introduced "my friends". I ignored their lack of discernment. I understood why these team members were joining so I tried to accommodate and make it as comfortable as possible for everyone, especially the man. Within minutes another person popped up beside us and listened in. We must have looked hilarious and intimidating, the four of us all crowding around the man as I explained the answers to questions he had. When I was done, the man said he agreed with me. Then one of the new team members turned to me full of excitement and said for all of us to hear, "I think he is ready, he is almost there, he's almost ready to do it!!" Inside I groaned at how strange that must've sounded to the man but also inwardly chuckled at this newbie. I sympathetically smiled at the man and continued the conversation. Eventually he ended up giving his life to the Lord. All three of the new team members offered much advice about looking for God that week and the things he should do. I translated their well-meaning "christianese" terminology for the man into the straightforward instructions: read your Bible, pray, and come back next week to learn more, ha ha.

When the night was over I processed the conversation with the new team members. They are great brothers and sisters in Christ who wanted to observe and learn, and I love that. It was also quite obvious that they had not been out of church culture for some time and it certainly showed.

I saw how desperately people in the church need to learn how to relate to people outside the church, just like I did years ago. It was like seeing deer caught in headlights. I was again convinced of the need for believers to have encounters with strangers and not just cling to relational evangelism. Both are good, both are powerful. One is not more valuable than the other. But as we learn how to speak and minister to strangers, we learn discernment spiritually and socially.

On a different evening a friend and I were talking to a random man at the hospital when some new team members approached to listen. The guy started to feel a bit uncomfortable as he was suddenly surrounded by five people instead of the original two of us. When I asked him if I could pray for him he said yes. Suddenly arms flew at him from every angle and touched him. He jumped, "Whoa! What's going on!?" It was a little difficult to explain.

From my own experiences and observations it often seems Christians who are new to evangelism can be very socially inappropriate in their zeal. And I get that, it's new and they are not used to having spiritual conversations outside of the church. I find it a bit troublesome though, that Christians tend to be awkward about their faith outside of the church. It's actually a big part of what drove me to get involved with evangelism. I realized how socially awkward ***I*** was in the past when I shared my faith with someone because of my own lack of confidence and not knowing how to engage. Awkwardness can definitely occur when sharing our faith or when discussing uncomfortable issues or truths when evangelizing as I have demonstrated in many ways in the previous paragraphs. What I'm addressing here is social inappropriateness that lacks discernment and respect when we are sharing our faith. There's a difference. Just because we are evangelizing doesn't mean we stop honoring people. We always must honor the people we engage with. Social inappropriateness that lacks wisdom and humility comes at a cost and it hinders our witness. I believe the reason is that many believers are not used to talking about their faith. The more a person does something, the more natural it becomes. Of course, the opposite is true as well, the less a person does something, the more unnatural it becomes. Praying for an unbeliever, talking about Jesus with them, and listening to the Holy Spirit are very hard, awkward things for many believers to do. Did you just read that last sentence? I'll say it again. Praying for an unbeliever, talking about Jesus with them, and listening to the Holy Spirit are very hard, awkward things for many believers to do. Sobering thought. So we must rise and change this in our church culture.

CHAPTER 9

JUST DO IT

"It should be considered illegal for a follower of the Lord Jesus Christ not to be burning with passion for our Lord and burning with passion for the lost."

- Mark Cahill, The Watchmen

FEAR. REJECTION. Yes, those are two huge things that we must face when talking to someone about Jesus. We must decide if we will give in to those things. Will you be ruled by fear? Fear of the unknown, fear of not having control, fear of not knowing enough, fear of other's responses. Will you fear rejection? Or are those just common feelings we all must face? If that is the case, then we must face fear and rejection, then choose to just do it anyway. Why are we letting our emotions rule us? More often than we would like to admit, we become slaves to our emotions, allowing them to dictate our decisions, following them right into retreat, even if it means missing out on something good. I love Isaiah 61. In verse one it says that Jesus has come to "bind up the broken hearted". As I researched the Hebrew words of "bind" and "broken hearted" I discovered some interesting things. The word bind in the Hebrew is: a meaning that conveys putting pressure on a wound to stop the bleeding. It also means "to govern and rule". To govern and rule what? The broken heart. Broken heart in the Hebrew means - to be smashed to pieces in the innermost, deepest place of a person. Here is a more literal meaning to this verse according to the original Hebrew word definitions: Jesus has come to stop the bleeding and to govern and rule over the devastated part of our most inner places. I am so thankful for this revelation. I can't handle my brokenness. I need the Restorer, the Healer, the One Who loves me, to handle my brokenness. I actually need Him to govern and rule over all my emotions. Whether it is hurt, anger, anxiety, fear or rejection, I can't handle these emotions in my flesh and I often respond to them in ungodly ways. We've had this pendulum shift where in generations past, emotion was seldom acknowledged, but now in our present generation emotions are often the deciding factor of what a person does and doesn't do. The world will tell you to live by your emotions. I now pray on a very frequent basis, "Lord, govern and rule over my emotions, bring them into alignment with Your emotions and perspectives of the issue or person." Then I take captive every thought and make it obedient to Christ. (2 Corinthians 10:5) That is, every thought that is not in alignment with the character and Spirit of God, every thought that is cooperating with something that Jesus died to set me free from, I make it obedient to Christ by rejecting it and replacing it with truth. Then must I act in line with the Holy Spirit regardless of how I feel, until my feelings come into submission to my will, which is under submission to my spirit, which is under submission to the Holy Spirit. This is walking in the Spirit and not the flesh. It is a daily surrender.

I was asked to preach to a crowd downtown. The platform where preaching would occur from was up on the box of a pick up truck. I was new to evangelism and the thought terrified me. I told the leader I would need a month to prepare my twenty minute message. I had done public speaking many times before in front of all sorts of church crowds but this was an entirely different scenario. I had watched hecklers yell and swear at the preachers. The crowd might be interactive or may totally ignore the speaker, choosing to talk amongst themselves. I prayed and fasted. I pleaded with God to show me what topic to speak on. The following is what I found in my prayer journal lest you think it came easy:

"O Lord, I must confess I'm terrified of having to speak on the truck to those on the street. Lord, the very thought makes me go weak and fear wells up within me. My first impression is that I would be disobeying You if I do not do it so I must empty myself of my flesh and allow Your Spirit to fully take control in order for me to do this. O

Lord God! What should I even speak about? May it be Your timing, Your words, Your everything. Grant me peace and let Your power flow through me for I can do nothing without You. Oh Lord, You must speak to me, through me, guide me, lead me."

I tossed and turned the night before. The day came, I went over my notes and felt weak every time I thought of facing a crowd of approximately one hundred street people. I had diarrhea all day . . . hey, just keepin' it real. I got up on the back of that truck and heard my voice project loudly in the night air. The crowd went silent and listened. The Spirit of God took control of my tongue. When I came to the end, although fear invaded my thoughts and I wavered for a few seconds, I invited anyone who wanted to surrender to the Lord to raise their hands. Several did! As I climbed off the truck there was a line of people waiting to talk to me. I had the most amazing conversations and was able to pray with so many people. I remember thinking at the end of the night, "I think I could do that again."

Fast forward years later: I have faced so many situations when the preacher scheduled for the night cancels at the last minute. I have literally five minutes to prepare before I have to deliver a message, sometimes to a rowdy crowd. The Lord always comes through and amazes me at what He speaks through me. How different things would be if I would have given into the fear that grasped me at first. I could have justified all my feelings and never have stepped on that truck, but then I never would have experienced the intimacy of the Holy Spirit the way I did that night and the way I do countless times I take the mic. I would have never grown in that way. It's the same whenever I say no to fear and take the risk of speaking to someone about Christ. It's the same whenever you say no to cooperating with fear and instead step into the Kingdom perspective of the living, all-sufficient God.

I was going to go for a run, as I do that for exercise. I walked to the park which is close to my house, I did a few stretches and used the playground equipment for some sit ups and chin ups. A mother was there with her kids. It was early in the morning so there was no one else around. She was super friendly and chatty. She initiated conversation and I listened half heartedly as I did my thing. I was kind and polite. After about ten minutes I was ready to go on my run and said goodbye. As I ran, listening to my worship music, I clearly heard the conviction of the Holy Spirit. "*Val, if this was a planned evangelism night, you would have jumped at the chance to start a spiritual conversation with that lady.*" I felt very uncomfortable, not because I felt godly sorrow at my lack of action but because this was nearly in my own backyard. What if the lady lived nearby? What if I'd feel obligated to continue a relationship with her? What if I see her around town? What if she asks for my phone number and becomes clingy? While running and wrestling with the Lord, I prayed, *"Well Lord, what would I say to her if I went back? What do You see about her?"* The Lord began to give me pictures of her heart. She truly wanted to do what was right and she wanted truth, and I saw that she wanted to do good things. An image of her doing some sort of exercises came to my mind. The Spirit also showed me that I was to pray for something in her life that was causing her to be in turmoil. After thirty minutes of running I was rounding the corner where I could turn left to go home or turn right and return to the park. I heard the Lord, *"I told you before, don't ask Me to show you things about someone if you are not going to obey."* I instantly turned right. By now the park was quite busy. There were kids and people talking and running all around. The woman was still there. I was totally sweaty and out of breath. If I would have just been more attuned to the Holy Spirit earlier I wouldn't have had to return like this. I sheepishly approached the woman panting. She was surprised to see me and said, "You're back!?" I wiped the sweat from my forehead and said, "Yeah, I had a good run." She replied, "Oh that's great. Good for you, how long did you go for?" I knew I could either continue in small talk or make a decision to dive in spiritually. "Thanks, I went about thirty minutes." Just do it, Val! "But while I was running, I was praying and God showed me some things about you." She again looked surprised and said, "Oh wonderful! That's so nice. I'm very spiritual, I do yoga." I was about to open my mouth to address that comment but I sensed the Holy Spirit saying "No, just speak what I showed you." So I did. She listened intently. She began to cry and asked, "Can I hug you?" I, of course, said yes, sweat and all. She shared with me she had just received a phone call earlier that morning before she came out to the park. Her mom, who lived in India, had cancer for the second time. It was stage 4. She had to make a decision whether to fly to India immediately as well as advise her mother what medical procedures to take. I listened to her concerns and fears regarding the ramifications of the choices she had to make. I shared with her that I believed in a God who heals, Jesus Christ. He knew what she was going through and that's why He wanted to send me over to her. I asked her if I could pray for her and for her mom. She accepted and when I was done thanked me over and over. I gave her my phone number . . . because I actually wanted her to have it. She never did call me and I never saw her again.

When it comes to evangelism there are so many excuses and inner dialogues as to why we don't apply the popular phrase - Just Do It! I think sometimes we in North America just don't get it, myself included. We want comfort and applause, recognition and convenience. We put value on the silliest of things and don't take time to value the most important things above ourselves. We think our gifts and abilities are not for evangelism. Again, you tell me your gift, I'll tell you how you can use it in evangelism.

As I have asked Christians to come join in evangelizing, discipling, providing administration, to sing worship on the streets, and I've asked. . .and asked . . . and asked . . . I listen to typical uneasy responses: "I'll pray about it", "Yeah, maybe, I'll get back to you", "I'm really busy right now with stuff in the church", etc., I've realized that many times it's actually not about busyness or about praying. It's a matter of the heart. With street ministry there is no applause, no lights, no platforms, or furthering personal aspirations. It's scary and has no worldly recognition. It's on a sidewalk, praising God, doing spiritual warfare, changing the atmosphere, ministering to hearts where you may or may not even get to know the impact of your efforts. In evangelism anywhere it means taking a risk. If you are blessed with the talent to sing and have a heart to worship, if you have any kind of skill set, gift, strength, ability, a heart to serve, if you simply have two ears to listen, or the resolve to simply be kind, then I urge you to find an evangelism team and be intentional with the gifts and talents the Lord has given you. There was a man sitting and listening to amazing worship that was happening on the downtown sidewalk. I sat down with him and introduced myself. His name was Max and he was Ethiopian. He shared his story. He was adopted by a Christian family as a child, who brought him back to Canada. He had been doing drugs for ten years and just recently came to the homeless shelter. He was now living for a period of time clean from taking drugs. He told me that he had mental issues and I asked, "Do you mind if I ask what are they?" He listed depression, anxiety, PTSD, ADD, ADHD, on and on. A doctor told him it was because of the things he saw and the trauma he experienced before he was adopted and this was how his body and mind had responded. His doctor just gave him pills to control it. He pointed to a window at the shelter and said it was his room. Four weeks ago he heard the music on a Monday through his open window. He hated and feared crowds so he couldn't bring himself to come down but still listened. The next Monday he was feeling very depressed and had high anxiety. He was ready to relapse, overdose and take his life. He had the drugs prepared and was ready to take them in his room, but then he heard singing from our team again. He told me the girl just kept singing. As he listened, her singing so affected him that it stopped him from taking the drugs. He just couldn't bring himself to doing it. He decided that even though he disliked crowds he would come down to us. As he came, I was preaching. He listened and stayed for the music which continued after. He had come three weeks in a row and had not relapsed. That was very encouraging for me to hear. We ministered to him and had much discussion.

I wonder what would have happened to that man if we had not had music that night or even just plain didn't show up. What if we decided it was too scary or we were too tired to be there? What if we felt we were not good enough or talented enough so we stayed home? What if the singer felt like her talent and ability was not an evangelistic gift?

At the transit station I was drawn to a gentleman standing waiting for the train. I pressed into the Holy Spirit for a few moments. I approached the man and asked, "Hi, how are you?! As I was standing over there, God drew my attention to you. He showed me a picture of you playing a guitar. I'm not sure if you play guitar or not (the man gave me no indication one way or another), but as you played you were pouring out your heart to God and it was like music to God, it revealed the openness and vulnerability of your heart before Him.

I'm not sure if that means anything to you." The man nodded his head and responded, "It does." That was all he said, so I asked, "Do you have any spiritual beliefs?" His train pulled up and he said, "Yes, I do." Then he let down his guard a bit, smiled and said, "Thank you for sharing that with me." Then he got on his train and left.

Now the way he responded was a bit of a vague response at first. I could have watered the message down or just smiled and left it, but I'm glad I followed up with the question.

We have to trust Jesus so much. Although we may never know what He's doing in a person, we resolve that we will still follow through in obedience, to go as far as we can in conversation. When it comes to revealing Jesus to people, put yourself aside and just do it.

CHAPTER 10

PLANS FOR WORLD DOMINATION

"There is nothing in the world or the Church - except the church's disobedience - to render the evangelization of the world in this generation an impossibility." - ***Robert Speer***

I could see a man sitting on a bench. I stopped and wanted to listen to the Lord before approaching him. I got a quick picture in my mind of a white pearl necklace being placed around his neck. I didn't know what it meant but went to approach him. There is always a moment of decision where I choose to throw away fear and push myself to follow through. When I approached him he looked skeptical, like I was going to try and sell him something. I said, "Hello, how's your night going? My name is Val and as I was walking toward you the Lord gave me this picture about you." He looked at me as if I was the strangest person. I sent a quick, silent prayer for God to give me some revelation as I began to talk, "It was of Jesus putting a necklace of white pearls around your neck . . . (and then instantly, as the words came out, I knew what it meant) . . . the pearls were things of God's kingdom, things like joy, peace, and love that only come from God. He was giving the things of His kingdom to you, but you must decide to receive it. If you do, these things will be placed upon you to have and keep. Yet, the choice is up to you." The man thought this was really interesting and he shared with me that he has been reading the Bible and researching Christianity for some time now, he was carefully considering it but had not been ready to receive it. I always find it fascinating when the Lord shows me something about a person that I didn't know before and it becomes an amazingly accurate message for them. I found out his name was Henry. I asked him what was holding him back. He said he just couldn't bring the scientific viewpoints together with biblical viewpoints on the origin of the earth. As well, there were many things in his life that would not coincide with Christianity. He was quite intelligent and we discussed many things regarding science and Christianity and how they coincided with one another. Henry then told me a definition of sin he liked. It went something like: Sin is the failure to thrive. I asked him where he had heard that from and he responded it was from an author who wrote horror novels. I laughed and said that perspective and source were interesting but not very biblical. I explained to him the biblical definition of sin, to miss the mark, and what Jesus did. I shared many verses in the Bible so he would know the truth about the decision of coming into a relationship with God that he was actually trying to make. He mentioned that he had had a few supernatural experiences and he didn't know what to make of them. I told him God was getting his attention. Henry told me he just kept asking God to show up and give him a sign. It seemed every time he would get one he could somehow explain it away, which made him doubt that there was actually a God. I smiled "Yes, and then God highlights you to a complete stranger who tells you about a picture from God that completely fits where you're at in your spiritual journey." He smiled and slowly said, "Hmmm, good point." We talked more about having a relationship with God. I offered him prayer and he said he thought prayer was best done privately. I respected his wishes and did not pray right then for him but I also explained that prayer was talking to God and could be done anywhere, anytime and that I would pray for him later in the week. "Well, only at your convenience", he responded. "Prayer is not necessarily something convenient. Just like communication in all relationships, prayer is a choice, as is the relationship with God." He processed that and said he would need to think about his choice. I closed by saying, "That is wise. It is the most important decision you will ever make. Don't wait too long."

I had a friend once say to me, "It's going to be so awesome when Jesus comes back. Why are we as Christians so afraid of the end times when we know what it'll bring?" My response was, "Well, it probably has something to do with persecution like the world has never known and you know, maybe getting beheaded for our faith in Jesus." (Rev 20:4) We laughed, but not because it's funny, but rather in a nervous sort of way. Many believers don't count the cost and the scriptures do say that many will fall away from their faith and not follow Jesus (Matthew 24:10-12, 1 Timothy 4:1-3). I know that in our present physical, natural realm as we look at our fallen world, things look pretty bleak. We as believers are and will be hated by the world as it inevitably falls into moral decay. We will certainly struggle with holding onto hope.

When shopping, I saw a shiny notebook at a bookstore that had the words, "Plans For World Domination" on the cover. I instantly thought of Jesus' plans of bringing His Kingdom to reign in full on the earth. How exciting and honoring it is that we have been trusted with the insight and knowledge of what the God of the entire world, universe and beyond, is planning to do. As co-heirs with Christ, we are invited to join Him in bringing His Kingdom on earth now. We get to *bring* light into the darkness. We get to *be* light in the darkness. It doesn't depend on our race, economic status, education, gender, age, talents, abilities, or gifts. As believers we get to be children of God. I thank God for the opportunity to evangelize everywhere, whether it be in a distant country or region. I love that I can also be on mission every week, in various areas of my city, in fact, every day.

So with a smile, I bought the notebook, inwardly giggling as I bring it to meetings wherever I go. As eyes sweep over it and faces try not to show puzzled expressions, I wait for an opportunity to respond to any comment. You see, if the words are read from a worldly, fleshly point of view, it may seem arrogant, power hungry and ridiculous. Yet from a spiritual viewpoint they should be inspiring words and challenge us to rise up to be the person God created us to be. We should be so aware of our identity and what we carry spiritually that when Jesus says in Matthew 5:14, *"You are the light of the world"*, we believe it. When He says in verse 16 *"Let your light shine before men"*, we do it.

After a long, powerful conversation about the Lord, I prayed over a gentleman. When I was done, he asked if he could pray for me. I knew he was a Christian, just struggling, so I said yes. He prayed a beautiful prayer and then during it he said an interesting thing, “Lord, I can see a white light in Val’s eyes and I know it is Your Spirit in her.”

Another time, while I was standing among a crowd on the streets listening to someone share about the gospel, a lady looked at me and said, “You have good energy”. Surprised and not surprised, I responded, “It’s the Holy Spirit in me. It’s Jesus you sense.” I smiled. The lady and the people around her looked quizzical but accepted my answer as I turned my attention back to the preacher.

One night during an evangelistic outreach, I grabbed the pizza plates and began handing them down the line, greeting people as I went. When I came to one man he said, “Why are you so joyful?” I laughed. There were many around us listening and I said, “Jesus!” I could see he was actually really serious. He said, “That’s what I thought. . . .I’ve been watching you and I can see there’s joy in you. It’s different, and I want it.” I studied his face and said, “Seriously, if it wasn’t for Jesus I would not have joy. The joy in me is not because of circumstances. If it wasn’t for God, life’s trials would have destroyed me and I would not be smiling.” He nodded and said, “I believe in God and know Jesus is Christ. I’m trying so hard but I need that. I need what you have.”

Still another time in a conversation, I was talking to a man and woman who were living together. One claimed to be a Buddhist and the other a Christian. I was passionately discussing with them scripture and truth. As we discussed many things one of their friends spotted them and came over to greet them. After I was introduced, the friend said to me, “Wow, you are glowing! Whatever you’re doing, I want some!” I was taken aback and then laughed, “Well, it’s the Holy Spirit.”

Now, just ask my family, it is clear that I am not always glowing! I have many weaknesses, flaws and failures. However, I find it amazing that people sense the Spirit of God inside of a person. I wonder how many times this happens without us ever being aware. I wonder what it would do for the identity and life of believers if they could “see” what they look like in the spiritual realm. How do we look to the demons, to the angels, and what are we radiating to people? What if we could see the light of the Holy Spirit within ourselves? On the opposite side, what if we could see what heaviness, doubt, fear, anxiety, despair, etc., look like on us when we cooperate with it? Does it blanket us, does it cause us to look dim, or dark, or repulsive, causing people to want to keep their distance from us but not knowing why? When we speak words of life what do they come out looking like? Are they like beams of light, sparkles, glowing air? What do words of condemnation, negativity and judgement look like? Are they dark drippings from our lips, ugly poison, or sharp arrows? I know if we could see, we would live differently. If you knew that you "glowed" with the light of the Holy Spirit for all the spiritual realm to see, and perhaps even all of mankind to see, would you live differently?

We need to understand more and more the presence that we are carrying and resolve to follow Jesus, no matter what the cost. He is coming back. He will bring justice and every knee will bow, every tongue will confess that Jesus is Lord. (Philippians 2:11) There will be judgement. All will be held to account, resulting in their eternal destiny sealed. Let's live intentionally, fully committed to the Lord in all that we think, say and do.

I have been thinking and praying about Wally all week. I've been thinking about Susan from last week in the hospital and Zander in his wheelchair being back home for Christmas and the transition with his family. I've wondered about many from past encounters - Norman, Ken, Fred, George, Verna, Darcy, Barb . . . their faces pass before me at times as I bring them to the feet of Jesus and wonder if I will get to see them in heaven. How incredible that will be. Then I turn to all the faces in front of me: family, neighbours, friends, acquaintances . . . our whole life is just one big mission field. Through Jesus, every conversation is an opportunity to minister and evangelize. The word minister is defined: to attend to the needs of someone, to tend to, care for, take care of and look after. As you will remember, to evangelize is to proclaim the good news, to reveal Jesus. People say we go as believers to do "ministry" and do "evangelism" and make it a compartment of life. I think we just need to live ministry and evangelism. Let's make it our life and live purposefully. Let's ask Jesus to enable and equip us to have faith, to obey Him and to cooperate with His plans for World Domination.

CHAPTER 11

THE WORLD NEEDS OUR HOPE

"If sinners be damned, at least let them leap to Hell over our dead bodies. And if they perish, let them perish with our arms wrapped about their knees, imploring them to stay. If Hell must be filled let it be filled in the teeth of our exertions, and let not one go unwarned and unprayed for."

- Charles Spurgeon

I decided to go to the public transit station platform. People were coming and going onto their train. In between trains there is about five to eight minutes where people wait, usually in silence. I've nicknamed this "fast-food gospel". There's no time to ask about the weather or get into a long conversation. When I first began, I simply gave the biggest, friendliest smile and said, "Hello, uh, hi, my name is Val, and I know this sounds weird but I love Jesus and I was wondering if I could pray for you for anything?" What shocks me is that 80% of people will say yes! I don't know why that just blows me away but I've come to realize the world just needs hope. The very first lady I said this to responded, "Oh I'm not religious . . . but my dad is in the hospital and has cancer. Can you pray for him?" Absolutely! When we get permission to pray for someone, oh what a powerful opportunity to pour out our hearts to the Lord on their behalf. It doesn't need to be lengthy, just full of truth and love. What a fantastic opportunity to get to ask the Lord to rend the heavens on behalf of someone He created, loves and desires to rescue.

It was a quiet night at the transit station and not too many were riding the train. As soon as I stepped onto the platform, I saw an elderly gentleman sitting on the bench. I said a friendly hello and asked him how he was doing. He told me he had just been visiting his wife in the nursing home. As he spoke his dentures rattled around in his mouth. He had such a thick accent that I had a hard time understanding him. His eyes were full of sincerity and . . . well, pain. I asked him why she was in there and he told me she had a blood condition that her mother and grandmother had. That's all I could understand. I asked him how her mind was. He did a thumbs down and mentioned that many times she didn't even know who he was. I acknowledged how difficult that would be. His train came and I quickly said, "I will pray for your wife." His eyes were so surprised and full of desperate hope. He literally fell into my arms and hugged me. He said, "Thank you, thank you so much for taking the time to talk to me and for caring." The train door started to close and he stuck his hand in between to open it up again so he could get on. He turned back to me and I called, "Jesus is the One who heals." He nodded, smiled and got on the train.

On a night when we were out intentionally ministering on the streets, I saw a man standing from afar and watching our team handing out food. He was curious and I was drawn to talk to him. Sam had a plan for suicide that night. Two weeks before he had overdosed and had an outer body experience where he smelled sulphur and experienced a darkness that terrified him. He said he was suffering from all the things he saw and did while serving in the military. He shared how many people he had killed during his time of military service. He felt like he had broken God's command "Do Not Murder" and therefore he was unforgiveable. He cried as he shared that he prayed everyday from the heart for God to forgive him but he felt like it was hopeless. The night was getting late, I had a team of people waiting for me to close the night as well as a street guy to clothe. I got really firm with Sam. "Sam, do you believe that God is God?" "Yes!" "Do you believe that whatever God says is true? Like, if God says something, then you are going to believe it no matter what?" "Yes!" He shared he had a

Catholic background and he seemed to know stories in the Bible. I said, "Ok, well do you remember Moses? He was a murderer. King David? He murdered an innocent man. The Apostle Paul? He murdered Christians and had them cruelly stoned to death. All of those men were murderers. All confessed, repented and asked for forgiveness. God gave them forgiveness and did amazing things in their lives. You are not worse than them, and if you ask for forgiveness, you will be freed from the guilt of these sins. God has promised this and will do this for you." He asked me why he had that encounter of smelling burning sulphur and experienced darkness? I asked him if he had ever surrendered his life to God, confessed that Jesus was Lord, believed that he died and rose again, and asked for forgiveness? Had he ever committed to having Jesus as Lord of his life, completely surrendering to Him? Sam thought about it for a few seconds and said, "I pray from the bottom of my heart to Him, but I have not done anything like what you said, not that way." So I explained to him that unless he did this, he was not saved and had not made a complete decision to serve God. He had not acknowledged that Jesus was the Son of God, nor had he entered into a relationship with God the way God requires. He was simply asking God for help when he needed it and then having nothing to do with Him when things went well. I quickly explained the cross and the gospel and asked him if he wanted to make that decision tonight, right now. He said he did! I asked him to talk to God with me. He sincerely and thoughtfully followed me in prayer to give his life to God through Jesus. As he asked for forgiveness, tears streamed down his face. We gave him a Bible and prayed over him. I cast off all spirits of heaviness, suicide, condemnation, despair, and self hatred. I declared him a new creation and a son of God, forgiven and free. I prayed that God would protect his life and that the seeds planted in him tonight would not be taken away or snatched by the enemy. I told him his life had just begun and that God had a lot of adventures in store for him. He smiled and exclaimed, "I'm excited". I laughed and said I was excited to see what God was going to do in his life. I encouraged him to come back next Monday and to tell me what he had read in his Bible. I was still a bit worried about him taking his life. Apparently he had a package of heroin in his backpack which I found out from a team member once I got into the motorhome. I marched back outside and called him. "Sam, do you have heroin in your backpack?"

He answered, "No, I just threw it in the garbage over there." I smiled, nodded and shouted, "Good job!"

I don't know if all that he told us was true about his past, nor if his conversion was sincere or not. I don't know if we will ever see him again, nor where he will spend eternity. However, I can't help but rejoice that lines were drawn in the sand spiritually that night and that he chose God. I have great expectation that the direction of his life was changed from suicide to hope that night.

Romans 15:13 says, " *May the God of hope fill you with all joy and peace as you trust in him, so that you may overflow with hope by the power of the Holy Spirit."*

Did you catch that? God *owns* hope. Hope has no other master. Our Father is the "God of Hope". In this passage we do not *choose* hope, we *choose* to trust God. This results in peace and joy which *produces* hope from the power of the Holy Spirit. If we are to bring hope to the world then we must trust God. Only then will we overflow with hope supernaturally. We must trust Him to speak to us and through us when we ask Him. Then we need to trust Him enough to believe what He has said and be obedient in sharing it with others.

Today I received a call from a gentleman who has been successful in his career but has struggled with much inner turmoil, especially since getting divorced and being estranged from his family. He has struggled with alcohol, has gone through the AA program a few times and is 95% clean. Today he relapsed and was in the depths of despair. I spoke to him about his value in Jesus' eyes and Who God was. He wept, shared his hopelessness and suicidal, emotional state. Then he said something that surprised me, "I'm sorry I'm calling you, Val, I just . . . I just had no one else I could call. I was thinking about that night when I met you in the darkness (during street ministry) and after speaking to you, you gave me such hope. I just knew I needed to call."

The lost are at the core of my heart but not because I'm naturally this way. In the flesh I actually have a "suck it up, buttercup" attitude that flares quite often. I have to ask the Lord to let me see people the way He sees them. The lost are at the core of my heart because they are the core of Jesus' heart. That's why He gave His life for them. You and I have been one of them. He pours His love for the lost into us, and then out of us to them. I have become more and more grieved, even devastated over what a person can become: rebellious, proud, wild, unpredictable, tempered, depressed, full of anxiety, hopeless, angry, evil, numb, etc. - all out of pain, brokenness and ungodly choices. I know that's not who they want to be. It's not as if as a child they dreamed of having those things enter their life. Nor is it who they need to be in the future. Only, only, because of Jesus can they be free from these things and have the fruits of the Spirit flow out of them. This moves me to act out of intense compassion, love, and urgency to hold out Jesus to people. He is the ONLY One who can heal, who can bring freedom, who can redeem. If we, as people in the Kingdom of God, really believed that God can do this, then we would not be able to stop ourselves from evangelizing. It would be our very life!

Our team had just finished our outdoor Christmas celebration that we put on every year for those who are without families or homes. I was bent down cleaning up and I heard, "Do you remember me?" I looked up and it took me a few seconds as I studied the familiar face. "Dan?!" I shockingly exclaimed. A grin came on his face, "You remember me!" I had thought he may be dead. I hadn't seen him for two to three years. He looked much older than last time. His hair was grey and cut short. He was dirty as always, no teeth in the front and rotting ones in the back. His hands were like I remembered, huge, red and swollen. He had a bag of bottles in one hand and all his belongings in a backpack on his back. I found out he had been in prison. He told me he really liked prison and it was better than being out of prison. We chatted and I asked if he was still selling drugs and doing drugs. He sheepishly said yes. I studied him while we talked. I saw what I have always seen in him; a gentleness and sweetness underneath all the mess and yuck. He rarely looks a person in the eyes. He was not on drugs or anything so he was clear minded at this moment. He told me he was out and about biking and realized it was Monday. Then he thought, "I wonder if that group still comes to that spot on Monday nights and if that woman is there". So he came. I was thrilled to think he remembered our group and me. I realized it had only been a couple weeks ago that he had come to my mind and I had prayed about him, wondering if he was dead. Prior to that, I hadn't thought of him for months, if not years. The back story is this: I met Dan about four years ago one summer Monday after I had preached off a pickup truck in the downtown core. He approached me and told me he really wanted to follow Jesus and give his life to Him but asked if he could do that and still sell drugs, because that was his way of life. At that time, I told him no, he couldn't. I explained that to repent was to turn away and change. That he had to count the cost of following Jesus and be willing to give up the things that were against God. I said it would be like slapping Jesus in the face after what He did on the cross for him by saying, "I want your benefits but not anything else". We had a good talk and then he left. I saw him every once in a while after that. He would bike by and stop to talk, usually while on a drug run. I would put my hand on his shoulder and pray for him out loud, knowing there were drugs in his backpack that he was going to deliver. I'd often stick a Bible in his backpack and give him a big hug. He shared with me many things over the different encounters. He grew up in a small town. His mother got pregnant with him at age fifteen and in those days you needed to get married, especially in a small town. His dad and mom got married but it was a terrible marriage, full of alcoholism and abuse. His mother hated and resented the baby (Dan) as she blamed him for ruining her life. He was abused in many ways and the only time he ever remembers being told she loved him was one night when he was a young boy and his grandma burst into his room at two in the morning, dragging his mom by the hair. His grandma was yelling at his mom, "Tell him you love him! Tell him you love him right now!" Then his mom would fight back, "NO! I won't and I don't!" As a little boy he was frightened and startled as he watched his mom and grandma fight, both physically and verbally over this. Finally, his grandma threatened to throw his mom out of the house and his mom finally said, "Fine! I love you." and stomped out of the room.

He was always open to me praying for him and God continued to give me an agape love for him, as I saw something very special in him through the grossness of his appearance and lifestyle. The last time I saw him was two years previous. At that time his hair was long and stringy, sweat was pouring down his forehead, spit was dripping down his lip and he could not stand still. I knew he was on some sort of drug and for the first time I felt very uncomfortable with him. I called a male teammate to come and stand with me as I spoke with Dan. As Dan would speak he would come close to me and then back away and then close again. At one point when he was close and speaking, the drool on his lips projected as he spit out his words. Some landed straight onto my lips. I froze as I realized what just happened. I didn't want to move my lips or risk getting anything in my mouth. Within a few seconds my husband happened to walk by and I excused myself from Dan to grab my husband. "Get me some hand sanitizer right now!" I whispered. He looked at me confused as I talked oddly, trying not to move my lips too much. "I just got that guy's spit on my lips. Get me the hand sanitizer before I get it in my mouth!" He ran and got it, and I rubbed the sanitizer all over my lips. I sent up a quick prayer for God to protect me and thought, if Jesus could touch the lepers, then He could also protect me. I then resumed the conversation with Dan and prayed over him. That was the last time I saw him until now.

As he stood in front of me, he looked older and tired. He told me he had just turned fifty years old. I would have guessed he was in his seventies. He had absolutely no one in his life. I shared with him that I remembered what he told me about his childhood and his not so pleasant life with his mom. He looked down, paused and smiled gently, "I told you because nothing phases you and you are only one who believes in me." I was totally shocked and saddened to hear that I am the only one, especially since I don't see him much nor am I involved in his life. I suddenly remembered the very first conversation we had. "Dan, do you remember when I first met you? I was preaching and you came up to me and asked me if you could have Jesus and still sell drugs." He shook his head and quietly said, "Oh man, that was stupid of me. Of course I can't, I'm sorry I asked that." I jumped in, "Dan, I have something I need to tell you. Look at me!" As he raised his eyes and looked into mine, I took his face in both my hands and said, "I was wrong. I'm sorry. The truth is, you can have Jesus. You don't have to stop selling drugs, you don't have to DO anything. All you have to do is make a decision and choice that you want Jesus to forgive you. You must believe He is the Son of God and surrender your life to Him. It's a free gift. All other religions say you have to do something or be good enough. God said He did it all and made the way. Jesus will do the changing after you make the choice. As you follow

Jesus, your desires and lifestyle will change but the change doesn't have to come before the choice." Dan looked at me and said, "I know I'm not good enough, I know I'm not worthy. That seems so . . . . simple." I smiled, "I know . . . God made it simple." As we continued to talk, I explained the gospel more and more. He felt like he could not receive God's love or mercy because of how bad he had been and still was. I spoke with him further about the truth, what the Bible said, and asked if I could pray for him. He gladly accepted and I prayed. He was very moved by the prayer. I gave him a big hug. He asked if I had any food. I ran into the ministry motorhome to see if there was anything. I found a leftover Christmas gift bag and grabbed it. When I gave it to him, he was so happy and said it was the only gift he had received this year for Christmas. I told him to come back and see me again. I told him that God loved him and had poured out His love for him in me, that I could see a gentleness and sweetness in him. I encouraged him to make a choice and we parted. I was so thankful to see him again and will be battling in prayer for him.

It is not that I have some sort of valuable, long term relationship or even spend much time with all those that I meet. I don't do life with them, nor have I poured hours into discipling them. I just ask the Holy Spirit what He wants me to say to them and what He sees in them. Then I speak words of truth, life, hope and love into them. I choose to see them in the Spirit and not the flesh. Unbeknownst to me, words I have uttered at times have gone down to deep parts within some of the people I talk to and are planted.

Could it be that it really isn't me at all that they connect to but the Spirit within me? I am fully convinced it is Jesus in me that they sense and that causes them to trust. It is Jesus who sees and knows them. It is the love of Jesus they feel and remember. It is the hope of Jesus that makes them spiritually hungry for what I carry. If I took on the weight and responsibility of being the only one in their lives to truly care about them, it would be a very heavy burden. I would want to do more and get involved in a greater capacity. With the amount of people I meet and that I have in my life, I simply can't do that. I would become overwhelmed and exhausted. There is a time and place to get involved in people's lives and a time and place to direct them to others who can invest. This is discipleship and should not be confused with evangelism. When we truly *see* people through the Holy Spirit and speak life, we give them hope for the future, for their lives, and direct them to a God Who is real, active, and loves them. This reveals Jesus to people.

A lady came to our team and asked for mittens and socks. I could only give her socks. We had no mittens left. She explained that her hands had gotten frostbite at one point and now they hurt very badly in the cold. I had a pair of mittens on my hands, took them off and gave them to her. I held her hands in mine until they warmed up. As we talked, she shared she had been married for twenty two years, had a very good life full of money and luxury. When her husband left her, things went downhill fast. I could tell by the look of her droopy eyelids that she used drugs. She wasn't on them while we talked, but the signs of her lifestyle were there. She said she had a boyfriend now who had a home but would leave her on the streets. He would just come pick her up when he wanted to be with her. Eventually she shared that she had been abused as a little girl by a family friend. Her father refused to deal with it and was still friends with the man to this day. Ugh! Such heaviness poured out of her with tears. I asked her if I could pray for her and she said yes. I prayed and afterwards she commented on some of the things I said that had resonated with her. She believed in God because she had overdosed multiple times and each time was revived. She believed God was keeping her alive. She also believed in karma. Two other ladies joined me and we shared with her about forgiveness and healing through Jesus. We wrapped a scarf around her and put a toque on her head. I hope she comes back.

Four of us decided to go share Jesus with whoever God put in our path. On our way we came across an older homeless man, completely drunk, sitting on a bench. He looked like he was talking on a phone but there was no phone in his hand so I said, "Hey sir, are you okay?" He told us to leave him alone and he was fine. So we left. On our way back he was on the cement sidewalk, with a bloody gash on his forehead. He had urinated on himself as well. We gathered near him and crouched down. He was scared, completely drunk and incoherent. I asked him what happened but he responded by asking us to leave and to not take his stuff. He was terrified of us. He was so drunk he couldn't pick himself up. He said he was trying to get to the homeless shelter. We called 911. One team member corresponded with them on the phone while we tried to comfort him. He did not want us to call an ambulance and he kept freaking out. Another team member tried to sing to him which calmed him for about thirty seconds and then he begged her to stop. I prayed over him. Finally the EMS came and we left. I thought, "When he was a boy or even a young man, if he could have seen himself that night, he would have been horrified and made different choices." It made me wonder about what choices I am making now that in five, ten, twenty-five years how will I reflect on them, will I regret my choices or be thankful for them?

This week, an unknown number texted my phone, looking for, well, sexual services. I have no idea how the person got my number. I let the person know that he had the wrong number. However, ten minutes later, he texted again asking me to outline my service options and if he could call me. I know this is a very common method for prostitution or escorts to connect with clients. I was about to delete the message and block him but then I thought, no, this is a great opportunity. I texted back: "Your loneliness won't be filled by sex. It'll leave you empty over and over. You need Jesus. He can set you free from your addiction and heal the pain that is causing you torment."
Ha Ha, I didn't hear anything from him after that.

May the Lord increase His Spirit in you and me, flowing through us and from us. I am so disheartened by the ways of the world, but so passionate about Jesus. Let's get passionate about Jesus. Fan the flame, fast, pray, go on a retreat to seek the Lord, read His word, engage in worship, get ministered to, forgive, serve others and get free from the things that hinder you. Do whatever it takes to revive love for God and love for people. Understand when Jeremiah says, *"His word is in my heart like a fire, a fire shut up in my bones". (Jeremiah 20:9)*
Let this be our heart cry.

"For the sake of a world that so desperately needs Jesus." - Henry Schorr

May God be glorified in all we say and do.

CHAPTER 12

BE READY

"It is the great business of every Christian to save souls. People complain that they do not know how to take hold of this matter. Why, the reason is plain enough; they have never studied it. They have never taken the proper pains to qualify themselves for the work. If you do not make it a matter of study, how you may successfully act in building up the kingdom of Christ, you are acting a very wicked and absurd part as a Christian." - Charles Finney

It was near the end of the evening and a new team member needed to go to the train station. Knowing that another part of our team was still at that location, I walked with her the couple blocks over to it, and planned on walking back with the team. Right at the station there was a crosswalk. I saw the team crossing the street towards us and the lady I was with said goodbye, crossing at the same time. There was a bit of a crowd of people crossing towards me. I looked at the team members and said a big, friendly "Hello!" There was a man directly in front of them who greeted me back with an equally friendly, "Hello!" I shifted my gaze and in a split second knew he thought I was greeting him. He thought I was looking at him. I paused for a moment, then decided to go with it. "Hi . . . How are you tonight?" He said, "I'm good how are you?" He looked very curious as to why I was greeting him. I realized my team members thought I knew him and he had no idea that my team members were behind him. I asked him, "Uh, are you going this way?" He said he was so I began to walk with him, my team members trailing behind in their own conversation. Ha ha, I didn't have the heart to tell him I wasn't really saying hello to him so I just awkwardly said, "I'm out praying for people, can I pray for you for anything?" He thought this was very interesting and said, "Yes, you can." I asked if there was anything specific and he surprised me by saying his ankle had pain and he needed healing. I told him I would pray for him right then. This again surprised him and he agreed to let me. I crouched down and placed my hands on his ankle. I felt that familiar warm, hot feeling in my hands that I sometimes experience as I pray. When I was done I asked him how it felt. He said it felt better. I asked him if it felt completely better. He laughed and said it felt better but not completely better. So I told him I served a God of 100% healing, not partial and could I pray again. He told me it was okay, I didn't need to but I was already down again and began praying. When I was done he said it was actually feeling really good so I told him the Lord had begun a work and to pay attention to it. We kept walking and he asked what church I went to. I told him that it did not matter what church I went to, but what matters is that I loved Jesus. He told me he too loved Jesus. I was surprised and happy to hear that. I'm cautious to tell people what church I attend in certain conversations because I don't want it to come across that I'm recruiting members for my church, or that a certain church is my identity. I like to find out where they are coming from spiritually first in order to know how best to handle the conversation about it. He told me he went to an evangelical church and that he was from Germany. I was glad to hear it, yet a bit puzzled and asked, "Do you mean you moved here from Germany or you are just visiting?" He told me he just arrived the day before and would be leaving again on the weekend. He was downtown for work attending some conferences. Wow! I thought this was very cool, so I said, "Welcome to Calgary! You are my brother in Christ! How cool is it that God wanted to bless you tonight while you are here." He too was excited. His name was Martin and he had questions: Where did I work? How often did I do this? Would I be here more this week? What was the name of my church? Did I work for the church? I told him I do not have a career, that I am a mom of four children and I am married. I explained that I am in this area with others on Mondays. He thought this was amazing that I would approach a stranger and offer prayer. He thanked and hugged me. I told him to enjoy his stay and perhaps God wanted to get his attention to reveal something to him in his relationship with God. He went into the fancy hotel where he was staying and I went to find the team. I thought that was a pretty cool encounter, all starting from a misunderstood "hello".

One summer day, I was in a rush getting groceries with my toddler. As I walked out the grocery store doors to my car, I noticed there was an elderly lady waiting in a wheelchair at the curb to be picked up. As I went past her, a very small thought went through my mind that I should pray for her. I went to my car which was about fifty feet away and began the familiar wrestling conversation with the Lord. *"Lord was that You? Do you want me to pray for her? I don't know why she's in a wheelchair. Lord, it could be something major. If I pray for healing for her, will you heal her or will it be embarrassing if she doesn't get healed? Do you want me to pray for her healing or just for her in general? I have my toddler with me, I'm kind of in a hurry. This is really awkward now because I already walked by her. If I have to go back, well, she will think I'm weird . . ."* I scanned my situation. I was easily able to keep my eye on my vehicle so I put my toddler in the car seat, windows rolled down, gave her some snacks and toys then walked back to the woman. "Hello, how are you today?" She looked up a bit puzzled and said she was fine. I said, "I know this is really weird but when I came out a few minutes ago from the store, I just really felt like I heard God say that I was to pray for you. Do you mind me asking what happened that caused you to be in this motorized scooter?" She was polite and I found out that she was eighty-one years old. About six weeks before, she had been hit by a car that was backing up and broke her hip. The recovery was long and painful. She said it was extremely frustrating to be so confined and not be able to get around except by the handibus, which she was presently waiting for to come get her. She did not have a very warm personality but I realized she was processing my engagement with her. I asked her a few questions and empathized with her situation. I noticed in the distance that the handibus was pulling in the far end of the parking lot. So I quickly said, "Well, I really feel like the Lord wants me to pray for you before you get picked up, is it okay if I do that before your ride gets here?" She responded yes and so I put my hand gently on her leg and prayed over her and her injury. I said, "Amen" and the handibus pulled up in front of us. I smiled and was about to walk away when she grabbed my arm, "By the way dear, you heard right." Wow! Incredible confirmation and her words boosted my faith to not be so hesitant. I don't know what all was going on in her life but God does. We simply need to obey to reveal the Father to people.

On the streets during an outreach, people were going through the line to get food. I stood half way down the line and greeted each one as they came by me. During this particular season there were so many new people living on the streets, most of whom I do not know. As I greet them, I'm listening to Holy Spirit, I'm watching and waiting for the Lord to highlight one to me. One man stuck out to me (I never know why) and I started walking down the line with him. Once he got his pizza, we stood and chatted. I waved a new team member over to join us. I learned that this man, Hank, had not been at the shelter long, he had his own room (paying resident), and was from Michigan. He had a chunk of money saved up to have his own place, but his twenty year old daughter back home needed a car and so he bought her one. She didn't know that by doing this he had to go live at the homeless shelter for a bit. As I asked questions, I found out that his sister was murdered by her husband through domestic violence. That had been very hard to deal with. He was struggling with alcohol. He went to a party one evening where a bunch of guys beat him up pretty bad and he was hospitalized. He had a bad concussion and was still dealing with symptoms, so much so that he had been put on disability and hadn't been able to work. I asked him why the alcohol. Hank told me it was cheap and a way to deal with the depression and the PTSD that he was dealing with. He shared that he used to go to church, a Pentecostal one, but through life's difficulties just kind of stopped and hadn't thought much about it since. We talked about Jesus a bit, then I asked Hank if he had ever actually decided to surrender to Jesus and make Him Lord of his life. He said yes, he had so I put my hand on his shoulder and told him, "Then you are my brother in Christ. I am your sister and the Lord has sent you here tonight. God drew my attention to you and He wants to let you know that He knows all that is going on in your life." Hank appreciated that. A team member had joined us and wanted to read him a scripture. It was about sin in a person's life. Hank thought and responded, "It is funny you read that. Just two days ago I was standing in the shower thinking and just a faint thought crossed my mind about God. I thought, 'I've done so much, I have so much sin, how would God ever want to have anything to do with me?'" Instantly, the Lord gave me the words to respond to Hank's thought. I shared with him that there was a time in my life where I had asked for forgiveness for a sin in my life. I was so grieved about it that I'd ask God for forgiveness and then a couple days later ask again, then a week later, and again in another week and again a month later and on and on. Then one time the Lord said to me very vividly, *"Val, when you ask me for forgiveness, when do I forgive you? Is it immediately? Is it in a couple of hours? A week? A month?"* I was totally taken aback with the question. I answered, *"Well, I guess, it would be immediately."* He answered back, *"Then why haven't you received it?"* Hank listened intently and nodded his head. I began to talk to him about the word sin. "We often think of sin as doing bad things and then needing to be punished for them. But the actual Greek word for sin means 'to miss the mark'. We have missed the mark in what God has said is right and wrong according to His standards. When we repent, we are saying that we are not only regretting what we've done, but want to turn away from it and live differently; we are coming back into agreement with God in what He says is good and evil. He forgives us and because of Christ, looks at us as pure and holy in His sight." Hank's eyes brightened and he said, "That was so beautifully and clearly explained, thank you!" I asked him if he had a Bible. He said yes and I encouraged him to read it in order to clean his mind and put truth into the deep parts of his heart and soul. I asked him if we could pray for him. We prayed and then I told him, "We give hugs around here!" He received hugs and I encouraged him to continue coming on Mondays to hang out with his family in Christ because we'd love to talk more with him.

I was sitting at the food court in a mall when a janitor came walking by and began mopping the floors. I felt strongly that I needed to talk to him. The Lord gave me pictures in my spirit right away for him. I saw him holding rosary beads, then dropping them into the dirt and getting covered up. Jesus was in front of him. I was a bit puzzled and asked the Lord why the rosary beads in the dirt? Was the man covering them or was Jesus covering them? The Lord showed me that the rosary beads were precious to the man and held much value, but Jesus wanted to show him they were nothing but symbols, and instead He wanted the man to behold Jesus as precious and valuable. I walked over to him and said, "Excuse me, I was just wondering, are you Catholic?" Yeah, I know, kind of blunt. He said "Yes I am! I am a very pure Catholic. I go to St. Mark's." That was so cool for me to hear because the picture the Lord gave me was so applicable. I explained it to him and he received it well. We talked about Jesus and the importance of a relationship with Him and not just following a bunch of rules. He shared with me that he was now divorced and his wife had custody of their kids. He asked me for prayer for them and his involvement with them. He did get to see them every weekend and financially supported them. He had other staff janitors working around him and he did not want me to pray right then as he was supposed to be working. So I once again repeated the message about valuing Jesus over symbols, and we parted as he continued working.

I was on my own in a mall which was actually pretty fun as I had no distractions and could just focus on who the Lord wanted me to talk to. The mall was pretty quiet as it was almost closing time. I went to a store and began a conversation with the large tattooed guy at the counter. I inquired about some of his products then asked him about the tattoo on his arm, "Hey, I love finding out why people get their tattoos and what they mean. I'm curious about the one that is of the knife with a skull on it and the word 'hope'. That seems like a strange combination. Tell me what it means." He was more than happy to share with me about it. He told me that the basic meaning is that sometimes hope hurts. The handle on the knife had spikes and so when you grabbed it, it would cut your hands. I studied it and said, "Hmm, interesting, but, like, what does the skull mean? To me it symbolizes death and well, evil. So why is it on the knife with hope?" He shrugged and said, "Yeah, that's what the skull would mean, I just think it's cool and wanted to have more skulls in my tattoos. I try to put skulls on several of them." He proceeded to show and explain to me every tattoo that had a skull in it. At this point there was another customer who was examining the stuff around us and listening in. It was sort of a distraction and I knew the conversation would be over if he went to serve him. I ignored the customer and kept the conversation going. "Tell me why you have the tattoo that says 'moms', not just mom?" He explained his mom and dad got divorced. His dad remarried and his mom remarried another woman. I responded, "Wow, how was that as a kid to experience such a shift?" He said to be honest, the divorce was worse than when he realized his mom was a lesbian. He shared a bit about that situation. I continued to get a tour through the rest of his tattoos and at this point the male customer was standing right beside me looking at items in the glass countertop. I could tell he wanted the cashier's attention but I felt like I had got so far in the conversation and I hadn't yet been able to turn it spiritual. Even though it was awkward with the customer beside me, I said, "So do any of your tattoos have any spiritual significance?" He said no. I asked him if he had any spiritual beliefs. He told me he was raised a Catholic because of his dad but only went to church on Easter and Christmas and it meant nothing else. The customer was ready to make a purchase and we were all aware my conversation needed to end. As I departed I said, "Well, thanks for sharing with me about your tattoos, it was fascinating . . . I just really sense that you have a resiliency about you." He was a bit surprised and said thank you. I walked out of the store and felt frustrated that was all I was able to say. The guy was super friendly and talkative. I just needed a bit more time. I walked around the mall a bit and after five minutes saw the customer leave the store I had been in. I felt like the Holy Spirit was giving me words to say to the cashier so even though it was weird, I went back to the store. He had already closed the store and was vacuuming. So I pushed aside the metal curtain on the storefront to make a small opening and called to him, "Excuse me," He turned off the vacuum, came over to me and I continued, "Uh, I just again wanted to say thanks for sharing with me about your tattoos but as I've been walking in the mall I just felt like I needed to come back. Sooo . . . I love Jesus and He wanted me to tell you that He knows you deep down. He sees the depths of who you are and He knows the areas nobody knows about. He loves deep parts of you. He also wants me to tell you 'it wasn't Him'. Uh, yeah, I don't know what that means, but maybe you had a situation in the past that you just need to know, 'it wasn't Him' meaning, it wasn't God's fault. Lastly, you're precious to Him and He sees you." The man looked at me shocked and he stammered, “Okay thank you.” I smiled and said, “Have a good night,” and I walked away.

Our team was being the church without walls by singing, sharing testimonies, praying for people and serving in whatever way we could on a sidewalk. His name was Eric and he just happened to be walking by and asked what we were doing. He shared with me that he had been to many Christian churches and he enjoyed them. He had also worked with Christians. He told me he had one job where for hours every day he was in a basement with a Baptist, Pentecostal and a Jehovah Witness. I told him that sounded like the beginning of a good joke. We laughed. He said it was really interesting listening to them all debate. I spent the next hour with this fellow in spiritual conversation. I could have used him as an object lesson for Evangelism. He respectfully and sincerely asked me every typical question I have taught on. Things like: If God truly cares, why is there evil in the world? What happens to those people who live in far off places that never get to hear about Jesus or the Bible? How do we know the stories in the Bible are actually true? Why so many denominations? etc. He asked, I answered and we made our way through many issues. At one point he said, “I’m sorry, I shouldn’t ask so many questions, I don’t want to make you question your faith.” I laughed and said I love questions and that there weren’t many that I hadn’t heard before. It would also take a lot more to shake my faith than questions. He mentioned that he’s never been able to ask his questions to Christians before because it either makes them uncomfortable or fearful. The conversation gets awkward and he feels like he’s damaged their faith in some way or sometimes they get angry and defensive making the conversation tense. I sighed at the truth of his observation and assured him questions were good and important. At another point of the conversation he told me about his co-worker who was a young Christian guy that came to work on the oil rigs. They were a rough group. Eric told me the guys ridiculed the Christian guy for his faith mercilessly. The poor guy even cried one day because the crew was so aggressive. Eric felt bad for him and took him out for lunch to talk. The Christian told Eric he believed God was putting him through this to strengthen his faith and grow him. Eric gave me a funny look and said, “I don’t know if God would do that. I was thinking, ‘these guys have been terrible, maybe you should just quit and go home.’ ” I laughed as Eric told me things that Christians had said to him that didn't make sense. It was so insightful to hear his perspective. He said a Christian told him once that he didn't know what job to take so he sent out resumes. The job he got hired by was the one he believed God chose. He, therefore, believed God had spoken to him and put him at that specific job. Eric was puzzled as he thought that was a pretty normal way to get a job whether you're a Christian or not. How could a Christian think it was God speaking to them? Then he asked me straight out, "Does God talk to you?" It suddenly felt very difficult to share with him that yes . . . God does speak to me and how that looked. I think it was because I was trying not to freak him out, nor sound like a New Age - type religion and I found myself giving Eric shallow answers. Then finally I just said, "Okay, this may freak you out but God gives me . . . well, pictures in my mind, but it's different then just my mind, it's like an imprint in my spirit. And I know I'm not making them up, it's not just my imagination. He does speak to me in many other ways, too. Through having other people speak to me, through reading the Bible, 'highlighting' verses to me, and even through dreams. However, I always make sure that anything I think is from God also must be in alignment with the truths of the Bible. If it's not, I throw it away." Eric handled it pretty well and kept asking question after question. Finally the night was completely over and only a few team members were left who were going to ride with me back to the church. I asked him if I could pray for him and he said yes. I asked him if there was anything specific, he said his knee was hurting and he was concerned it was an old injury that had returned. I told him I would pray for healing but when it got healed he had to acknowledge it was God who did it. He agreed. I crouched down and put my hand on his knee and prayed. When I was done I asked how it was. Eric was a bit nervous and said it felt really good. I pushed further and he said it was an 8/10 of pain and had gone to a 7/10. So I prayed again. Eric encouragingly told me I "had done real good" and it was feeling better. I said, "Eric, I don't want you to feel any pressure. I don't need to defend God or think my prayer is 'working'. My God heals. But He is also not a genie in a bottle. He chooses, when, where and how. I don't need to make excuses for God. So be honest, did the pain change?" He laughed and admitted, "No, it didn't". I laughed with him and told him to pay attention to it today and tomorrow. I continued to pray over Eric's life. When we were done I encouraged him to come back next week when our team would be back.

My conversation with Eric was so full of topics that clarified for him many things he had been pondering. I hope we as Christians can always be ready and available to answer such questions. We have to be so willing to examine how we make others feel. Do we make them fearful to ask questions about our faith? Are we fearful to be asked? Are we angry and defensive, causing tension? Do we put pressure on them to say what we want them to say? I know I've been and done all these things at one time or another. It is simply not the way Jesus engaged the lost. Yet it is very common.

Barna Group research recently came out with a study that revealed that Christian Millennials felt conflicted about evangelism—and almost half believe it is wrong to share their faith, especially with someone of a different faith with the intent to convert them.

I believe these findings are for a number of reasons: cultural spiritual climate, influence from media and education, lack of training and modelling from the church, to name a few. I think a big part of this is that when we do evangelism the way Eric has experienced it, it makes him feel bad and scared to ask the questions. Millennials, as well as all generations, hate making people feel anything negative and hate having negative feelings themselves from a situation. So the solution for them is to not share their faith at all. It's better to avoid the topic than to cause damage to the relationship or feelings.

It is true we can't control the emotions of others and how they react, nor should we fear, take responsibility or avoid what gets stirred up in them. If through our evangelism, we as believers <u>respond</u> with fear, get angry and defensive, or pressure people to say and do what we want, then we are doing it wrong. Christians sometimes get very nervous of other Christians bringing up God to someone as they think it will be a horrible experience. In the Bible, when the tax collectors, the prostitutes and the thief on the cross had an encounter with Jesus, it wasn't a horrible experience. Ha ha, that was saved for the religious leaders who leaned on knowledge, rules, judging and controlling others, and being self-righteous. Unbelievers often felt valued, loved, and joy in the engagement. I definitely am not saying that unbelievers won't ever feel negative when the gospel gets brought up. We know that at times people get angry, defensive and offended. I do, however, think that we as believers, need to learn to be unoffendable, be willing to answer messy questions, receive challenging statements and questions, resist temptation to get angry or arrogant, and then remember that we are carrying the Presence of God and get to bring to the lost an encounter with Jesus who works powerfully through us.

I was getting a massage from a new therapist. I haven't had a massage for a very long time but recently had a running injury I wanted to get worked on. As I lay there I began to think about how many massage therapists have told me they often can sense things about the person they are massaging. They have told me they can often tell if a person has sadness, or darkness, peace, turmoil, joy, etc. It just oozes out of a person as they work on them in such close contact and many therapists will do some sort of a physical shaking off after working on someone because it affects them emotionally and physically. These are unbelievers who have told me this. I wondered what I was "emitting" to the lady massaging me. Did she sense the fruits of the Spirit or just things of my flesh that I wrestled with? I began to pray and ask the Holy Spirit to radiate from me so that the lady would feel something spiritually amazing from the Lord's presence in and on me. I asked the Lord if there was anything He wanted to show me about her, since I had ample time to listen to what the Holy Spirit wanted to say. I wrestled with it a bit as I wondered how awkward that would be for this therapist as she couldn't just walk away from me if she didn't want to hear what I had to say. The Lord gave me an instant picture of Jesus handing her a bouquet of flowers, with many blue ones in it. He was showing me that by me sharing with her a message from the Lord, it was enabling Jesus to give her a bouquet of flowers, spiritually. The Lord showed me a few pictures and the meaning behind some of them. I shared them with her. I wasn't able to see her face, or read her facial reactions to what I was saying. She thanked me for sharing and was silent. I was hoping to have more conversation with her about it. The Holy Spirit gave me such peace, however, and I sensed I was to just be silent and let it roll around in her head and heart.

- Are you ready to give an answer to the hope that lies within you? (1 Peter 3:15)
- Are you ready to let your light shine before others? (Matthew 5:16)

Be Ready.

CHAPTER 13

OUR DEAR BROTHERS AND SISTERS

"The greatest blessing in the whole world is being a *blessing." - Jack Hyles*

Oh how I love to ask the Lord who He wants me to speak to and, after stepping out in faith, find out it is a brother or sister in Christ! How loving our Father God is that He would love His children so much that He would send one to go encourage, strengthen and build up another even though they are strangers. I don't know about you, but if some stranger approached me and told me they loved Jesus, that God had highlighted me to them and they had a message to give me - I'd feel very valued and loved. I would, of course, test, weigh and measure their words. I have found when I do this for others, the Holy Spirit bears witness and lands the words straight on their hart so that they end up in tears or with immense joy. The Spirit in me is the same Spirit in them and we spiritually recognize it.

I told a team member I was really drawn to a man that was standing over in a corner away from people by a wall at the train station platform. He was tall and looked a bit intimidating. We took a minute to hear from Holy Spirit. I got the word *"hope"* very strongly, and then a picture of hanging chains and a sword. He had his headphones in his ears so I tapped him on the shoulder. I introduced myself and said, "I know this may seem weird, I love Jesus and as I was standing over there He drew my attention to you. Would it be okay if I share with you what I believe God would like to say to you?" He grinned, told me his name and mentioned that his mom was a Pentecostal but that he didn't go to church. He explained that at one time he had a very personal and active relationship with Jesus. I shared with him the word "hope" and that God would equip him to get rid of the things in his life that were holding him back. He responded by telling me that things at his job hadn't been going well and in fact he was just thinking about it moments before I came along, and was feeling very worried. He shared he was actually baptized at the church I attend in 2002! However, he had found that he had been in a desert ever since. He reads scripture every day, prays, and he even shares Christ with others. Once I heard all this I decided to share with him the images I received of the chain and sword. My teammate added, "The sword is your tongue, your words." We asked if we could pray for him and he said yes. As I prayed, I felt like I needed to declare it was the end of the desert season and time for a new season spiritually, to rise up; a time to listen to the voice of Christ calling him. God was getting his attention to go to new depths of spiritual intimacy. We hugged him and he departed very grateful and full of hope.

How different the Bride of Christ would be if we would be so attuned to the Spirit, aware of who He is drawing our attention to and willing to speak what the Lord lays on our hearts. We would unite in comradery. Jealousy and judgement among believers would be disarmed. We would be strengthened and refreshed by offering one another a drink of living water. We would know God's love at a different level.

I took a lady who wanted to learn how to evangelize to the train station area. As we walked on the platform I asked the Lord who we should talk to. He highlighted a woman to me. I could only see the back of her. The wonderful thing is that my companion was very attuned to God's voice and when I pointed out the woman I was listening to God about, she too had sensed God highlighting the same woman! The only picture and sense I received was like pieces of metal, sharpening on each other. I asked the Lord what it meant and the Holy Spirit revealed, *"She is sharp (mentally) and very smart. Go tell her I made her that way"* So not wanting to miss my opportunity before her train came, I approached her, introduced myself and the lady I was with. As I spoke, the Lord gave me a fuller revelation. "I love Jesus and as I was walking by He highlighted you to me. He showed me that you are very sharp, and very smart. He made you that way and He wants you to be confident in that. He has given you these things and loves that about you." She was surprised and smiled, "I love Jesus too! I'm a Christian, what are you?" We shared that we were Christians as well. She was so delighted and we joyfully interacted. I told her the Lord obviously wanted to bless her, His daughter. My companion then shared, "I actually was also shown a picture. I saw a daisy flower, that God delights in you, and the colour pink, that His Spirit rests upon you." We hugged her and she was so happy to hear from us. I said, "Well, as your sisters in Christ, can we pray for you?" Her name was Rhonda and she said yes so we both prayed over her.

When we were done she told us to not stop what we were doing and that this had made her day. She was actually a teacher at the nearby college (which fit with what God showed me) and was just on her way home. She also told us she couldn't wait to tell her sister about our encounter to encourage her. Her sister, Carol, had just been diagnosed with cancer and is trusting God to heal her. We said we would pray for Carol too. Rhonda's train came and we hugged goodbye.

A friend and I were walking at the mall and there was a man texting on his phone leaning against the wall. He was Asian and was highlighted to me by the Spirit. We stopped a bit away from him as we pressed into the Holy Spirit for direction. I was blank at first and my logical mind was thinking he was probably into a traditional Asian spiritual belief system. I had to force myself to stop jumping to conclusions based on stereotypes instead of relying on the Holy Spirit. I cleared my thoughts. I brought him before Jesus and I sensed that he had such a hunger to hear Jesus. Jesus showed me this man was humble and really wanted to hear what Jesus had to say. I was a bit surprised but thought, "Okay, here we go". I approached him and said, "Hi, I was just walking in the mall with my friend and God drew my attention to you and showed me how He sees you." Before I could continue the man looked like he wanted to shut the conversation down and said, "I know God, I go to church and am just waiting for my wife." In split seconds the thoughts went through my mind, "I wonder if my approach was awkward or weird? Since he is a Christian, isn't he curious?" I'm not sure if my approach is awkward anymore because it has just become natural and normal for me. Is it a weird thing for Christians to hear? And if so, I think that is kind of sad. Shouldn't it be a more common occurrence? Anyway, I quickly said, "Oh ok, that's awesome that you are my brother in Christ, I guess God wants to share something with you," He was still hesitant and said, "I am ok, I go to Centre Street Church." I broke out into a smile and eagerly said, "We do too!! I've been going for years, with Pastor Henry, right?!" Instantly his defences dropped. He smiled warmly and was a bit relieved, now happy and willing to talk to me. My message from the Lord seemed more relevant now so I shared with him what the Lord showed me and it blessed him. Then he said, "Now I have a prayer request . . ." He went on to share that his daughter needed prayer as she was going through a hard time. Just then his wife came out and after we caught her up on who we were I asked them if I could pray for their daughter with them right then. All four of us bowed our heads and I prayed. After praying together the man was excited and exclaimed, "The Lord is good! He works in surprising great ways! Thank you for stopping, thank you for praying! Maybe we'll see you at church." We hugged them and went on our way.

A teammate and I walked by two women on the sidewalk who had three young children between them both. Suddenly my teammate swung around and said, "Excuse me, I know this is weird but we are out here talking to people about Jesus. Could we pray for you for anything?" Even I was a little surprised but jumped right in. The two women were taken aback and asked him to repeat himself. One of the children, who was about three years old, began wandering away causing a brief interruption and the mom apologized. I said, "No worries, I have four kids and totally understand." Once she gathered her child, to my surprise, the woman said, "Yes, I need prayer." She went on to explain how her ex-husband was trying to take away her kids. She shared he was very violent and had already taken their daughter but she had been able to get her back. Now the courts were getting involved and he had more money than herself. The situation looked grim for her and he was a dangerous man to their children and to her. I knew now was not the time to start discussing theology or the wages of sin. Instead, I approached her with compassion. Her name was Serena and I said, "Serena, that is so difficult. How are you doing with all this?" She burst into tears and shared with me that she had been in three shelters escaping his abuse. He abused her physically, emotionally and had even violently raped her several times. She believed in God and had faith but since she had to go to the shelters and suffered so much, her faith had really suffered as well. I said, "Serena, out of all these people, God got my friend's attention here and He highlighted you to him, in order to stop you and to pray for you. God sees your heart, He sees your pain and what you are going through. He has not abandoned you, He will not forsake you." I held her while she sobbed on my shoulder. I prayed over her and her young children. Then my team member prayed for her and I hugged her again. The other woman with her had been listening. I hugged her as well and she thanked us for stopping. My team member gave them a Bible, we encouraged them more and Serena thanked us so much for taking the time with her.

I love going up to a long line of taxi cab drivers. They sit in their cars and do not want to leave the line up. They wait for people and I can talk to them while they wait. On one occasion I approached an open window. "Hello! How are you? I'm not needing a ride but I'm just out here because I love Jesus and was wondering if I could pray for you for anything?" The driver looked confused. He asked me to repeat. So I explained further and asked him if he had any spiritual beliefs. He was an orthodox Christian from Ethiopia. I asked a further question, "Who is Jesus to you?" He wholeheartedly proclaimed Jesus as his Saviour. So I enthusiastically said, "Well, as your sister in Christ, is there anything I can pray about for you?" He was still a little hesitant but asked for prayer for his two adult children in their twenties, that they would follow the Lord fully. So I prayed for him and his family. When I walked away, he leaned out his window and called after me with a huge smile, "Thank you so much! I really, really appreciate you coming and talking to me. Keep doing it! It really means a lot to me!"

As I served pizza on another evening of street evangelism, at a table set up on the sidewalk, a man came up to get some. He told me he was staying at the homeless shelter. He said he grew up Christian and although he was not living the way he should, he knew enough to know the difference between Christianity and religion. His name was Danny, so I asked him where he was now with God. He told me he still believed in God but was just not really close to him. He seemed a bit antsy to get going so I asked, "Danny, as your sister in Christ, can I pray for you before you leave?" He answered yes; for his family, his mother and sister. I asked him if he had contact with them and he said not for quite some time. I laid my hand on his shoulder and prayed for them while I asked the Lord what He loved about Danny. I sensed Danny was a man of strength and a defender so I told him that and prayed into who the Lord showed me he really was. As I opened my eyes, I was surprised to see he had tears flowing down his face and he couldn't speak. I grabbed his shoulders and said, "I am a hugger." I gave him a hug and said, "Danny, you are who God says you are." He still could not speak because of his choked emotions. After a few moments he choked out a thank you and walked away, not knowing how to handle it. I turned to my team member who was standing with me and now emotions rose up in me. I needed a second, as it was a very powerful moment to watch the Holy Spirit touch a soul so deeply. I can still see those eyes of Danny.

Oh that we would bless our brothers and sisters in Christ, whether they be strangers, friends, acquaintances or family! Wouldn't it be such a sweet fragrance among God's family?

CHAPTER 14

THE MESSY

"In vain I have searched the Bible, looking for examples of early believers whose lives were marked by rigidity, predictability, inhibition, dullness, and caution. Fortunately, grim, frowning, joyless saints in Scriptures are conspicuous by their absence. Instead, the examples I find are of adventurous, risk-taking, enthusiastic, and authentic believers whose joy was contagious even in times of full trial. Their vision was broad even when death drew near. Rules were few and changes were welcome. The contrast between then and now is staggering."
- Chuck Swindoll

One night I was hanging out with people on the streets and there was a woman there who was clearly upset. I sat down with her as she was crying. She showed me the inside of her arms that were freshly cut up from her own doing. There were so many cuts from the past as well. She had unsuccessfully tried to commit suicide a few nights before by jumping from a building but it had only resulted in her getting hurt. She was now planning to jump off a bridge close by that very night. I talked with her long into the night. She sobbed and I could see she was exhausted. Finally, I told her I would pray with her. I closed my eyes and she held my one hand with both of hers. She softly cried, and with both of our eyes closed, she bobbed my hand up and down close to her face. Suddenly as I was praying, I felt my finger go into her mouth! She had been so focused on the prayer and crying that she accidently had placed my finger fully into her mouth!

I pulled it out as quickly as she did and my praying stopped for a moment. I regained my composure and continued my prayer without opening my eyes. Once we had said good-bye I examined my finger for cuts. I applied hand sanitizer on and then thoroughly washed my hands once I got back to the church at the end of the evening. I prayed on my drive home, "Well Lord, once again, I know You touched the lepers and made them clean. I've touched the unclean . . . I'm going to trust you will protect and make me clean." My husband was fully grossed out and groaned when I got home, asking me to take one more step and take a shower. Ha ha, it's one of my favorite stories to tell.

During an evening of street evangelism, I was among our team looking to get into conversations with people when a man asked to use my phone. I wasn't ready to give him my phone since he was a stranger so I asked him why he needed it. He told me he had just gotten out of prison earlier that day. Someone had stolen his phone and he needed to get it back because it had evidence on it that would help him in his next court hearing. He was a tall, strong, middle-aged guy, with three crosses around his neck. He wasn't happy with my question so he turned away and began walking around asking others, very agitated. He was pretty aggressive with the men in the area. He was getting more and more worked up. I approached him and said, "Hey buddy, is there anywhere you can go and use a phone, like the Salvation Army?" "No!" he angrily groaned. He stood with me and further explained his situation. He was trying to control himself. He would make a fist, punch the metal building and then try to calm down while he talked to me. I offered him prayer but he freaked out and said no. He wouldn't tell me his name and said to call him "Marty McFly". He took off to follow and yell at some random guy. Within a minute he came back to me. I asked him why he was wearing the crosses around his neck. He told me he believed in God and they were very special to him. He took my hand and kissed it multiple times telling me he was sorry. Then he stood in front of me and put his head on my shoulder and gave a weak attempt to cry, telling me he was so tired and just needed some help. I stood my ground and did not move, not letting "Marty" fluster me. Inside I rolled my eyes at his efforts to play the victim to get me to do what he wanted. He then took two bracelets off his wrist and despite my objections placed them on my wrist and insisted I have them. They were cheap, worthless, ridiculous things. As his anger ebbed and flowed, I sighed and left them on my wrist. He went to rip his necklaces off to give them to me. I quickly stopped him, "No! Don't do that! You keep them. They look important to you." Thankfully he listened. He curled up in a ball on the pavement. I crouched down and said, "Look, I can see you are a man who can be very street smart." Before I could go on he said, "Are you kidding me? Have you ever slept out on the street?" I honestly said no I hadn't and then oddly enough he put out his fist to give me a fist bump and said, "Good for you. Don't ever if you don't have to." "Marty" stood up and then angrily began to yell at a guy to give him back his phone. A team member came up to me and asked me if I was okay. I waved my hand and replied that I was fine. It was the end of the night and I could see I was getting nowhere with this angry guy so I tried to wrap things up. "Marty" got louder and louder, swearing, chasing and threatening another street guy. A few of our male team members tried to calm him down but he just became more aggressive with them. I told the team that "Marty" could entertain us all night, so I ushered them into the ministry motorhome. The door remained open and a team member prayed a closing prayer for our night. As she prayed standing with her back to the doorway of the motorhome, another man from the street came and stood behind her. I had my eyes open and was watching him. Then "Marty" came over and started yelling at him. The man turned to him and strongly addressed him, "Hey, they are praying in there and you are interrupting. Stop being disrespectful." He said it so forcefully that "Marty" said sorry and both men stood silently until she was finished praying. I found this amusing and interesting. As soon as she finished praying, "Marty" and the stranger immediately resumed yelling at each other as the team and I drove away.

On another night, Kurt and Oliver sat down with me. Oliver was depressed and down because all his stuff had been stolen again. He felt like giving up on life, again. I asked to see his hands and wrists. He still had open wounds that I had seen on him about five days before when I was downtown and bumped into him. His fingers were swollen from infection. His hands and the one lower arm were no longer hurting but had gone numb. He had refused to go for antibiotics. He took off the bandage on his wrist. The sore was a circle a bit bigger than a toonie coin and yellow pus completely covered it. I sighed and told him he needed to deal with it soon. I remembered we had just been given a first aid kit and told him I'd go see what I had to treat the wound. I found some disinfecting cloths, antibiotic gel and bandages. I put some disposable gloves on, laughed and mentioned that Dr. Val was going to fix him up. I carefully wiped all the pus off and dropped the disinfecting cloth on the ground by my chair. Then I squeezed out the gel and put it on the wound, as well as four other ones. I was careful to use different fingers so as to not spread the infection between them. My gloves were disgusting when I was done. I carefully took them off the proper way my sister-in-law (who is a nurse) showed me and I threw them into the garbage. I put on a new pair and applied several more bandages. When I was done, his wounds looked much cleaner and sanitized. I carefully took off my gloves again, throwing them out. I sat down and started chatting with them again. "What am I going to do with you two!! When are you going to stop being so stubborn and give your lives completely to Jesus? Oliver, you wear those necklaces and rings on your body and they are symbols of what? Evil things, against God. How can you expect God to bless or protect you? You open yourself up to evil and then you want everything to go right." Oliver looked at his stuff and said, "What?! These are just dragons, I love them." "Well, what do they represent to you?" I asked. He pulled up his sleeves, "I have seven dragons tattooed all over my body. They represent power and each one represents power of something." I rolled my eyes, "Oliver, you know Jesus is the One who is ALL powerful. So why are you looking for power in a dragon? You are going after counterfeit power and it will never give you what you want. It will always disappoint you." As I spoke the papers from the bandages started blowing around so without looking down I began to pick them up and then my hand grabbed the wet, dirty disinfecting cloth with pus on it. I had forgotten to throw it in the garbage! Ugh, seriously! I had been so careful and now my fingers had pus all over them! I didn't show any shock and just told them I'd be right back. I tried not to touch any part of my body with my hand, went to the motorhome and found another disinfecting cloth, opened it up and scrubbed my hand with it. I sighed and said a silent prayer, "Lord, we've had this talk before. You touched the lepers, protect me again." I examined my fingers for any cuts and then went back out, careful not to touch my face the rest of the night, knowing it would be awhile before I got access to soap and water. I continued our conversation and Oliver told me about "crackerjack alley". Apparently even he didn't go there. He told me everyone there was on crack and it was very dangerous. I told him he needed to find me someone who would escort me to it, since he wouldn't, and to tell me what I could bring to be welcomed. He laughed and shook his head. Oliver and the other guy, Kurt, both told me they were exhausted. They said they could never stop walking. If they stopped to sleep, their stuff would get stolen. If they sat on a bench, someone would tell them to leave, whether it was a business owner or a city worker. Kurt told me there was a restaurant owner who would leave him scraps out at the back of the restaurant and sometimes leave the dumpster unlocked for him to go and get stuff from. They told me the nights were very long because they just had to keep walking. If they stopped, they could get stabbed or beat up. Oliver had been sitting with me for about thirty minutes and said he hadn't sat this long in four days and it felt good. They also told me that some new gangs had moved into the city. One was Russian and the other was Asian. They said it was crazy how violent they were. They were selling their own drugs and that street people like themselves had been warned to not stand on certain street corners or blocks because the territory belonged to the gangs. Kurt did not drink nor do drugs but Oliver did drugs as he was in constant pain with his back. I prayed for healing every time I saw him. I challenged them about who they were and what they were living their lives for. I told them that they had so much potential and I knew God had a bigger destiny for them. Then I said God loved them so much and that I couldn't help but love them both because of that. I offered to pray over Oliver. Kurt piped up, "Well I want prayer, please pray over me too." I put one hand on each of them and I poured out my heart to the Lord over these two. I held nothing back and didn't care that they heard me praying for things perhaps that neither of them wanted. When I was done, Kurt had a big smile on his face and said, "Yeah, that's what I'm talking about. I love it when you pray for me, it always makes me feel so much better and is so, like, powerful or something. It really means a lot to me. Thank you!" Oliver was starting to fall asleep even though he was sitting upright. I told Kurt to watch over him so he could sleep for a little bit. I drove away feeling like I didn't accomplish much tonight. However, I felt I had discovered a little bit more about what it is like being on the streets. I also felt a little bit more agape for those men and I pray someday they will be all in for Jesus. Washing my hands that night felt really great!

I was simply walking in a small town and a gentleman who looked a little rough was walking towards me. I greeted him, "Hello sir, are you from here?" He was a jovial man and totally sober. "No, I am not." I asked, "Well, where are you from?" He smiled, "I'm just a guy not from here." I smiled back and laughed, "Well I'm a gal not from here. What's your name?" He said, "Gus." "Hello Gus, my name is Val! So what are you doing here?" He continued with his joking, "I'm here to try and get drunk." I smiled and played along, "That doesn't sound so great. Where are you headed?" He said, "To the hospital, I have a cut above my knee I need to get looked at." Concerned, I asked, "How did you get that?" Gus explained, "Last night I got into it with the cops and they did it. They also sprayed me with mace and it really stung the skin on my arms." "Hmmm," I said, "Well, you must have been a bad boy. What did you do that was so bad to have that happen?" He grinned, "I dunno, I was drinking." I nodded and said, "I am out here praying for people and I would like to pray for you. What can I pray about you for?" He was a bit surprised and then said, "Pray I can get more beer." I laughed, "Oh I will pray about the beer." I put my hand on his shoulder and began praying for this man, that his addiction would be broken and he would no longer depend on it to give him joy. I prayed he would become a man of integrity, of truth, of compassion. A man who people could trust and find safety in. That he would be a man who would stand up for those who could not defend themselves, such as widows and orphans. I prayed that most of all Gus would truly serve God with all his heart and impact many for Him. When I was done, the man shifted back and forth and looked down, his jovial demeanour turned somber. He didn't know what to say, "Oh . . . hmmm . . . Oh . . . thank you." I patted his shoulder and told him I hoped his knee healed soon. He turned, wanting to get going, and off he went.

It was a freezing night and I had forgotten my toque. I hadn't mentioned it to anyone but was shivering in my conversations with others. Rex suddenly came over and interrupted me as I was talking to someone, which he never does as he is a quiet, shy man. He handed me his toque. I was surprised and said, “Rex, what are you doing?” He just motioned for me to put it on. I protested but he insisted. I studied the toque for a few seconds. It wasn’t the cleanest! It had pieces of his hair on the inside of it and it didn’t even look that warm but it was such a kind thing that he was doing for me. A group of street people were all watching. Determined to show appreciation, I decided to put that toque on my head. It was a bit big but it was warm. A quick prayer escaped my thoughts that I wouldn’t get any weird things living in my hair. I smiled, he smiled, all those watching smiled, and I continued my conversation about the Lord.

I was standing near a homeless shelter. I had a box of pizza in one hand and a stack of plates in the other. I handed out pizza to those who came up to me. A man came up and was extremely thankful for the pizza. He took a slice and went to eat it. A little while later he came back and asked if he could have one more piece. Since everyone else around had eaten a slice I agreed to give him a second piece. He leaned in, placed his hand in my coat pocket and said, “I really, really appreciate this. I have just been so hungry.” He pulled away and smiled. I was puzzled and asked, “Did you put something in my pocket?” He quietly said, “Yeah, just a little thank you. It’s good stuff. Thanks again.” My eyes went big and I said, “Is it drugs?” He kindly smiled and nodded, “Yep, just some coke. I appreciate what you’re doing.” My hands were holding items and I couldn’t do anything to pull it out. I looked around at the area and saw security cameras pointed at me and thought, “Oh great, this probably is going to look like I’m doing a drug deal with this guy.” I said, “Uh, you’re welcome but this pizza’s totally free. I don’t want anything for it.” As he ate his pizza he said, “Oh no, I want you to have it.” I smiled and laughed (because sometimes I laugh when I get nervous), “No, really, take it out of my pocket. You can have it back, I don’t want it. The pizza is totally free.” He asked, “Are you sure?” I eagerly nodded yes. So he reached back into my pocket, pulled out a small bag of white powder and shoved it into his pocket. He thanked me again and left. I had to chuckle and shake my head.

As a friend and I walked along the sidewalk, there was a man off to the side scraping his drugs together on the cement and burning it with his lighter. I don’t really understand the drug world, nor what he was doing but we stopped and went over to him. (Later I found out that was how you do crystal meth.) "Hey, are you okay?" He looked up and stopped. He said he was. I continued conversing with him. Eventually I found out he was from Sudan. I asked him his name and he said it was Matthew. I instantly knew he probably had a Christian background. I inquired and he confirmed. His family was very orthodox. He said that when he was eighteen he was forced to join the army. He had come in contact with Pentecostal believers and he became a Pentecostal Christian for four years. His family was very unhappy about it. In particular his brothers told him it wasn't right and to stop. Due to political upheaval in Sudan, he came to Canada. He ended up living on the streets and turning to drugs. I looked at my brother in Christ who was so damaged by the world, his poor choices, and the devil to the point where he had given up. I said, "Matthew, you are my brother in Christ. You are doing drugs to numb pain but it will not work. Return to the Lord. He loves you and is waiting. Read your Bible once again. Get free from all this. You are doing drugs to numb your pain but you know it will not last. Let me pray for you." I prayed over him and gave him a big hug. When I looked at him I could see a glimpse in his eyes that he actually had been a different man than how he was now. I could sense he had been a godly man who had once sought after the Lord. I told him I could see he had been a man passionate about the Lord in the past. He appreciated our prayer. Matthew understood what I was saying and his eyes held regrets and sadness. His drugs sat on the cement by our feet awaiting for him to finish heating and inhaling. We left him to decide his next step.

What can I say?! Evangelism can be messy, the world is messy and not every conversation results in healings, miracles, salvation and repentance. Am I willing to get messy and love people again and again regardless of the outcome? Or do I need safety and positive outcomes in order to be obedient to Christ's commands? No, I love the intimacy with Jesus and because of that I won't stop His love from pouring out of me for people. In fact, I desperately pray for it. The messiness is a privilege and the outcome is His dominion.

CHAPTER 15

"WHAT IFS"

"Something is wrong when our lives make sense to unbelievers." - Francis Chan

As we gathered at the hospital to begin evangelizing, we first prayed over our team member for healing and over my headache that had returned. Again it lifted. As the other team members were chatting, I noticed two young men in the entryway of the hospital, sitting on chairs in conversation. I couldn't hear them but the one man really stuck out to me. I pressed in to the Lord and I sensed this young man was gentle and kind. However, he did not look like it. His hair, clothing and attire looked more like I'd be able to purchase illegal substances from him (that's my unfiltered analysis). I waited a few more minutes and really felt the nudging of the Lord to go talk to him even though it did not seem inviting. The spot he was sitting at had a very high traffic volume of people coming and going. I wondered if I approached him how he would respond and if he would cause an uncomfortable exchange, telling me to mind my own business. I have found if I just start walking, my courage will catch up when I open my mouth. I got up, walked through the doors and sat down beside the young man. His buddy had gone out for a smoke break. I greeted him and told him, "I was sitting over on those chairs inside and Jesus got my attention to show me you were very gentle and have a kind heart. The Lord knows this about you and in fact has deposited it in you." I was almost grimacing as I said it as it just didn't seem to fit his outward appearance and I didn't know if he'd reject the words "gentle and kind" to describe him. His eyes went big and he said,

"What?! He told you that!? I do have a gentle and kind heart! I too believe in God." I was surprised and learned that he had some sort of a Christian upbringing. His name was Mitch. He respected all faiths and had even sat and talked with Jehovah Witnesses who he respected. He told me he was a good person. He had done some jail time but was now trying to be really good. He had gotten very sick with pneumonia and had now been in the hospital twenty-six days recovering, but his organs were swelling. I asked him if I could pray for him and for healing. He said yes and held out his hands for me to hold them while I prayed. Ha ha, so I did as we prayed. Since we were right at the entrance, a constant flow of people went by us. The Lord gave me the words to pray and I prayed passionately for the young man. When I was done, my team member, who had joined us, was about to say something and Mitch said, "Whoa, wait . . . I just need a moment. Man, I wish I would have recorded that prayer on my phone. All those things you said, well, I have never heard someone pray like that. That was smart, logical, powerful, deep and well, that just blew me away! You're the real thing!" I laughed as he responded in such a non-churchy way. It also demonstrates why I encourage every believer to pray out loud with people. This models a whole different way of praying for most people and they get to witness the relationship we have with Christ. I asked him how he knew he was good with Jesus. He told me because he tried to be kind to everyone and love everyone. So I explained to him the difference between other religions and Christianity. I went through the gospel very quickly. At one point his buddy returned and interrupted, telling him he was going back up and wanted him to come along. I was dismayed as I wanted to continue the conversation. I wondered how to ask Mitch to stay but then unexpectedly Mitch answered. He was not shy or embarrassed but said, "Bro, I'm talking here about important stuff, you go without me. I need to hear this." I tried to get through as much as possible without losing him, as Mitch was distracted easily. He told me it made sense to him and then he asked what church I was from. When I told him, he became very excited. He used to live near the church and would go play basketball in the gym on youth night. He said he never heard any of the "sessions" as he called them, which I think he meant Bible studies, but really liked to hang out there. As our conversation wrapped up, he took a Bible to read and said, "Hey if you're back here again, come talk to me. Even if you see me on the street some time, come up and talk to me, I'll talk to you more about this anytime."

I am asked a lot if I am afraid, especially when engaging with street people. Every time I'm asked, I feel caught unprepared to answer. I think it's because I want to try to calm their fears and also relate to them. For example, I was asked this question by a pastor in front of an audience of around eighty people. I felt like the right answer should have been, "Yes I do, but I do it anyways with God's help." Ha ha, that seems like the correct Christian response, but to be honest, I'm not scared on the streets. I really don't have fear. Part of the reason is that we have set up wisely so we are in groups or at least with one other person around but even so . . . I know I have not always been street smart in situations I have found myself in. The fear that needs to be conquered is more so the inner fear of actually speaking about the truth and not fearing the response. In regards to physical harm, I feel like a baby in relation to what believers in other parts of the world have to face. I have also resolved that I won't love my life so much as to shrink from death (Revelation 12:11). Is that not what should be normal? Is that not to be the call and position of every believer?

After I preached on the street, I turned and there was Robert, the atheist, whose dad had been a pastor. Robert was very angry at God. I didn't know him all that well and he has avoided me since our last conversation where I really pushed hard at exposing the root of his unbelief. This time he was very friendly and with another gentleman that comes often. Robert said, "Hey Val, I brought you a cookie for Easter!" I looked and he held a seemingly store bought, clear plastic packaged cookie in his hand. He went on, "It's After Eight chocolate melted over an Oreo cookie. It's very gourmet." It looked sanitary enough since it was sealed and I thought this was very nice. I said, "Oh wow! Thank you so much, that was so kind of you!" He again expressed it was for Easter and he wanted me to try it. I was squirming because I really wanted to eat the cookie to be kind but for Lent I had been off of all dairy, wheat and sugar. There were only three more days of Lent and I wasn't about to break my fast now. I apologetically and almost embarrassingly said, "I'm so sorry Robert, I'm off of wheat, dairy and sugar. I . . . I . . . just can't eat the cookie you brought me right now." They both looked at me stunned and Robert said, "Whaaat? Are you serious? Is it an allergy thing or by choice?" I told them it was by choice and they asked why. So I explained I was doing it for Lent and why. Robert tried once more and said, "Yeah but it's so good. It's amazing and delicious." I declined again and thought about suggesting I take it home in order to eat it on Friday when my fast was over but the thought passed through that I shouldn't. After a bit more trying, Robert finally said, "So there is no way that you are going to eat this cookie, even just take a bite?" I shook my head no and again apologized. The men looked at each other and Robert made a comment, "Okay then, it has a lot of good stuff in it. It's got a special ingredient of THC in it, just the right amount." I suddenly stopped and in a moment of realization exclaimed, "Is that a marijuana cookie!!??" They both chuckled and Robert said yes. They explained they had made a bet to see if they could get me to eat the cookie. I said, "Guys!!! I have to drive that motorhome tonight, then drive home. Were you going to let me eat it and get high?!" Robert said, "It wouldn't have kicked in for an hour. You'd just feel really relaxed by the time you got home. All your muscles would have relaxed and you'd be just chilling on the couch. You'd feel great!" I was still in a bit of shock, and I turned to the guy beside him and said, "You wouldn't have let me take a bite would you have? Like you would have stopped me if I went for it, right!?" He gave a nervous smile as he didn't want to give an answer and I slowly, disbelievingly got the feeling he would've let me eat the cookie. Then Robert said, "If you would've just taken a bite it would've been fine." The other man said, "It's a pain killer. It's pretty strong, Robert, if she would've eaten the whole thing." Robert looked at me and said, "How much do you weigh? Oh, uh, with the amount of THC, " he laughed, "Ya, you would've been real (messed) up. Eating the whole thing would have (messed) you up real good. You would have been just jelly on the couch but you'd be fine by the morning." He gave a deep laugh. Maybe out of being naive or innocent or wanting to see the best in people, I was still believing they wouldn't have actually let me eat it so I laughed and said, "Oh great Robert, now I'm not trusting you at all! Don't be offering me candy or food because now I will always be wondering!" I was then pulled away from our conversation by another lady who wanted a hug and some brief attention. By the time I was finished with her, Robert and his friend had walked away.

I realize now it was actually not funny at all. I was and still am in such amazement, awe and praise to God that the timing of this was when I was doing a fast for Lent. I had been complaining the last few days how I couldn't wait for Lent to be over. I wonder if thirty-seven days ago God put it on my heart to do this fast knowing it would protect me that very night. I would have totally eaten that cookie, totally. I would have done it to not be rude and to show gratitude and kindness. I have now had my eyes opened and have added that to the list of don'ts on the streets: don't give out personal info, don't give out money . . . don't eat or drink anything offered to me. Ugh, that night I may not have made it home as my nights often go much later than expected and that night I didn't start driving home until one and a half hours after the cookie incident. This, however, did not give me anger or fear or anxiety. I learned. I actually feel more confident than ever when people ask me if I'm scared on the streets, I just know from experiences over and over God's protection and have the confidence to say, "My God will protect me, He just does!"

There was an older lady who lived on the streets for twenty-eight years. The first time I met her she was pushing a cart and looked ten years older than she was. She was pretty cold to me and didn't really care about engaging with me. As she went to push past me, ignoring my attempts to talk to her, I suddenly noticed her hat and said, "I really love your hat. It looks pretty on you." It was like I had unlocked the door to her heart and her face brightened. She began talking to me and introduced herself as Barbie. I started to see her occasionally when I was downtown in that area. I learned she was thought of as the street mama. Everyone on the streets knew her and gave her respect. She shared with me she was in a lot of pain because she had stage 4 cancer, therefore, she drank a lot to deal with the pain. She was a very hardened woman and spoke with such foul language that I often had to laugh as it was hard to decipher what she was saying between all the swear words. She took a liking to me and started to seek me out on nights she knew I'd be there. I would talk about God and she would agree with everything I said but then she would mix her spiritual beliefs into it, which would muddy up the gospel. I always showed her a lot of respect but had a difficult time getting her to correct her theology. I knew she was not in alignment with the God of the Bible, nor in obedience to Him. I would always ask to pray with her and she always wanted me to. One night she took me over to a group of street people and introduced me, "Hey, this is Val, she's my favorite Christian. She'll probably pray for you. Now everyone tell her your name." All of them looked at me cautiously. They shifted their weight and looked at each other, but Barbie had authority and she demanded, "Come on, tell her your names!" One by one they muttered their names to me. Conversations resumed and I watched them interact with her. Suddenly, right beside me, a young man came running up and before I knew what was happening one of the guys from the group smashed him in the nose multiple times. The young man yelped and ran off holding his face. It happened so fast and all I saw was the back of this young man running away with a pizza box that was from our team. I thought it was one of my team members who had come to offer pizza. I freaked out and exclaimed angrily, "What!? Why did you do that!?" I was about to go after the young man to help him and the group looked at me and said, "Didn't you see? He had a knife in his hand and came running up behind you at us." Barbie nodded. I looked at the young man running off and realized he had received a pizza box from my team but was not one of my team. In shock I said, "Oh, I see . . . good job." I'll never know if that young man was coming after me or the people I was with but I do know the lightning responses of the street people was God's intervention.

Some months later I found out that Barbie had died from her cancer. The news shook me and I cried. I was not so much crying about her life and missing her. I cried because I shrank back from pushing deeper to sort out the gospel with her according to the Bible. In the name of friendship and respect, I didn't plainly lay out God's way of salvation and that it was Jesus alone in whom we can be saved. To be completely honest, even though I did not conscientiously think this through until after, I did not love her enough to tell her the truth. I loved myself more and catered to my desire to not have confrontation or uncomfortable tension. I cried because from my knowledge of her mixed beliefs, opinions and according to scripture, she was spending eternity in hell. I, of course, hoped that someone else had shared it with her before she died and that she had turned whole-heartedly to God in the end. I also hoped that somehow through my kindness she was impacted and wanted to turn to the God of the Bible. But how silly that sounds now. My kindness made her like me but probably also made her feel her beliefs were acceptable as I did not fully correct her. I thought I had more time, I thought I would get there in conversation eventually. I now look at people I engage with as divinely arranged encounters. If I ask the Lord to lead me to the people He wants me to talk to about Him, then I will trust that He is doing just that. I must then be intentional to not waste the opportunity to reveal Jesus, to share truth with gentleness and respect but to also be bold, to take risks knowing the Almighty God has entrusted me to speak into a person's heart and soul. Could I have been stabbed that one night when I was hanging out with her? Possibly, but I wasn't. I was being given the opportunity to share the gospel with people and God was taking care of the "what if".

Once I had engaged in a spiritual conversation with a man when we were feeding and encouraging the homeless population. He explained to me that his father had bipolar and that he too now had bipolar. He asked me if someone who had bipolar could be a Christian. I handled this conversation very carefully as we discussed the gospel laid out in scripture. I asked him why he was asking me the question if he believed he was a Christian. He told me he was two people: Jeremy and Jack. Jeremy was the Christian who was kind and good. Jack was terrible. Jack wanted to kill Jeremy and said all kinds of terrible things about Jesus and Christians. He couldn't control when Jack manifested.

Now I know it is a delicate subject; when bipolar is considered a spiritual problem and not exclusively a medical condition. I am not a doctor nor do I like flippant spiritual labels. I'm merely telling the story of what happened, so here goes.

I asked him "who" I was talking to right then and there and he responded, "Jeremy". However, he mentioned Jack was speaking to him in his mind telling him to pounce on me, put me down on the ground and do hurtful things to me. I said, "Oh wow, well, don't do that!" Jeremy said, "I don't want to do that to you! See it's terrible and that's why I don't know if I can be a Christian." I said to him, "Jeremy, I know why Jack is telling you that. He doesn't want me to tell you how to get free from him. Jack sees the Holy Spirit in me and he hates me." I went on to explain more of how to get free and told him I could give him some resources that I had with me. I went over to the motorhome. Without realizing he followed close behind. I went into the motorhome and suddenly there was Jeremy in the motorhome right behind me. It startled me a bit. I quickly grabbed what I needed and ushered him outside. I looked around and saw that my team members were pretty far away. Knowing there was a demonic spirit wanting to hurt me, I very casually and discreetly said, "Oh look, there's some of my friends." I beckoned for them to come over. My beckoning caught their attention. They looked at me a bit puzzled, then smiled and waved back at me, not realizing I was hoping for them to join me. Ha ha, I laughed inside, breathed a quick prayer and said, "Jeremy, I'm going to pray over you." I did just that, rebuked any ungodly spirits and finished off a great spiritual conversation, equipping him to make a choice of fully surrendering to Jesus. I thank God for His protection. We are to be wise in our actions, however, I have also learned that the Lord alone is the One we must trust in to protect us when we get into situations that leave us vulnerable.

We often get the plague of the "What ifs". I get asked: What if you get stabbed? What if you would've gotten hurt? What if you would've eaten the cookie? Well, I didn't. I could ask the same questions for other parts of my life. What if I fall off the horse? What if I get hurt while motor biking? What if I run into a bear when hiking? What if the plane crashes? . . . What if the sky falls down? You get the picture. I think there are better "What if" questions. What if that person dies lost? What if Jesus returns tomorrow? What if I trust Jesus with my whole life? What if I obey him? What if I love God with all my heart, soul, mind and strength? What if I love others as I love myself? Those are the "what ifs" worth answering.

CHAPTER 16

TRUDGING

" 'Not called!' did you say?
'Not heard the call,' I think you should say?
Put your ear down to the Bible, and hear Him bid you go and pull sinners out of the fire of sin. Put your ear down to the burdened, agonized heart of humanity, and listen to it's pitiful wail for help. Go stand by the gates of hell, and hear the damned entreat you to go to their father's house and bid their brothers and sisters and servants and masters not to come there. Then look Christ in the face — whose mercy you have professed to obey — and tell Him whether you will join heart and soul and body and circumstances in the march to publish His mercy to the world." - William Booth

Have you ever walked up a hill, pulling a sled in deep snow up to your knees? Or perhaps you've walked upstream against the current with water at your waist? I've done both. Neither are pleasant because of the resistance each has and the effort it takes to keep trudging. I can't wait to get to where I'm going. That's how I feel sometimes when I repeatedly talk to people who hear the truth over and over yet will not choose to cry out to the only One who can change their lives and bring them healing.

Once again out on the streets of the downtown core, I had conversations with the "regulars". A young man who had only been in Canada for eight months came over to me. I recognized him but had trouble placing him. He reminded me that I had talked with him several times eight months ago and I had prayed over him. When I realized who it was I was instantly saddened. He had lost a lot of weight and looked pretty rough, so I told him that I noticed these changes. He nodded and said he was struggling with an addiction to opioids. I threw my hands up and said, "Eric, when I met you in the summer and you had just arrived in Canada, you were fresh and weren't on drugs or anything! What happened??!!" He nodded in agreement, explaining he had been doing great. He had been hired with a great company, loved his job but unfortunately ended up with a health issue. He had to get surgery and afterwards the pain was so bad that he was prescribed powerful and addictive painkillers. He struggled to get off of them. With continued pain, he ended up turning to street drugs, eventually getting involved with a bad crowd. He checked himself into monitored housing accommodations in order to get away from the bad crowd and enroll into a treatment program to wean him off the opioids. He was receiving a prescribed drug that wasn't addictive and helped him get off of the other drugs. As he spoke I noticed he was shifty and couldn't stand still. I had to keep turning as he circled around me while we talked. I asked him where he was with Jesus. He repeated the same answer He gave me eight months ago. He believed there was a God but this point he did not want to pursue spirituality. He wanted to see what he was made of, see if he could get out of this himself and if he was strong enough. I challenged that mindset. I shared with him that God wasn't some sort of crutch to turn to only when you need help and can't make it on your own. I explained the whole meaning of life was to make a decision whether you were going to have a relationship with God or not. He told me he understood but he was determined to do this himself. I shared God's heart with Eric. God wanted to not just give strength, but to reveal Who He was to Eric, as well as, who Eric was to God. I told him that by making a decision to do life himself he was making a decision to reject God's presence in his life. The street preaching from our team began and I wanted Eric to hear it so I ended our conversation. He kindly thanked me for caring and we began to listen. I saw Eric a few more times and each encounter was the same, except his eyes were darker and his weight loss continued. No matter what I said, Eric continued to refuse to turn to God.

Suddenly, Joseph came straight to me. Whenever I see him I think he looks worse than the time before. I've probably known him for five or six years. I never know if I'm going to get the joking, cocky side of him, or the broken, desperate side. Tonight he was broken and desperate. When I greeted him, I could sense it and I had this weird feeling that I did not want to let him leave. It was like a deep part of my spirit wanted to beg him to change. He immediately began telling me how he almost died. He pulled up his shirt and showed me a huge fresh scar that was a long vertical line on his stomach. I listened to Joseph tell me that something had collapsed internally and he was able to phone 911 before he blacked out. They had to GPS his phone to find him. The paramedics had to work on him for forty minutes before they could transport him to the hospital because they kept losing him. He woke up in the hospital not remembering much. I noticed his necklaces had changed from skulls to a cross and a tree of life. As he finished telling me his ordeal, how he still was not feeling good and hadn't slept for five days, I asked him, "Joseph, when you realized you almost died, what were you thinking?" He knew me well enough by now to know why I was asking. He looked far away and got choked up and quickly said, "I wondered if I was really forgiven." I studied him, half frustrated and half grieved, "What are you going to do about it?" I asked. He forced a smile, "I don't know." Just then his buddy rushed up to him and said something I couldn't hear. Joseph's eyes went big and he said, "Oh I forgot! Sorry Val, I have to go, I have a meeting I'm supposed to be at!" He began backing away, truly sorry he had to leave so fast. I watched him sadly, shrugged and said, "Come back." Come back someday soon and finish this conversation. He knew what I meant. I hope it's soon enough.

Jan was a well-spoken Christian woman I have known for months. She moved off the street ten months ago, had a job and was now in subsidized housing. She had been married and had kids, attended a church, got divorced and was asked to leave the church as it was too difficult for both her and her ex-husband to both attend a small church. She struggled with alcohol. She had participated and led many Alcohol Anonymous groups. She had been sober for a good amount of time and then one day phoned me in a relapsed state. She was crying and ready to commit suicide. I talked her through it, spoke truth into her, declared who she was in Christ and prayed for her over the phone. She did not commit suicide that day and I texted her later to check in with her a few times but received no response. Everything about Jan went silent for about six months. When I saw her next I felt such relief. I had this feeling overcome me, like I wanted to just fall on my knees and thank God for sparing her life and giving her more time. I approached Jan and said, "Jan, it is so good to see you!" We got straight to deep issues as I inquired where she was living at, if she was working and if she had further relapses. I mentioned her phone call and she looked puzzled. I asked her if she remembered calling me. She looked horrified and said no. Apparently she was a "blackout" drunk and she usually didn't remember much. She asked me if she had said anything offensive to me. I said no but that she had been in a pretty low spot. She was so ashamed and apologized sincerely. I told her I was actually really thankful she called me during that time as I was able to pray for her during and after the phone call. I was honored I was the one she called. I really do believe it was an intense spiritual battle over her life. She shared with me she had been in tears every night for the past couple of months, grieving her losses and dwelling about where her life was at. She acknowledged that she knew I had set up all sorts of opportunities for her with the church and for discipleship with our team, yet she hadn't followed through with any of them. Her doctor had recently given her a new diagnosis, post traumatic syndrome disorder. I listened and said, "Well, I'm sure the stuff you've been through has been traumatic and it's a relief to have acknowledgement that it has been seriously hard. But be careful not to take that identity on." She agreed and again apologized, "Val, I am absolutely tired and done with all this." I said, "Good." Jan continued, "Val, I know I don't deserve it but if you're willing, will you please set me up again with the church? Will you let me know the opportunities again and help me get involved with whatever you think I need?" I said, "Of course, Jan." She told me she planned on moving out of the subsidized housing and closer to the church as she wanted to get involved. In six months, she was planning to take some time off and put herself in some sort of a program to finally get free of her alcohol problem. She was currently going back to AA even though she really didn't like it anymore. She said there were street people there but also judges, lawyers and the like. She was frustrated because people were making their "higher power" ridiculous empty things. She knew without God it was impossible to get free. The more she talked the more I could see she felt her problems could be solved by external changes to cause internal changes. I knew the opposite was true, she needed internal changes which would lead to external changes. I asked her, "Jan, what if nothing changes? What if you don't get to move closer to the church, and you don't get to take time off in six months? What if circumstances in your life don't change?" She looked at me seriously and said, "I will die." I looked at her and asked, "Why?" . . . Are you depending on circumstances to change in order for you to get healed and be free?" She was puzzled and said, "Well yes, I have to have it change, or I can't go on." I thought carefully and said, "You're being tormented, Jan. You know that satan wants to destroy you. He will do everything he can to keep you depressed and self-medicating. You don't need to wait for circumstances to change to get involved with the church, nor to start discipling. You don't have to die if things don't change. You need to speak to your heart, to your soul, and tell them it's time to heal as you submit them to God. Be led by the Spirit of God, not your heart and soul. Decide with your will that you are not a victim anymore, throw off the identity you've taken, and take on who God sees you as. Get your identity and your changes from Him. You have to deal with the internal before the external." She considered what I was saying, agreed and said, "I do feel like I'm being tormented. I guess I don't know how to change in this circumstance. I know . . . I know . . . you've offered me ways and I am ready to do them." I told her I wasn't trying to belittle her pain or circumstances but that eighteen years was a long time to sit in it. We chatted more and then I asked if I could pray for her. I prayed over her and when I was done she wiped her tears, saying I prayed exactly all the desires that were inside of her, she just wasn't able to put them into words. I asked her to do some homework, To write out one thing she was thankful for everyday. She said she would. She had done an exercise like that once for AA. I told her that was good, but I wanted her to think of one thing she was thankful to GOD for. Then I wanted her to come back and read them out loud to me. The reason I asked her was twofold. First, I wanted to give her a simple invite and challenge to see if she would follow through. This would allow me to see if she would follow through on future opportunities I would provide. Secondly, I wanted to begin working with the Holy Spirit on renewing her mind and changing her thought patterns from despair to thankfulness and joy. Jan agreed and we parted. To this day, Jan continues to drink, continues to apologize but never completes the homework, nor follows through on her relationship with God.

As I arrived downtown, Lane was waiting for me as he had recently completed reading the book, More than a Carpenter by Josh McDowell, that I had given him. He thought it was a good book but was very upset at the references for explaining the disciples' deaths. We discussed the accuracy and evidence provided regarding the martyr accounts of the disciples and if it can actually be proven? We went around and around the sources and debated reliability and accuracy. Finally, I asked, "Why does this matter so much to you?" Lane responded, "Because people can't go around saying this happened if in fact it didn't, and then claim it helps prove that Jesus rose from the dead." I asked, "Do you believe Jesus rose from the dead?" He answered, "Well, I hope so." I told Lane, "If he didn't then there's no point in being a Christian." Lane knew that and it was bothering him. I said, "Why does it matter to you that the disciples were martyred? Let's say they weren't; the historical sources are wrong. Does that then mean Jesus didn't rise from the dead?" Lane stammered, "Well no, I mean, maybe . . . I don't know?" I said, "So if someone came to us right now and said to me, 'If you believe Jesus is the Son of God and was raised from the dead I'm going to blow your head off', and I responded, 'I know He lives and I cannot deny Him' and then he blows my head off, would you then believe more fully and follow God without any hesitations because I was martyred?" Lane looked at me disturbed and said, "Uh, I don't know . . ." I continued, "It doesn't matter if I die for my faith or don't die for my faith. The history of the disciples' deaths is interesting but it doesn't determine the truth that God is God, Jesus is God, and that Jesus died and was raised from the dead. There is a lot of evidence you need to continue looking into. It's good to ask questions but eventually you have to decide whether you are going to believe or not." Lane inquired, "Well, I mean, take Noah for example. That didn't really happen, I mean two of EVERY animal in a big ark? That is totally not real?!" I asked Lane, "Have you heard of or seen the life size ark they built in the U.S.? I've been there! There's incredible information and scientific explanations as to how it could have happened according to the Bible. You make judgements and opinions based on your current understanding, but once you actually research it, you will realize the amazing possibility of it all. Lane, you have to decide if you are going to serve the 'god of understanding' or not. If you say to yourself, 'IF I understand this passage of the Bible, or this story, or this principle or command, THEN I will follow God', then you have put an idol in your life before God. You are making a 'god' of your understanding. Whether you understand every part of the Bible or not shouldn't keep shaking your faith. There is much in the Bible that when it was written did not make sense to the people of that time. They just had to trust that what God was saying was true. We now have hindsight, science, and knowledge that proves the Bible was accurate in those things. Even though you may not understand everything now, you may understand it later, plus you need to take the time to study the basics before trying to understand a bunch of things without foundational biblical knowledge. Stop trying to prove the Bible wrong. Instead, pour yourself into knowing God and learning about the things in the Bible, especially the things that don't make sense to you. It is good to question but don't just stop there. Research and find out the answers rather than forming opinions based on your lack of effort." We discussed more as I pulled out my Bible. I told him there was a chapter I was memorizing and I wanted to read part of it because it really spoke to me for him.

Colossians 1:21-22 *"Once you were alienated from God and were enemies in your minds because of your evil behavior. But now He has reconciled you by Christ's physical body through death to present you holy in his sight, without blemish and free from accusation - if you continue in your faith, established and firm, and do not move from the hope held out in the gospel. This is the gospel that you heard and that has been proclaimed to every creature under heaven and of which I, Paul, have become a servant."* We discussed the meaning. Every week he continues to question, doubt, criticize and make excuses for his lack of faith and spiritual fruit in his life .

I asked for the hundredth time, "Joey, have you read Psalm 1 and 139 yet?" He told me no and I said, "What!? You told me you would, and it has been weeks. You've had enough time." He raised his hand in defence and told me his Bible did not have Psalms in it. It was the one I had given him, a little New Testament and unfortunately, it actually didn't have the Psalms included. I asked him if I could give him a Bible with the Psalms in it and he said no, he didn't want two Bibles.

Then he said, "Can't you give me something else to read that's in my Bible?" I thought for a moment and said, "Why don't you read 1 John, it's a very short book of the Bible but it is so good." So he shook my hand and promised me, once again, that he would read it. As he turned to leave, he looked back and meaningfully said, "Thanks Val." Sometimes I just want to look up and say, "Lord, Joey's heart is so dead and his mind is so lazy. This man better be worth it!" Ha ha, a very "untheological", unchristian prayer that I already know the answer to.

I saw Tyler on the street. I've known him for a couple of years. I have watched him deteriorate and I suspected he was on some drug. I told him he looked pretty rough. I asked him how his pain was in his leg and mentioned he just didn't seem right. I asked him if he was taking any street drugs and he confessed to a bit of marijuana on top of his prescribed pain meds. I asked him if he had done any drugs that day and he said he hadn't. I asked him how he was doing with the Lord as he proclaimed he was a Christian. He told me he was doing really good and that he prayed to the Lord every day. This answer frustrated me as he was obviously not doing well with the Lord, with life or with anything. I suppose I needed to ask Tyler different questions. I spoke to him about a few things but because his demeanour just didn't seem right. I asked him if I could pray over him. As I prayed, my disappointment with him fell away, my heart posture changed and I began crying out to the Lord over this man, once again. When I was done, Tyler had tears streaming down his face. I love how the Holy Spirit can minister to someone when I can't.

Nine months later, I was talking to a man, looked over and again, saw Tyler. I hardly recognized him and went over to him, "Tyler?" His legs were shaking from his past injuries and he held onto a table for support. I immediately picked up in my spirit a heaviness on him. He shared with me that his family had just found out that he was living on the streets. He had been hiding it for the last two years. His sister came immediately, got a room at a fancy hotel and had him stay with her as they discussed his situation and what steps he needed to do to get out. I asked him how his relationship with Jesus was. He gave me a pat answer and said he was doing good. I looked at him. His eyes and body told me otherwise. I said, "Tyler, I know you're trying to be positive, but I understand that what has happened in your life is difficult and must be exhausting and disappointing. I'm going to pray for you." I put my arm around him. His body was so weak, he leaned on me. I prayed, "God, have mercy on Tyler. He's not innocent, he's done lots of things he shouldn't have and his life is such a mess. I know he actually doesn't deserve it but You are our only hope. I don't even know what to pray for, but, Lord, have mercy and deal with the mess. Restore, raise up and bring him into the destiny that You created him for. May he be a man after Your heart . . ." Tyler shook with sobs. I can't describe the feeling it was to intercede for someone in his weakened state with a raw, deep pain and a mess that seemed impossible to get out of. For moments as I stood with my fallen brother in Christ, I felt the weight of sin and trauma. I continued to pray and when I was done I gave him a hug as he thanked me. I encouraged him more before he left. I have had countless discussions, times of prayer, and pointed him to the Lord over and over. I am thankful to serve a God that does the impossible because Tyler really does seem impossible.

It was Jordan! I hadn't seen him since the summer. He shared with us that he was stabbed in the chest while he was sleeping on the street. He flatlined for four minutes and was on life support. He had the scar to prove it. As we listened to him tell this horrific story and asked him questions about what he was doing now, we saw that he was having memory issues and had changed. I had known Jordan for eight years now. I prayed for him but his hard heart caused him to interrupt and argue with my prayer, of all things, saying he was basically fine and he was surrendered to God, which he clearly was not. My friend and I later discussed his behaviour. We agreed he was not quite right. My friend is a nurse and told me that if he had flatlined for four minutes he most likely did not get enough oxygen to his brain which would affect him. That really bothered me. He's had so many chances to turn to the Lord. I have had countless deep conversations with Jordan and the Lord has spoken clearly to him. He has been to tears many times as the Holy Spirit touched his heart, but as the years had gone by, he continued to say no to God and live in disobedience. I have had a front row seat as to what it looks like to watch a heart harden, eyes turn blind and ears go deaf. It's sickening and compels me to continue reaching out to the lost.

I once again brought up the topic of God to an individual in my life. We have had hours and hours of conversation about her rejection of the Bible, rejection of a relationship with Christ, and unhappiness with life. She keeps running to all sorts of other things to find happiness; men, alcohol, activities to distract her. Of course, she remains empty and full of despair. I've reasoned, I've begged, I've sent information, I've given examples, I've prayed but to no avail.

I have tried running on sand a few times. Ugh! It zaps my strength, takes the spring out of my stride, and slows me down. BUT . . . it develops stamina, strength and endurance. Similarly, we must not give up on those who are still this side of eternity. Why? Well, it certainly isn't because they deserve it, none of us do. Frankly, most people and their situations really are hopeless and there is nothing that can fix it. That is, of course, apart from Jesus. Our Jesus is the Redeemer, the Restorer and the One who saves. Trudging reminds me that I cannot save, it is the Holy Spirit who changes hearts and minds, whether it is in a moment, or over a long span of time. I don't get to determine the way someone responds or how someone receives. I just get to listen, to trust, and to obey the Life Giver, the One who fills me with determination not to quit.

CHAPTER 17

FLYING HIGH

"God forbid that I should travel with anybody a quarter of an hour without speaking of Christ to them."
- George Whitefield

I love taking trips in airplanes. I love the surprise of who God is going to sit beside me.

A young man was sitting in the airplane beside me. He was playing video games on his phone. For the last hour I had been sensing the Holy Spirit nudging me to speak to him. I kept coming up in my mind with excuses as to why I shouldn't, "He's probably another religion, he can't escape from me if I talk about Jesus, that's not really fair." But the nudging was growing. I put the book down that I was reading and listened to the Lord. He showed me the young man had a softness and a sensitivity to the things of the Spirit. I was to share with him that the Lord wanted to reveal things about Him that many cannot be shown. So I turned to him and said, "Hey, just have a strange question for you, were you raised in a church?" He looked at me and said, "No." I continued, "Have you ever been to a church before or have any spiritual beliefs?" He answered, "Well, my wife is a Christian." I said, "And are you one as well?" I think I had startled him with my questions and he was trying to know how to answer. "Yes, I am too." I smiled at God and him. Then I said, "I am a Christian too. This whole flight He's been showing me things about you." I went on to explain what I had sensed. He shared with me he was a fairly new believer and was still growing a lot in his faith. They went to church every week. I encouraged him to read the Bible and seek Truth. We had a great conversation. He thanked me for sharing with him and I went back to reading my book.

I love how the Lord wants to speak to His kids, encourage them, tell them how He sees them. What if I had not been obedient? Well, the young man in the plane would have missed out on an identity statement and invitation from the Lord. Now the Lord can show him truths in other ways but I was able to be part of it and experience watching the Holy Spirit work. The gentleman was able to hear from the Lord, and now the Holy Spirit will take the seed and grow it.

I had a seventeen hour flight ahead of me and to my delight I got a row with three seats across with only one other gentleman, making an empty seat between us. This enabled me to sleep a good portion of the trip. When I was awake I read, ate and asked the Lord about this man beside me. I noticed the man had his arm in a tensor bandage. I engaged in conversation with him, just asking him where he was from. I eventually turned the conversation to his arm, asking him what had happened. Once he shared, I told him I believed in a God who heals and asked him if he had any spiritual beliefs. I found out he was raised in a Christian home but hated going to church. He had married a strong Christian woman and she went to church but he didn't. I asked him why and he squirmed a bit. He told me he felt most connected with God when he was out in nature. It became clear through conversation that he had no idea what being a Christ-follower truly was even though he thought he did. I was able to share with him what my faith looked like. I then shared a couple words that I had gotten from the Lord beforehand which communicated how God saw him. All were received well, except one, which didn't make sense to him at all. I simply shrugged and said, "Well, keep it in mind. Maybe God will reveal it to you later." I encouraged him to pursue a deeper relationship with the Lord. I asked him if I could pray for his arm. He said, "If this arm gets healed I'll remember that Val from Canada healed it!" I just about choked on my drink. I laughed and said, "NO NO!! I can't do anything. Healing would be from Jesus!" I prayed for him as the flight was descending. Nothing visible happened at that moment. Later I wished I would've remembered to ask him to move it around and test it. We said goodbye and I prayed for him that night. Again, I must leave the results and fruit up to God.

On another flight, I sat beside a gentleman from Germany. He spoke English and we got into a discussion about politics in which we had opposing views. I tried to keep things light and friendly, waiting for an opportunity to lead the conversation toward spiritual things. He shared with me that he was put in a Christian school as a teen but saw so much hypocrisy he completely turned away. He did not know if there was a God now. I gave him a message and explained a picture that I felt the Holy Spirit was showing me but it didn't seem to really land on him. I discussed with him aspects of my Christian faith and acknowledged the hypocrisy he witnessed but also shared with him that did not mean God did not exist. We had a friendly conversation but to be honest, it was really hard. Although respectful, he debated with me over things regarding the validity of the Bible and the church. We discussed many issues that he was angry about Christianity. He eventually turned the conversation back to politics before the flight was over. We departed on friendly terms but I had to wonder if anything impacted him. I asked the Lord to use the discussion for His glory.

I could simply read a book or watch a movie the whole time on a flight but I choose to first listen to the Lord and engage. I can't control people nor their responses but I can be willing to be obedient and pour out the love I have for Jesus and for others. Flying high is never boring for a believer ;)

CHAPTER 18

HOSPITALS

"Our prayers may be awkward. Our attempts may be feeble. But since the power of prayer is in the one who hears it and not in the one who says it, our prayers do make a difference." - Max Lucado

The following accounts are a collection of experiences in a hospital setting.

I paired up with a fifteen year old team member and we had so much fun. I saw an older gentleman sitting in the hospital lobby and I asked him if he was visiting someone. He said he was a patient just getting a change of scenery. He was dressed in normal clothes and reading the newspaper. I asked him if he had been in the hospital long. He said he had been there for a few weeks and would likely be there a while longer while they tried to figure out all that was wrong. I sat down beside him, introduced myself, and shook his hand. I asked him where he was from and he told me that he was originally from Romania. I told him I was at the hospital praying for people. At the mention of prayer, he told me he was raised in an orthodox church. Just at that moment, a bunch of security personnel came charging in response to a man who was yelling and being quite disruptive. I wanted to wait for the drama to end before praying for this gentleman as I didn't want to draw any unwanted attention or get kicked out or something. I asked this gentleman all sorts of questions about his life. When the security team left I immediately turned the conversation and said, "Okay Dorin, I'd like to pray for you. God heals and I know He can heal you." He agreed to it, so I prayed for him, closing my eyes. My team mate said she watched him and he kept his eyes open while I prayed, studying me intently. When I was done I encouraged him and left.

We walked down the hall and saw three men sitting with an individual in an intense conversation. We heard the words "God", "Holy Spirit" and "prayer". We were pretty sure there were other Christians who were in the hospital evangelizing! We didn't interrupt but decided to go down to the cafeteria. We sat at a table and asked the Lord who we should talk to. There was a man hooked up to an IV sitting at a table working on a computer. I was really drawn to him. So we pressed into the Holy Spirit regarding what to say. My teammate got a picture of a lighthouse, she sensed that God was the Lighthouse and He was shining his light looking out into the dark waters for this man. I was sensing this man had anger and disappointment. I pressed into what the Lord wanted me to say about that. We approached him. I said, "Excuse me, but I love Jesus and as we were sitting over there He highlighted you to me." The man waved his hand and said, "I am really not interested. You are the third person to approach me about this." I was surprised and thought, "Oh no, all us evangelists have approached him tonight." I asked, "Three people tonight?" He answered, "No, in the last two days!" I was excited and said, "Wow! Well, we aren't going to keep you long but God wanted me to come over and tell you that He sees the way you feel about Him, the turmoil, anger and disappointment. He wants to remove those things from you and give you peace inside." I turned to my teammate and she told him about the lighthouse which was very accurate to what this man had just shared. I smiled, "God is obviously wanting to get your attention." We said goodbye and left, respecting his desire to not want to discuss anything. We thought that it was amazing that God had sent three people to this man already. We walked to the other entry way and there was a couple trying to get in through the locked doors. We let them in and the woman was very pale, walking with difficulty. We followed them from a distance and again asked the Lord if there was anything we were to say to them. I was getting a distinct picture of a waterfall. They turned a corner and I knew the opportunity for talking with them was closing. I sped up after them and called out to them. They turned and I said, "Excuse me, I love Jesus and when I passed you back there God gave me a picture for you. It was of you in a waterfall. You were standing in it and drinking from it. It was very refreshing and revived you. This is a picture of how God wants to heal you and refresh you." They were a bit startled and I knew I had delivered it pretty abruptly and bluntly. I find when this happens there is always a processing time that needs to occur and so I don't get too caught up in responses. However, they were listening intently and then the woman responded, "Well, I hope He will heal my hip." She started to continue walking. I called after her, "He does heal . . . we will pray for you." They called back, "Thank you!" and kept walking. We prayed for them as we walked away. My young team member said she felt she had a word for one of the workers back at the coffee cafe. We turned and headed to the cafe listening to Holy Spirit. I dug in my pocket and found some money so we decided to go buy drinks while we delivered the word as we weren't sure which woman the message was for (there were two workers). As we got our drinks, I saw the joy of God the Father over one of the young women, but I waited for my teammate to lead and to speak. Once we got our drinks, she chose the same woman and shared many things. She finished with, "And I see the joy of God over you." I smiled as that is exactly what I was shown. When we walked away I confirmed to her that she heard the same thing I had. We walked with our drinks back to the front door. It was a really busy night and many people were coming and going. As we stood at the front door discerning who to talk to next, a young man walked in and looked at us. His shoulder was wrapped up and he stood beside us waiting for the person who had dropped him off. I greeted him and said, "What happened to your shoulder?" He told us he hurt it snowboarding that day. I winced for him and said, "Well I believe in a God who heals. Can I pray for you?" He was shocked and said, "What?" I repeated it and he said, "Uh, okay," So I prayed for his shoulder and when I was done he asked perplexed, "Are you just standing here to pray for people?" My teammate and I looked at each other and laughed, "Yep, pretty much." His girlfriend walked in at that moment and he began to go with her to emergency. He stopped, turned back to us and said, "Uh, thanks." We waved and immediately to our right a woman pulled up in a wheelchair with a friend pushing her. She was waiting for her ride. I turned to her and said, "Do you get to go home?" She was happy and replied, "Yes, finally!" I asked, "How long have you been here?" She said a few days.

I smiled and offered, “Can I pray for your recovery? I have no idea what you've been in here for but I believe in a God who heals.” She said, “Yes, you sure can.” I put my hand on her shoulder, closed my eyes and prayed for her. When I opened my eyes her husband was just walking in the door with the vehicle parked outside. He looked at me, then her and was confused. I smiled and said, “So you're the one warming up that vehicle for her!” I said goodbye. When they left, my team member and I giggled. We looked like we were the welcoming and send off committee. Many people had been standing and watching us pray for these two individuals right in a row. People seemed to be unsure if we were officially assigned there to do that or not.

We walked back down the hall and there were the four men who had been talking to people about God. They stopped us and asked, “Hey, are you here praying for people and evangelizing?” We joyfully met our brothers in Christ who were there as well, doing what we were doing. We found out that one of them had actually served with our church at an outreach event. We exchanged contact information and were happy to know we were brothers and sisters in Christ.

The night was over and we headed back to our vehicles. It was so fun to do prophetic evangelism; just listening to the Holy Spirit and sharing with people His thoughts about them. Just praying for people is a huge act of evangelism as people listen intently to how we pray and what we pray for when we pour out our hearts to our God. It is usually very different from the dry, memorized, ritualistic prayers many have heard, and I know the Holy Spirit is impacting them and will stir them after.

One time, two other team members and myself met Rusty, a gentleman with diabetes, in the hospital cafeteria. He was missing his one leg from above the knee down and the other leg from the thigh down. His hands were swollen and he shook. He was sitting with his wife and three children. I found out they were Christians and actually led a street ministry in another city a few years ago. His wife loved going to Bible studies and they had been really struggling with his severe illness. They had been transferred from their city to ours and had all been staying at the hospital. As the team members spoke with him, I listened to the conversation but also tuned into the Holy Spirit, asking Him how to pray, what to pray and to take notice of. Both team members prayed over him and while they prayed, I kept my eyes open, continuing to listen to the Lord. I sensed demonic spirits ravaging his body and anger rose up in me over it. I sensed a need for him to purify his relationship with God at a deeper level. Because I had come in part way through the conversation, I did not know exactly where he was at spiritually. When they were done praying, I quietly asked one of the team members if he was indeed saved. She said yes and then asked him where he felt his relationship with God was. From his answer we could tell that yes, he definitely was a believer but then he said he felt like there was a wall between him and God. So I gently told him, "Rusty, since you are a believer, and understand the things of the Bible, I was wondering if I could pray against any ungodly, any demonic spirits that could be attacking you?" He nodded very quickly. I began to pray and rebuked every spirit that the Holy Spirit brought to my mind for him. I asked him if there was anything that perhaps he needed to repent of that he had not. He thought and said no, he felt very free in the Lord. I took a moment to go to the Lord again for direction. I then prayed out loud for healing, and commanded demonic spirits to stop their assignment and go. When I was done, Rusty said, "I am so glad you did that. I have been praying that God would send someone to come pray for me, and to also pray in that way against the demonic." That was incredible to hear. While he continued chatting with the others, I was very drawn to his wife. My heart went out to her. She was skin and bones, messy hair and looked so worn, yet I sensed such gentleness, a quiet strength and a need for encouragement. Her name was Lily. I stood up and walked over to her and put my hands on her shoulders. I asked her if I could pray for her. She nodded and as I began to pray, the Holy Spirit showed me things about her that I was able to speak to her. I told her God saw that she poured into everyone else and put everyone else before herself. She had a strength in her that God had given her. She chose to persevere, to not give up and her gentleness was evident to all. The Lord delighted in her and saw her as beautiful. Lily burst into silent tears as she buried her hands in her face. Deep, quiet sobs shook her body. I prayed fervently for her as the Lord filled my heart with love for her. When I was done, I gave her a hug and held her for a long time as she cried on my shoulder.

As the team members continued to chat, I noticed a man who worked at the hospital and was changing the garbage. He was a very tall man and I asked the Lord what He wanted to say to him. I walked over and greeted him. I said, "I just wanted to thank you for what you do; I'm sure it is a thankless job, but it is so important and I really appreciate you doing it." He was surprised and thanked me. I continued, "I love Jesus, and as I was watching you do your job, God just revealed to me that you are a man of strength in here," and I pointed to my chest, "and there is a quiet, yet very strong part of who you are." A smile broke across his face as he wiped the sweat from his forehead. I found out he was a Christian from Ethiopia. He was married and had a family. He had worked doing this janitorial job for eleven years. Currently, there was no other option for him to work in another job. This is what provided for him and his family. I asked him if I could pray for him. I did not close my eyes, as he was working and I did not want other hospital staff to notice that he had stopped working. He kept his eyes open too and I prayed fervently for this man, for his future, for more opportunities to provide for his family, for deeper intimacy with Jesus and that the destiny God had for him would go forward. Afterwards he was very happy and thanked me.

We went to the lobby of the hospital. There was a lady hooked up to an IV. She was with her husband. I greeted them and asked them what she was in for. She explained that she was just about to have her gallbladder removed and was waiting to be called to go into surgery. I asked them if I could pray for her surgery and they said yes. I quickly prayed for wisdom for the surgeon, a quick recovery and protection for her. They were very grateful and went back to her unit.

Another time, we were visiting the hospital, asking the Lord who He wanted us to talk to. We turned down a hallway and one of our team members greeted a young man. She asked him if he had any physical pain and he said yes, his back was very, very sore, so we prayed over him. He was with two young women who sat back and watched us. When we were finished, he told us that they actually came to visit a mutual friend who was a patient in the hospital. However, they realized they were at the wrong hospital and were on their way to the other hospital. Surprised, we laughed and suggested to him that perhaps the reason God brought them to this hospital was so that we could pray for him.

As we walked away, I caught a glimpse of a man and woman in a private waiting room. I felt the Lord wanted me to go in and bless them with prayer. I turned back, took one team member with me and peeked in the door. I introduced myself, explained I loved Jesus and as I had walked by, God had really urged me to come and pray for them. I found out they were cousins and were waiting for the one's sister to have her baby. They were also Christians. I joyously prayed over the baby, for protection, for the baby's destiny and the Lord's blessing on the baby. I also prayed for the influence these two adults would have in the baby's life. When I finished, the man said, "Wow, thank you. That just means so much to me that you would do that."

We sat in the lobby to go over our night, there was a lady there and I went over to her. She spoke poor English but when I said "pray" and put my hands into a prayer position, she said "church, Catholic" and pointed at herself. I again used my hands to indicate I believed in Jesus and asked her if I could pray for her. She said yes, so I did.

I just have to shake my head in awe at how much opportunity there is to minister and evangelize at a hospital. I could sit there all day and have constant conversation. I don't know how we as believers can unashamedly live a non-evangelistic lifestyle. We spend countless hours in front of computers, movies and pointless activities. I really do love mission trips and if possible, I'd love to go on one every year. I have to wonder though, how can we justify the time and effort of raising/saving money to go, and then temporarily take time in some other city or country to do a good deed, and if really intentional, actually share the gospel and minister, but then come home to do . . . nothing. We may share how much God showed up and what He did through us while we were in another country. It really is great and again, I love missions. Yet, could it be that we are walking around blindly, not aware of the opportunities in everyday life, and while we wait for the next "evangelism event" we miss out on watching God work in our everyday regular life. There is SOOOO much opportunity all around us, if we would just say, "Here am I, send me. . . send me

. . to the hospital, send me to the mall, send me to the streets, send me to the park, send me to the gas attendant, send me to my neighbour, send me to my co-worker . . . I am willing."

We were in a town that we had never been before. We were walking and looking for the hospital and came across a building that looked to me like either a nursing home or palliative care. I googled it and saw it was a nursing home. I thought, well, that could be fun. We went in and I introduced myself, "Hello, my name is Valerie and these are my friends. We have about 45 minutes of free time. We would like to come in and encourage your residents." The lady said, "Well, I don't know why not! Come on in." We signed in and one of the nursing home staff came to me and brought me to a table of six seniors, men and women, who were visiting with one another. They were very sharp mentally. I greeted them and sat down. I shared with them I had just come to visit with them. Our conversation went to where I grew up. This was great for creating conversation for a bit. I found they were very eager and friendly to engage. We laughed a lot and enjoyed chatting. There was a man beside me in a wheelchair, so as the conversation continued I just turned to him and said, "I see you are in a wheelchair. May I ask why?" The others all listened as he told me he had three ruptured discs and was in much pain. I asked him how long he had been in that condition. He told me it had been one year. I responded, "Well, I believe in a God who heals. Could I pray for your back to be healed?" He studied me and said, "I believe in a God who heals too. Yes, you can pray for me." I put my hand on his shoulder and began to pray. Everyone in the whole place went silent and listened. I prayed for the man fervently. As I was praying I became aware of all the people listening and the Lord stirred me to pray for all of them. I turned and prayed loudly for this community. I prayed and declared that this season in their life was not in vain and that God has a plan for them every day. He gave them breath and until that last breath, they had purpose. That every day has potential to have an impact for a thousand years because a day is like a thousand years to the Lord. I prayed they would encourage each other and that the Lord would shine His light through His people. Finally, I prayed that they would know Him deeper than ever before. When I was done, they all sort of just looked at me. And then the man in the wheelchair said, "What are you? What denomination do you belong to?" I said, "Well, I love Jesus and to tell you the truth, I really don't like all this denomination stuff. I think there is much division over silly things in the Christian church. As long as a person is a follower of Jesus and follows the Bible accurately, then I think we are all part of the Kingdom of God, with diversity. So I follow Jesus. But if you want to know what church I attend, it is part of the Evangelical Missionary Church of Canada. Do you go to a church?" He nodded, "I am a Pentecostal and was one of the founders of the Pentecostal churches here in town. I agree with you about the denomination thing. I was part of the Ukrainian Pentecostal church here in town. Years ago there was a dispute over which language to have the services in, English or Ukrainian. We ended up having a split. I was on the side for English and helped found the new church." I listened intently and responded, "That was a pretty stupid reason for the people of God to split over." He thoughtfully and slowly replied, "Yeah, it was pretty stupid now that I look back." We smiled at each other and I said, "What's your name?" He told me it was Jack. We shook hands. The others at the table and in the room had been listening but now began chatting amongst themselves about other things. I was able to focus on Jack. "Where would you say you are now Jack, in your relationship with Christ?" He answered, "Oh Jesus is everything to me and I pray all the time. I just . . . I just. . . I guess I haven't had the faith lately to ask for healing for my back." I smiled and loved this man so much. "Well, isn't God good! He sent your sister in Christ to come with faith and stir up yours. He wants to encourage you, Jack. He sees the pain and the place you're in. He is not done with you! Are you in major pain <u>all</u> the time?" He said yes. "How does it feel right now as we are talking?" He held up his hand and put an inch between his thumb and pointer finger. "Just a little bit better." "Well, we believe in a God of a 100%. Can I pray for you again?" He said yes, so I did. I prayed for his full healing. I asked him again how he felt. He said "good". I got more specific. "Do you still have pain?" He said, "A little, less than before." I told him that God was beginning his healing. I would continue to pray and have others pray for him too. We talked more about the Lord and then I could see we needed to get going. I went over to my other team member who was speaking to a 94 year old woman. This woman was seat belted into a wheelchair and was slouched far down because she did not have the strength to sit up. I crouched down and spoke with her. She was very sharp mentally with a huge smile and so in love with Jesus. I could clearly see the Holy Spirit's Light beaming out from her. I told her so and she was incredibly encouraged to hear that. I prayed over her, hugged her and then we left. I was so glad we had gone in there. What a difference we can make in someone's day, in someone's life, if we would just take the time and be brave enough to try different ways of revealing Jesus to people.

I bet when we get to heaven we will be embarrassed and grieving over what we all squabble over. How we should cherish one another. We must give one another grace, freedom and know we are going to be in eternity together. We must value, encourage and breathe life into our senior spiritual family. I love their insight and their life experience. We truly need to nurture them.

At a hospital, we went out to the emergency doors to see if there was anyone to talk to who was having a smoke break. A truck roared up to the doors. A man jumped out and ran around to the passenger side. He opened the door and helped a woman out, probably in her mid fifties, early sixties, who had a towel on her head covered in blood. Blood was splattered down her face, hair and clothing. I went over to them and said, "Hey, can I help you with anything?" The man's eyes were full of fear and panic. He held the woman, put her in my arms and said, "Please, please, take her to the emergency, get her in there, I need to park my truck!" I said, "Absolutely!" and began walking the woman slowly to the door. As we made our way, I asked her what happened. She told me she was doing renos in her basement and a piece of wood fell on her. I was hardly listening as we made our way through the hallways. I had my arms around her, walking her slowly and trying to keep her engaged in conversation. She said it was the fourth towel she had soaked in blood and that she was so embarrassed. We were walking past all the people in the waiting room. She was such a sight that everyone sat up to watch us. Suddenly, she closed her eyes and was starting to pass out. I kept calm, told her to breathe with me and then put her arm around my neck so that I had a better grip in case she went down. I told my young teammate to find out where the desk was for me to take her and to find a nurse. The lady recovered and kept walking with small steps. Two more times she almost passed out and I finally got her to the nursing area. They were busy and didn't see us. I banged on the window, calling out, "I have a woman here who's going to pass out and she has a head injury." They looked up and unlocked the doors to their area. I walked her in and sat her on a chair. I bent down in front of her face and she said, "Thank you so much! If I never see you again . . . have a nice life." She smiled weakly and continued, "It has been so kind what you have done for me, thank you! Oh! I hope I didn't get blood on your coat." I chuckled and said, "What is your name?" She said, "Hilly." I said, "Hilly, my name is Val, I will be praying for you. I'm going to go get your husband now and bring him to you." She thanked me and I turned to the nurse, "I don't know this woman. Her name is Hilly and that's the fourth towel she's soaked in blood, I'm going to go get her husband who has her health card. He's just parking the truck." The nurse was surprised and began to take off the towel. Hilly howled and they sprung into action. I went out of the room and found her husband running, confused and panicked. I waved and led him to her. I banged on the nurse's window again and called, "This is the woman's husband. Please let him in." They unlocked the door; he thanked me and ran to her. We walked away through the crowd in the waiting room and their eyes all followed us as they had just witnessed all our actions. We inspected ourselves for blood and then sanitized our hands, so thankful we could be there at that moment. We walked the main hallways of the hospital and it was very quiet. I saw a man sitting in a wheelchair, rolling really quickly toward the doors with his hands. He was wearing shorts and a light shirt. I called out to him when he went by, "Are you going outside in shorts? It's pretty cold!?" He smiled and said, "Yep!", then rolled quickly by. Much later on, our evening wrapped up and I still had not seen the man in the shorts come back in. On my way out, I looked for him. My team member and I found him in the entryway talking to another lady who also was in a wheelchair. I smiled at him and said, "I'm glad you're still not outside, you'd freeze!" He was friendly and invited conversation saying, "Oh, the cold doesn't bother me at all. I can't feel anything." I looked at his legs which had patches on them and I gently said, "Do you mind me asking what happened to your legs so that you are in a wheelchair?" Sid openly shared his story. Three years ago he came in for a simple, easy procedure that was supposed to have no problems. He was sedated and when the surgery was done, they had made a mistake which caused complications. They sedated him again to go in and fix it. The unthinkable happened; they accidentally nicked his spinal cord. He was put in ICU and heavily drugged. He said they woke him up after a month of being in a medically induced coma! He was told he was paralyzed. He said he didn't believe it at first and said "No, I'm not!". He was incredibly confused. But he was in fact paralyzed. Since then he has been in a wheelchair and will continue to be for the rest of his life. Over the last three years he had been in the hospital a cumulative of two years! His longest stay was nine months. He has had twenty-two surgeries. In his words, "None have been helpful." He was just finishing a six month stay and in three days he was going to get to go home. I asked many questions and found out he was married with four kids; 10, 12, 20, and 22 years old. I could just feel the pain and heaviness of this man's soul. We stood in silence and I stammered out very quietly, "Sid, I am at a loss, I can't even fathom how devastating this has been for you." Then with all the faith I could muster I said, "I . . . I believe in a God who heals . . . and I believe in a God who sees and knows us at our deepest parts. Could I pray for you?" Sid nodded his head, "I believe in God as well. Yes, absolutely, I would like prayer very much."

Suddenly Wilma, the woman in the wheelchair that he had been talking to and who was listening to all this, piped up, "Will you pray for me too??" We turned to her, said of course and asked her for her story. She shared that she had been on dialysis for ten months and had several heart issues. I could see that one of her legs had been amputated as well. Her other foot was wrapped up quite heavily. She pulled out her phone and showed us a picture of a huge area that was black with infection on her heel. It had appeared over a twenty-four hour time span, three weeks ago. There was no more blood flow going to her foot and the infection was climbing up her leg. I could see the swollen redness on her calf. Her doctors told her they were going to need to amputate her entire leg, although she was very against it. If they didn't though, the infection would continue to climb and she would die from it. The doctors were worried to do the amputation out of concern her heart was not strong enough and she had a high probability of dying during the surgery. In order to increase her odds of survival, she needed quadruple bypass heart surgery, which of course was very risky and not a great option because of the infection in her leg. Every option from the doctors ended in death and she was trying to hang on until after Christmas before going through any surgery so that fatal results would not devastate her grandkids and children during Christmas. She welled up with tears and said she hated to talk about it. We stood in a moment of silence. My team member turned and said, "Sid, you said you had a relationship with the Lord. Wilma, do you have a relationship with God?" Wilma shook her head no, "No, I don't, but I'm thinking I may need one." I said, "Let me explain it to you, Wilma. It is very simple, even a child can have a relationship with God." I explained the cross, sin, choice, other religions and heaven. When I was done, Sid said, "Tell her about the other place . . . tell her about where she will go if she doesn't choose God." Then he turned to her and said, "If you don't choose God, you'll go to the other place of fire and torment and you don't want to go there." I cringed a little. He spoke the truth. Nonetheless, I also didn't want her to make a choice out of fear and needing "fire insurance". I validated Sid's statement, "Yes, he's talking about hell. If you choose here on this earth not to have a relationship with God through Jesus then He will honor your decision and you will be separated from Him after death as well. God is everything good, everything perfect and right. He is true love, true joy and complete peace. If you choose to be separate from Him, you are also choosing to be separated from all those things as well. That is what is called hell." My team member jumped in, "Wilma, would you like to make that decision tonight? We can help you with that." Wilma said, "I don't want to say anything right now." I replied, "That is wise of you to think about it. And you can talk to God even when you are alone, in your room, in your bed or whenever you want." We began to pray over Sid and then over Wilma. It was a powerful time. When I laid my hand on Sid's shoulder it was completely skin and bones. When we were done, I asked Wilma if I could check in on her over the next few weeks. She gave me her full name and cell number saying I could text her. I hoped to follow up with our conversation after she had time to think about it. I knew that if the Lord did not heal her, she would not have much time left. I said to her, "Wilma, God made you and He knows the number of days you will live. He planned your birth and He knows the time of your death. No doctor knows that and so I want to encourage you that your life is only over when God says it's over, not before." She nodded and wiped her tears. Wilma went out to have a smoke. We were left with Sid. He shared a little bit more of the difficulties he faced. I said to him, "Sid, I really sense a heaviness on you. I can imagine this has also been very difficult stress on your marriage. I sense you're wrestling with some dark emotions." He got very serious and nodded. I encouraged him to worship God and fight to drive the dark, heaviness away. I explained to him a bit of what worship is and what the source of the heaviness was from. I asked if I could pray again for him and this time I rebuked the demonic spirits that I sensed were attacking him, speaking the things the Holy Spirit was showing me about how God saw him. We said goodbye and left the hospital.

As we walked down the street to our vehicle, I turned to my teammate and said, "And we were complaining about what??" She shook her head and said, "Yeah, no kidding!" We walked in silence as we rolled around in our minds the reality of the people we had spoken to.

This is why I love the hospital. I could just sit in a hospital all day long ministering to people. I feel sorry for those in the church who don't do stuff like this. They are robbed of the depth, richness and faith this kind of evangelism brings to a person's life. It brings everything into sharp focus and it just can't be replaced by anything else. I suppose that's why Jesus commanded us to do it.

CHAPTER 19

HEALING

"We are all faced with a series of great opportunities brilliantly disguised as impossible situations."
- Charles R. Swindoll

If I'm going to share about hospitals and people suffering infirmities in the last chapter, then I'd better write about healing. I've always been in love with the stories of Jesus physically healing people in the Bible. I've always been exposed to people calling Jesus the Healer. For years and years I just didn't really see many churched people actually pray out loud for healing or at least in a way that actually believed that healing would occur. My own experiences in praying for someone to get healed in a group setting would always cause me to break out into a sweat.

It was incredibly busy and a steady stream of people on the transit platform. My friend was needing to go buy a train ticket. I simply prayed, "Lord, while I'm waiting, is there anyone you want me to talk to?" I turned to scan the crowd and saw two young, tall men coming towards me covered in tattoos and piercings. They looked a bit intimidating. The one was limping. I wrestled for a few split seconds on whether I should engage them and the word "obedience" came to me. Then the question was posed to me from the Lord, "Val, when you say you believe that I heal, is it just words or will you walk the talk?" When they got close enough I took a breath, put on a big smile and said hi. The one man looked around to see if I was actually talking to him. Confused, he said, "Do I know you?" I laughed and awkwardly said, "No . . . I was just wondering what happened to your leg.

I can see that you are limping?" Through my questions he sheepishly and roughly explained he got shot seven weeks ago. A piece went into his leg and had caused infection. He was taking street drugs for the pain but then went to prison for thirty days and was forced off the drugs. Just recently released, he said his leg was incredibly painful as the infection was still lingering. I was not expecting that background story!! I mustered the courage to say I believed in a God Who heals and asked if I could pray for him. His quick and emphatic, "Yes!" surprised me. I got down on one knee and put my hand on his leg and prayed. It was really busy on the sidewalk and people were walking all around us. I didn't have words or how to pray planned out. As I prayed I wondered what I would say when I was done. The second I said Amen, he excitedly said, "Want to hear something interesting . . . the rest of the story?" Surprised, I said yes. He told me a couple years back he was in prison for a different reason and was in a rehab program. There was a Christian lady who came and did a "Sunday School" (I imagine this was a Bible study) and he regularly went. One time he was really sick for days and wasn't able to attend. The lady was able to come pray over him and he got better within the hour. He continued the story, "I've been walking downtown here for hours and my leg has just been killing me. I can hardly stand it. Just five minutes ago the memory of this lady came into my head and I looked up to the sky and said, 'God, can you send someone like that lady to pray for my leg?!' Then you came and stopped me!" He thanked me and started walking away in the crowd. In amazement I called, "He's trying to get your attention!" He turned and called back, "Yes . . . He just did!" I turned to my friend who had come and joined in halfway through. I was blown away and excited, "Wow! I'm sure glad I obeyed!" I don't even know if this man was healed or not because he disappeared into the crowd before I could ask, but I know both his and my faith were boosted that day.

I knew when I began doing street ministry that I was pretty scared to pray for healing for people and to be honest, for good reason. I don't think I had ever seen someone actually get healed in an instant. I had heard about it, read about it, but never experienced it. I decided to just start praying for people for healing, no matter the outcome, scared but wanting to be obedient. Here's how it went.

During my regular weekly outreach on the street, I prayed for a man who had back pain. When I was done, I made myself ask him how it felt, just like Jay, the former leader of the street ministry, had taught me and as a step of faith. The man said it felt the same. I asked him if I could pray again and he said yes. When I was done he said, “That’s okay, Val, don’t worry about it.” I found myself wanting to explain for God as to why he wasn’t healed. I wanted to defend that God really does heal. I fumbled through it. He showed up a week later and told me he got a place and was moving away. He just wanted to come tell me the impact I had in his life. The encouragement and prayers he received had really helped him get through a dark time.

I saw a man walking with a cane. I stopped him and asked him what had happened. Dan said both legs had been damaged from a bunch of accidents; he had been like this for ten years. I told him I believed in a God who heals and asked if I would be able to pray for him. He thought for a few moments and said yes so I bent down and put my hands gently on both legs and prayed for him. When I was done, I asked him how they felt and he said very sore. My team member asked him if he also had back issues, as she was sensing that from Holy Spirit. He said yes. She asked him if she could pray for him for his back and he said no, he had to get going. I don’t know why but I took a step in front of him to stop him and asked him a few more questions. He used to be a Christian but was now agnostic. I told him I could sense he had disappointment with God. I then asked him again if I could pray for his knees and back. This time he said yes, so I prayed. As soon as I was done he quickly said thanks and walked away.

I walked down the platform praying and a train pulled up and several passengers walked off. A tall man with messy hair and all dressed in camo came walking right towards me. I greeted him and asked, “Hi how are you?” He responded and stopped to chat. He told me he was on his way to get high. I said, “Oh really? Why are you doing that?” Through my questions, I found out his father was in the Hell’s Angels and raised him in that environment. He had a lot of physical pain (his shoulder and knee from fights) and the drugs stopped the pain. Then he asked me what I “do”. Ha, great question. I told him I prayed for people. He asked me if I was “born again”. I said yes. He said he didn't think any prayers for him would work because God would never help him. He began to walk away and I moved my body position to block him and said, "If God heals your shoulder and knee would you still use drugs?" He thought for a moment and said no. I said, "Well then, if that is true, let me pray for you. My God is a God who heals." He agreed to accept prayer. He told me his actual name was Angel but he went by Bert. I put my hand on his shoulder and prayed, having two conversations going with the Lord. The prayer from my mouth was for his healing. The prayer from my spirit was, "Oh Lord, please show up and heal this man. Show him Your power, show him Your glory, show him You are real and he needs You!!" When I was done he immediately started to walk away and I called out, "God loves you and He wants to get your attention." He shook his head and said, "I don't think so." I wish I could tell you he jumped in the air and shouted he was healed and then fell to his knees to declare Jesus as Lord. Sometimes when I think about these conversations I think about all the things I could've, should've said, but in the fast moments I just say what I can with the time I have. I do hope I run into him again sometime. . . I wonder if God healed him later that day?

As a friend and I went for a walk we saw a man and a lady pushing a walker. I approached them as we walked and asked her what happened to her leg or foot so that she needed a walker. She very willingly engaged and told us she has diabetes and has problems with her leg and her toes. Actually, she was going to have one of her toes amputated soon. I told her I believed in a God who heals and asked if we could pray for her. She looked at the man and back to me, then said sure. I prayed for healing and when we were done she asked what church we were from. We told her and she said, "Oh, I love that church! I'm going to go there again soon." We chatted a bit more, gave her a hug and then left. A man called to me during our regular outreach, "Val, I need you to pray for me before I head home." I stopped, I didn't recognize him but he told me his name was Ryan and he had a really bad chest cold. I was feeling rushed to get to the others waiting for me, so I grabbed a team member and without explanation laid my hand on Ryan's chest and said, "In the Name of Jesus, every virus, all bacteria, all infirmity, get off Ryan and leave his body! Jesus, bring his body, his systems and lungs under your authority. Jesus, You have the authority to heal because of the cross and so I ask that Ryan would have a deep sleep tonight and be healed. Holy Spirit, fall upon him from the top of his head to the bottom of his feet. Amen!" I opened my eyes and he said, "Whoa, I feel really floaty." FYI: this may be how people who are not in the church describe the Holy Spirit's presence coming upon them. I smiled and left Ryan to another team member.

I know, right!? Not very exciting or flashy. Certainly nothing that would cause people to run and ask me to pray for them for healing. I sure wish I was more like Jesus in this. Even so, my Jesus is the Healer and He told us to go and heal the sick. I continued my obedience, knowing He heals.

As my friend Jay says, "If you want to see people get healed, pray for them."

As I walked out of the homeless shelter building after inviting many to come out and join our team, there was Michael, the guy with a cane who we had prayed for healing several times. He usually got temporary relief after we prayed and then got worse again. He was sitting down and told me his leg was not hurting as usual but his feet were so bad that he couldn't walk over to us. He pulled up his pant leg and showed me a large red spot spreading on his calf. It didn't look good. I asked if I could pray and he eagerly said yes. I got down on my knees and put my hands on his shoe and leg and prayed. I felt when I was praying that I was battling the actual sickness and demonic issues behind it. I know not every health issue is linked to sin or the demonic. I also knew Michael didn't "deserve" to be healed. He definitely had a lot of issues that needed to be dealt with. But I had had enough with the infirmities destroying his body, sensed there were deeper spiritual causes and prayed against those. More than anything I wanted the man to be fully devoted to Christ. If his ailments were to be a way to glorify God to Michael then I was willing to pray however the Holy Spirit led me. I did not see any quick healing in that moment. I actually never saw Michael again after that. Whatever the results were, that was between God and Michael.

I was talking to a man all about the gospel; who I had just met through striking up a conversation. I asked him about the lady in the wheelchair who was with him, just listening to us talk. He told me she was getting surgery soon for her knee as it did not have any cartilage. I bent down and asked her if I could pray for her knee. She, Josie, nodded yes and I began to pray. As I prayed my hand became really hot, which, of course, was not natural as I had a thin glove on and it was cold out. I asked her if she could feel any heat on her knee. She said her knee was now very hot. I prayed again for her. When I was finished I asked her how her knee felt and she said really good. I was a bit puzzled, wondering how it felt before. I asked her if her knee had been in pain. She said yes. I wanted to clarify so I asked her if it was in pain before I prayed for her. She said yes it had been but now there was no pain! I told her that God was healing her knee. I told her to pay attention to it the rest of the night and know that God was touching her knee. Praise God!

I have a daughter who has special needs and I pray every night (I'm serious, that's not just an exaggerated statement), I pray every night for her healing. At the beginning of finding out there was something wrong with her development, so many questions around healing and God came. Well-meaning Christians made statements from both extremes. "What was your marriage like when you conceived?" "Is there any sin in your life?" "Do you have any sinful movies, books, etc., in your house that need to be removed which are blocking her healing?" "Put this anointed cloth on your daughter, it will heal her." "Maybe you should have someone who has more faith pray for her." "Don't say she has a 'syndrome', just say she's having 'difficulties' and God is healing her, otherwise you are causing her to keep the syndrome." "God is sovereign. Just accept He made your daughter this way and stop praying for healing." "This is God's gift to you, her syndrome, because He knew you could handle it." Oh, and my favorite in response to me explaining she has special needs, "That's Okay. Well at least you have three other healthy children. Be thankful for all things." Ugh! Please, don't. Don't say these things to people. It's just so damaging. I do understand the premise and theological stance behind each statement *and* the fallacy in the understanding of the scriptures. Here is some important wisdom: Unless you have spent days and nights in deep prayer and fasting before believing that the

Lord would have you say any of those statements, it's better to just send a casserole. Throughout my journey, which could be another entire book, I researched, listened to teachers, prayed and grew in my understanding of healing. Again, this is not a book on theology nor on healing. You can go find many books on this subject. This is my viewpoint: Jesus is the Healer. He heals yesterday, today and forever. He commands us to go and heal the sick. Nothing is impossible with Him. Jesus is also not a genie in a bottle and He has the sovereign authority to say yes, not yet or I have something better; and anything in between. I live with the reality of daily caring for my daughter who is precious, beautiful and I'm crazy in love with her. She brings our family so much joy and laughter. I will contend for her healing and have peace in the non-healing. <u>I won't let my experience determine my theology.</u> I will always pray for healing because Jesus died and rose to give me the authority to do so. I will pray for people to be healed, emotionally, spiritually <u>and</u> physically, as it is the very nature of my God. It's Who He is and what He is, the Healer. So whether I see the healing immediately, see it over time or never get to see it, I won't let results dictate my prayers.

We get so scared to pray for healing for others. What if they don't get healed? If we take the risk and actually pray for someone to get healed, will God show up? What do we say if they don't get healed right there? I wrestled with all of these things and at times still do. But then I met this guy named Jay Cooling. He was the leader of the evangelism group when I first began. I watched him intently as he just prayed for anyone to get healed. The crazy thing was the more people he prayed for, the more people got healed. He prayed with such boldness, as if he actually believed the things that were in the Bible could happen today.

One day a man in his eighties, a founding member of our church, asked to have his hip prayed for. He had hurt it quite badly and was in a lot of pain, limping. Jay turned to me and said, "Val, pray for him." I froze inside as I thought, "You don't know who my daughter is. . . uh, you should probably pray for him yourself because my prayers don't work." But I knew that would be super unchristian and unbiblical. Instead, I stood up, hesitantly went over, broke into a sweat and laid my hands on the man. I didn't know if I should put my hands on his hip or if that would be weird or if I should just put them on his shoulder. I thought I should probably touch his hip so I did, risking being weird. As I began to pray, I was thinking, "Oh Lord, I don't even know this man's name. I don't know how to pray. Please do something nice for this older man, I know he is such a pillar in this church." I don't know how I prayed but when I was done suddenly Jay asked him, "How does it feel?"I thought, "Oh no, don't ask him that!" The man began to walk around and move. To my surprise the man said, "It actually feels 85% better." I couldn't believe what I was hearing! I knew this man would not lie and he was too mature to feel pressure to say something happened. Jay said, "I believe in a God of 100% and so let's pray again." I joined Jay in praying for the 100%. Jay prayed with authority and assuredness. When he was done, he again asked, "How is it now?" The older man stood up, walked and said, "It's completely perfect! No pain!" I thought, "Wow, a man in his eighties does not fake healing." Then Jay said, "Does anyone else need healing?"

As I watched Jay week after week being obedient to Jesus' command to heal the sick, I was inspired and uncomfortably challenged to do the same. I began praying for people for healing. It was sooo incredibly hard to muster up the courage and face my distrust of God to show up.

I talked to deaf Drake on the streets. I had known him for years. The poor guy was a believer and had no addictions that I was aware of. He was deaf and just couldn't hold down a job even though he was a good worker. He had lived with five guys for the last nine months or so but he told me it had turned into a bad situation and they had been taking advantage of him financially. We communicated mainly by writing notes on my phone back and forth because he couldn't speak very clearly and I had a hard time understanding the sign language. He had trouble reading. He said it was hard to explain but ever since he was a kid it was like "something is blocking my mind". Because of this he has a hard time growing in Christ because he can't hear nor can he read. That just makes my heart break for him and so even though I have prayed for him before I decided to pray again. I once again put my hands on Drake's ears and head and prayed. Drake always keeps his eyes open as he wants to watch my lips to see if he can understand part of what I say. When I was done, he thanked me. I pray for his healing every time I see him. Drake has inspired me to be like the persistent widow in the Bible.

I began talking to a guy sitting on a sidewalk. I found out he was a Christian and throughout our conversation he kept rubbing his jaw. After the seventh time, I took notice and asked him what was wrong with his jaw. He explained that he had to have surgery on his jaw and that it had pins in it. It throbbed and ached. It bothered him a lot when he talked. I placed my hand gently on his jaw and prayed for healing. We continued talking and after ten minutes he began to move his jaw around in between sentences. Finally, I said, "What's going on with your jaw?" Puzzled, he said, "Well, I just, it's, well, all the pain has left and it feels great. I can move it all around!" I sat there stunned, wondering if it was true. Ha ha, what great faith, eh!? But then I saw he truly was getting excited and was not in pain. I praised God! His jaw was healed!

When we were ministering at a parking lot space near a homeless shelter, there was a man in incredible pain from both of his knees. As we engaged talking with him, he was grimacing from the pain. I asked him if we could pray for him and he said yes. I got down on my knees on the pavement and put my hands on both of his knees and prayed. When I was done I asked, "How do they feel now?" He groaned in pain and said it was the same. I asked him if I could pray again and he nodded. I prayed again with fervor and faith. When I was finished he again told me there was no change. I pleaded to pray for him a third time. I did and prayed passionately. When I was finished he said, "It's okay Val. That was really nice of you. But I can't stand the pain anymore. I have got to go and sit down." I watched him limp away and I was so sad for him. It was like the pain got worse the more I prayed. Later that night I was lying in bed and came with a huge heaviness before the Lord, "Lord, I keep praying for healing for people but I never see them get healed. Do I need to have the gift of healing and I just don't? Do You not want to use me in this way? Is this something I should stop? Do I not understand how I'm supposed to be praying? I feel like I'm embarrassing You and ruining Your reputation. Lord, if You don't want to heal people through me praying for them, then show me and I will stop." I fell asleep dismayed but really didn't think about it anymore until two weeks later. I was at the same location and I heard, "Val! Val!" I looked and saw a man jogging towards me across the parking lot. Yup, it was the man who I had prayed for about his knees! Out of breath, he excitedly pointed to his knees, "Healed!" I was in total shock, "What?! When?!" He said, "That night you prayed. I went back to my room and they started to get better. Then over the next day they got better and better and . . . healed." I suddenly got skeptical, "Wait, like what was wrong with your knees and how long had they been hurting?" I was thinking that if they'd only been hurting for a week and then after a couple of days started feeling better that would hardly be considered God's healing. He exclaimed, "I hurt them six years ago! I have had three surgeries on each knee. I had metal screws put in my knee caps. The reason I've been here at the shelter is that I have been on disability and couldn't work! But after you prayed and they got better, I waited a few days to see if it was real and then I started looking for work again. I got hired! I got a job and I'm out of here tomorrow! I just wanted to come tell you before I left! Thank you, thank you!" I threw my hands up, "Do not thank me! I can't heal anyone! This was Jesus getting your attention. He healed you and He wants to have a relationship with you!" We spoke more about the gospel and I prayed with him. When he left I turned to the Lord and we had our own little private dance party in my spirit. I gave the Lord complete glory and praise. I realized He was giving me my answers to all those questions I had asked two weeks ago .

There was a lady who had come to our ministry booth at a psychic fair. She was from the Hindu religion and was asking for healing prayer for her knees. She had incredible pain causing her to walk very slowly and had been suffering for years. We explained to her about Jesus and who He was. We knew she was receptive to add Jesus as another God to serve and worship, alongside her Hindu gods. We continued to share the truth that Jesus was the only God and the only One who had the power to heal her completely and permanently. We then prayed fervently over her knees. Eventually it was time for her to go and we gave her a Bible. The next day we were back. In the afternoon the lady returned, paid her entry fee again to get into the fair and came straight to our booth. She wanted to tell us that she had gone home and began reading the Bible we gave her. Her knees had been healed that evening, completely! She was so amazed she knew she had to come back and tell us. We celebrated with her and explained more about the God of the Bible who just healed her.

Jesus heals. I've learned to pray for healing not simply to be nice, not because of my ability or courage but because Jesus is the Healer. I believe Him. I continue to pray for spiritual, emotional, and physical healing for people. I can now testify I've seen Him heal and I trust His decision of how and when He chooses.

CHAPTER 20

GOD BLESS THOSE MOMS AND GRANDMAS!(Dads and Grandpas too!)

"Each day of our lives we make deposits in the memory banks of our children." - Chuck Swindoll

I often hear people say things like, "My mom is like you," or "My grandma is always praying for me." I love hearing that because I realize what an amazing privilege it is that I get to be a part of the answer to those mom's and grandma's prayers. I just know that they are praying for God to send someone to influence, remind and encourage their child/grandchild. I also know that I have the backing of their prayers as I speak to their child or grandchild. It has happened so often, that I confidently tell them that our interaction is not a coincidence.

We were standing by a guy in his thirties and I began to press into the Holy Spirit by asking if there was anything the Lord would have me say to him. I got the word "gentleness" and then a picture of a lamb. I began to ask Jesus questions: Does a lamb mean something to him? Is the lamb symbolizing gentleness? Symbolizing the man? I was aware of time ticking away with the train soon to arrive. It came to me that Jesus was symbolized as a lamb going to slaughter, but it took strength and courage to do it. Jesus was strong yet gentle. I approached the man. "Hi, my name is Val," (he shook my hand and told me his name was Carl). "I know this sounds really weird but I love

Jesus and while I was standing over there, He just highlighted you to me and showed me something He wants to tell you. The word gentle came to me and I was given the understanding that you were gentle. God has placed that in you and made you that way. God also gave me a picture of a lamb. In the Bible, Jesus Christ was described as a lamb who was led to slaughter when He died on the cross for our sins. (as I'm saying this, I'm thinking why am I saying this and does he even understand any of this or is it too deep). Jesus was very gentle to those who were hurting but it took a lot of strength and courage to do what He did. I believe He has deposited gentleness in you, and wants you to know it takes strength and courage to allow that gentleness to impact and help others. I'm not sure if that makes sense to you or what you believe and I know it's weird for me to tell you all that. What do you believe about God?" He thanked me and said, "I don't really have much to do with God, I believe there is a God but nothing else really. My mom believed in God growing up but my dad didn't. My mom still believes in God." "Well, I know there is a God and maybe He's trying to get your attention. Would it be okay if I prayed for you?" He said yes, I prayed for him and then his train came.

A young man came up and asked if there was any pizza as we were finishing up our evening of outreach on the streets. We were out of pizza but I was able to give him a muffin. I asked him if I could pray for him. I could smell alcohol on his breath but he was very coherent and not drunk. Through our conversation, I found out that Ted struggled with alcohol and drugs. He was staying at the homeless shelter but had not been there long and had never been homeless before. His parents died when he was thirteen and he was raised by his grandparents. His grandma prayed for him. I knew that there was a spiritual war over his soul and I got to be an answer to her prayers. He asked for prayer for her as she was struggling with stage 4 cancer. He knew there was a God and took Him very seriously. He was very ashamed that he had been drinking and that I would pray for him in that state. I assured him that God wanted him to come as he was. I prayed for Ted and he was very thankful. I told him he had to make a decision about who he was going to serve, and to think whether he wanted alcohol and drugs to be his master. I encouraged him that God has so many plans for him, but Ted had to make a decision. He agreed with me and said he did not like who he was. I did not want him to make any decisions at that moment as I wanted him to not be under the influence of alcohol at all when he made such an important choice. I wanted him to think about it and prayed he would remember my words. I gave him a Bible and urged him to read it. I could see God's potential for Ted . . . how exciting it will be when he fully surrenders to God.

I kept seeing a young man walking around near a bus stop. He had a big backpack and looked like a stereotypical rapper/drug dealer. He also looked intimidating so I had not been making much eye contact with him as I was spiritually drawn to him. I made my way over there and stood beside him. I turned to him and said, "How's your night going?" He talked in a very smooth, rapper style way and said it was going cool. I started with a lot of small talk and questions. He had done roofing as a job but was not employed right now. So I asked him if I could pray for a job for him. He said sure. I put my arm on his shoulder and prayed. I saw he had a cross around his neck and when I was finished I asked him why. He very quietly said he was a Christian. I actually had him repeat it. He was in a raised Christian home. I began asking more questions and noticed he had lost the smooth style of talking. He wouldn't look me in the eyes much. He shared he had so many difficult and painful circumstances, he just didn't know how to move on in life. I challenged him in his faith and shared with him some truths. I began to call him out and up into his true identity. I asked him if he had ever actually accepted Jesus as Lord and he said he had as a kid. I told him the Holy Spirit was in him if his decision had been sincere and genuine. I told him if he had not been following the Lord and been engaging in a lifestyle he knew was sinful, he grieved the Holy Spirit and was not cooperating with Him. He agreed and I asked him if I could pray over his hurts and his life. He agreed again. This time I stood in front of him and put one hand on his shoulder and one on his chest. He was thirty years old but I felt like he was a son. I prayed fervently into his life and when I was done he began to make eye contact as I spoke. I explained to him why he needed to read his Bible and that this was a time to rebuild and make Jesus the first priority in his life. I talked about forgiveness and how to lead his heart. We had spent about twenty minutes together and in the end I gave him a big hug. I am so glad I took time to spend with this young man.

His name was Gordon. He looked very familiar to me and he said this was his fourth time coming to our outreach but he hadn't been there since the summer. I stood with him in the pizza line. Through asking questions I found out he was from Eastern Canada and had moved here three years ago. He is twenty-four years old and his girlfriend of two years had just overdosed on heroin in August and died. This had really "messed" him up. He thought it was an accident and not suicide. He, himself, used to drink but had been clean for quite a while. He was living at a homeless shelter and wanted to get out as soon as possible. His mom had died of cancer when he was young. She was a Christian and went to church a lot before she died. His dad never went to church and abandoned the family. Gordon was raised by his grandparents after his mom died. His grandma went to church and had been fighting cancer for the last three years. He really didn't know how to handle it and had a hard time talking to her on the phone. So I told him, "It seems like there is a trend in your family with the men." He looked at me puzzled. I said, "They don't want to go to church. The women are the ones who want to serve God." Gordon said, "Well, do you go to church every week?" I smiled and said, "No, not every week but I go most of the time. It's not about going to church though. It's about a relationship with Jesus." He got excited, "Yeah, that's what I think!" I inquired about what his spiritual beliefs were. He told me he believed in God and "stuff". I asked him if he had ever read the Bible. He said just a little bit. I said, "Gordon, there's this verse in the bible and it sounds a bit harsh but it's so good. It says, 'You believe there's a God? Good! Even the demons believe that and shudder!' (James 2:19) So you can say you believe there's a God and that's great that you acknowledge He exists, but demons do that too. The important thing is what you are going to do about the fact that there is a God. You get a choice with that information. There is no neutral ground. Are you going to have a relationship with God or are you not? God wants a relationship with you, that's what He created you for. He knows what will give you true joy and contentment that nothing else in this world will give you. You will keep trying different things in life but it will always leave you empty. Jesus is the only one who knows what your purpose in life is and can show you what to do. I want to encourage you that maybe God brought you here so that He can get your attention. You need to decide who you are going to be and who you are going to serve." Gordon nodded and agreed that what I said was probably true. I said, "I bet your mom prayed a lot for you before she passed." He nodded again and said she prayed for him all the time. Then I said, "I bet your grandma has and still is praying for you." He nodded again and agreed she was. "The Lord has His hand upon you Gordon, because He wants you to know Him." Just then his friend came up and was like, "Hey, yo bro, are you ready to go?" Gordon looked at me apologetically and said, "I better go, but I'll come back next week and talk more with you." I smiled and said, "I want you to think this week about who you are going to be and who He is going to be to you." They walked away. I did hope this young man would come back. He was really not that much older than my own son. I thought about that dying mother's heart crying out to the Lord for her son's salvation years ago. Oh Lord, let my words land upon his very heart and soul and may he wrestle with them all week long.

There was a line of people waiting for a bus. I introduced myself to a guy with a backpack. His name was Nathan. I asked him if I could pray for him for anything. He told me his parents were devoted Christians and prayed for him all the time. I smiled and said, "Well then, that's why we are meeting. God brought me to you. I prayed that God would bring me to whoever He wanted me to talk to and I bet God's answering your parent's prayers." He ended up telling me he had a drug addiction and he just couldn't stop. He genuinely wanted to stop and I believed him. He told me he sold drugs right where we were standing to get money for his own drugs. He just wanted to stop and get free from it all. I asked him if I could pray for him. Even though there were people lined up on each side of him, he said yes. I prayed and asked God to release him from the addiction. His bus came and he left.

I simply greeted a man, who grabbed some pizza from our team out on the sidewalk, by asking him where he was from. I found out his name was Jaxon, he was originally from Manitoba but came to Alberta for work. He had just come to stay at the shelter that week. We chatted a bit more and I quickly went to some questions, "So what are your spiritual beliefs? Were you raised with anything?" He said he was raised Christian, went to church, Bible camp . . the whole thing. I asked him where he was at currently with his beliefs. He shrugged and said he hadn't really thought of it for a long time. I guessed he was in his early thirties and said, "So, obviously something has changed from the time you lived at home until now. What caused you to stop thinking about God and going to church?" He smiled uncomfortably and said he wasn't sure. I tried again, "Well, you went to church before and now you don't think about God. What happened?" He looked down, squirmed and kept his polite smile on. I could see this young man did not belong at the shelter and he wouldn't stay long. He said quietly, "I guess when I left home I stopped going to church." I asked, "Why?" He looked down again and said, "I guess I started doing a lot of things that, well, made me feel a lot of guilt and shame and I just knew I couldn't come back to God doing that stuff." I thought for a moment and asked, "What do you think you're going to do about that?" He said, "Well, I try to do good things and help people." I responded, gauging how much he would or should know about the gospel from his upbringing, "Jaxon, you know you will never be able to do enough good things to outweigh the bad things, right?" He looked up at me questioning and said, "I'm trying." I began to share with him, "It's impossible. There's a verse in the Bible that says all your good works are like filthy rags before God. Actually, if you look at the original language the word is that all the good deeds you try and do are like, are you ready for this, menstrual clothes to the Lord. (Isaiah 64:6) He wanted to give an example that was the most disgusting to show how worthless and meaningless it was for us to try and do good things in order to pay for the bad things in our life." I went on to share with him the entire gospel, the idea of the Ten Commandments being a mirror and not a cleaner and the verse about being neither hot nor cold or God would vomit him out of His mouth. (Revelation 3:16) There was no neutral position. "Jaxon, if I were to ask you if you wanted, say, a chocolate bar and you said, 'I don't know', then ultimately you are making a choice. You are choosing not to take the chocolate bar. It's the same with God. When you don't choose to reject God but you don't choose to make God the Lord of your life, then you are making a choice. The choice is to not follow God. There's a difference between believing there is a God, because even demons believe that, and then making God the

Lord of your life. If He is Lord then you come into agreement with Him on what He says is right and wrong. You realize you can't fix the mess in your life and you need to have a relationship with Him because only He can forgive you. When you confess with your mouth that Jesus is Lord and believe in your heart that God raised Him from the dead, you will be saved (Romans 10:9). What Jesus did was pay the penalty for your sin, which you know already. When a person is saved there is an exchange that happens between you and Jesus. The purity, the holiness, the perfection of Jesus is put on you. All your mess, sin, guilt and shame was put on Jesus and He took it to the cross. So when God offers you the gift to come into relationship with Him, through Jesus He will see you as holy and blameless." I went on to share with him about other religions of the world and the "do vs done" concept. I finished by asking, "You've heard all that before?" He shook his head, "I've never heard all that before, I never understood it like that." I was a bit stunned and yet, not. Jaxon shared with me he had been involved with Buddhism for about a year. I asked him how that had worked for him. He told me it was good and he liked it, but he couldn't shake the guilt and shame he felt. He was stuck in a rut. I explained to him that the whole meaning of life was to make a choice: are we going to serve God or not? We give an account directly to God when we die. I explained to him the reality of hell and what that meant: absence from everything that was God; no peace, no joy, no love, no goodness, no forgiveness . . . for eternity. He hadn't thought of it quite like that. I said, "Jaxon, I'm not pressuring you at all. I just have a question. If tonight you had to choose knowing what I just told you, what would you choose?" He said, "Right now I can see I've been thinking I'm neutral but as you said, that means I'm really not neutral. If I had to choose tonight from what you've said, I would choose God, but I don't want to make a decision or anything tonight." I said, "Well, that's wise because the Bible says to count the cost. There is a cost, Jaxon. You have to acknowledge you can't be the god of your life and do whatever feels good. So think about it." He said, "I will this week. My family has been super supportive and loving me with all of that I've been dealing with. I've got to do something because I'm really just stuck and I'm so tired of it." I shook his hand, "Go after Jesus Jaxon, you'll never regret it," and we parted ways.

I talked to a man who I had never seen before on the sidewalk. He told me he had only been at the homeless shelter for five days and was sharing a room with three other guys. He told me it was hell in that place. Today while he was working, he fell and really hurt his shoulder. It was black, blue and numb. I asked him if I could pray for it. He laughed and said I sounded like his mom, always wanting to pray for him and talk about God. I found out he was raised Christian and was from Saskatchewan. He was a rough character and swore a lot as he explained his situation. His roommate had kicked him out of their place which was why he was at the shelter. His friends were all into bad stuff. When he refused to do some activities with drugs and didn't have money to share, they all took off on him. I confronted him. "Okay, you know better so I'm going to challenge you. You know that nothing else matters in this world besides your relationship with God. What's stopping you from following the God you know exists? He is the only One in this world who will never leave you, never forsake you. Nothing can separate you from God's love for you. (Romans 8:38-39) Why are you choosing things and people that will abandon you? Everyone in this world is going to disappoint you and leave you, even if it's just in death." I continued to talk with him. I again asked him if I could pray for him. He said yes and I did. When I was done he said, "This has been such a weird day. I seriously almost died today when I fell, and then I hear about coming out here and now talking to you . . . it's just super weird." I said, "God has brought you here for a reason and perhaps He's trying to get your attention. He loves you so much He'll do anything to show you His love for you." As he left, I smiled and said, "Make sure to call your mom and say hi to her. I think I'd like her."

CHAPTER 21

CHAOS = JESUS HAS PLANS

"Satan is so much more in earnest than we are - he buys up the opportunity while we are wondering how much it will cost."
- Amy Carmichael

My van got its rear window smashed during the night when it was parked right in front of my house! The next day I found it. I was teaching and preaching later that day and needed time to prepare. Instead, my morning was spent reporting the incident, dealing with insurance and setting up an appointment for the next day to get it replaced. I took a few hours to prepare for the evening in between various tasks. My son lent me his older vehicle. I was given short notice to go pick up some socks for the homeless and anyone in need from some wonderful donors. I rushed around and headed out early, picked up nine huge boxes full of socks, drove to the church and parked in front of the main doors of the building. Now the church was locked but there were a few people in it. I had access to the security personnel to let me in. For some reason he was not answering his phone. I needed to unload the socks into the building and I just really needed to use the bathroom as well. I decided I would drive to the Tim Hortons, use their bathroom, come back and try again. I went to start my son's vehicle and it wouldn't start. I tried and tried - nothing. I phoned my son and he told me that this had happened before. I needed to find the tire iron and pop the hood. With the help of my other son through facetime I was guided to find a metal thing between the engine and the battery and then hit it. I tried a few times but couldn't get it right as it was hard to see deep down. Finally, I said to my son that I had to go to the bathroom so bad I just couldn't concentrate. I ran across the parking lot to some trees on the property, hoped I wasn't on any security cameras and relieved myself. Able to laugh again, I ran back and hit the metal box a few times, which I later found out was the starter, and got his van running. Just at that moment, some painters that had been working inside the church opened the door and I called to them to hold it open for me. After unloading the boxes I drove over to my team in the parking lot and was able to start the evening, albeit a little flustered. However, the moment the worship music began, I determined to fix my eyes on Jesus. I chuckled at the absurdity of it all. I taught the team, then preached to a crowd on the streets. After preaching, I got into a conversation with a believer who had just returned to the Lord. We talked for a good portion of the hour as we went over some strongholds in his life. I prayed for him, he wept and walked away refreshed. While I was talking to him, a gentleman who had come to be ministered to by our team for years interrupted and said, "Val, I just want to tell you, your preaching really touched me tonight and really meant a lot to me. Thank you." I got back to the church late at night and wouldn't you know it, the van wouldn't start again. I grabbed that tire iron, whacked the metal thingy and started it up. As I laid in bed that night, I thanked God that the conversations, preaching, and teaching had threatened something in the spiritual realm, enough so as to stir such chaos beforehand.

Do you ever just shake your head in moments of your life when you don't know whether to laugh or cry? When a time is planned for you to evangelize, don't be surprised if your day turns into several chaotic situations that cause you to question if you should go: headaches, sudden increased workload at your job, traffic is terrible, tension with family, out of the blue issues with friends, incredible weariness coming upon you, deep heaviness falling on your soul, unsure why you just feel so down, etc. This isn't a coincidence. It's important to recognize that most times this is the work of the enemy to stop you from going out and sharing the life changing good news of Jesus Christ. I've learned that the greater the chaos, the greater the spiritual battle going on. I've also learned to take a deep breath and get excited for the coming conversations the enemy is trying so desperately to stop.

The night was a bit crazy for me. It was cold and the motorhome that I drove which carries the food and supplies for the homeless was having issues. The signal lights wouldn't work, the heater wouldn't turn on, so I prayed silently as I drove that I would arrive safely. When I got downtown, I realized I had left my bag at the church with my wallet, license and gloves. We were also late getting down there. I took a deep breath and knew that there must be someone down there who I needed to talk to because of all the distractions. There was a man that I began to talk to on the streets. He sounded like he had a very messy childhood with lots of hurt and abuse. He was not raised with any religious belief system. He was told he was Catholic but that was the extent of his knowledge. He did not believe in a God and felt humans were the only ones around on this earth. He was in his twenties and found life very depressing, the world full of corruption and very hopeless. As he talked, I kept asking the Lord what to say. He asked me if there was life on other planets and inquired how that would matter with the issue of God. I told him God created all life and if He has created other life on other planets then that was fine, and if He wanted us to know about it, we would, and if not, we wouldn't. But it didn't matter if there was or wasn't because our existence and purpose didn't change. Nor did God's identity or validity change.

I asked him what he felt the purpose of life was and he said he had no idea. I shared with him who I thought God was and the purpose of life He had given. He told me he would need to see something pretty amazing to ever believe in God. I asked him to give me an example and he said, "Like a person floating or something." I said, "So you want to see some sort of physical sign that would be impossible unless it was God doing it?" He nodded. I told him the story of the Rich Man and Lazarus (Luke 16:19-31). When I was done, I asked him if he would believe there was a God if someone died, came back to life and said they had seen heaven or hell and that there was a God that he should follow. Or would he/we as humans explain it away saying that they were hallucinating, not really dead, unconscious, had lost their mind, etc. I challenged him to think about it and he admitted he probably wouldn't believe them nor would he follow God because of it. Exactly. I asked him, "If you could hear a message from God, like God wanted to say something to you, would you want to hear it?" (If he said yes, I would grab some team members and sit down with him and listen to the Holy Spirit and see what the Lord would say to him but I wanted to hear his answer first.) He thought for a moment, then said, "I would have to think about that, I'm not sure." "Why?" I asked. "Because it would have ramifications," he replied. I was surprised to hear him answer this way but so happy that he did. I went on to say yes, it would. It would mean he would have to make a choice about how he lived his life. Would he serve money, himself, drugs, women, popularity or whatever else as his god or would he want to have a relationship with the God who made him? Would he listen to how God told him to live? I was able to draw out the lies he was believing and present the truths of the Kingdom of God. When I offered him reading material he told me he didn't read much. I asked him if I could pray for him. He said yes, but he had no idea what I should pray for. Ha ha, I had lots that I wanted to pray for. After I prayed, I asked him if there was any way he would be open to reading a Bible. He said he actually had one and because of our conversation was interested in reading it a bit. I told him about Jesus' best friend, John, who wrote down the stuff Jesus did and said. He was very interested in reading that and I invited him to talk with me about it next week.

After we wrapped up by praying, a different gentleman who had been drinking stumbled over and announced he wanted to sing me a song. As the team watched, he sang a song through many missing teeth about saying goodbye but asking for a kiss before we parted. His spit hit my cheek as he belted out the tune. I waited a few moments before discreetly wiping it off, I smiled and swayed to his song, complemented his voice and clapped for him when he was done. I made a quick exit to the motorhome as not to encourage his request for a kiss. As we drove home a newer team member said, "I saw his spit hit your face tonight and I thought 'Oh! I wonder how she is going to deal with that.'" I was so glad I kept the man's dignity intact and was able to demonstrate the grace and love of Jesus, for his sake but also for this team member and whoever else was watching. When we got back to the church I found my bag with my wallet. I also jiggled the key in the ignition and the signal light and heat began to work in the motorhome. I was able to have some deep conversations with some team members. I finally drove home and I had to say, "God, You are truly amazing."

I can't tell you how many times over the years it has not been the ideal conditions to go out and evangelize. If you ask our Monday Night Evangelism Team they will tell you Mondays are crazy and there is always a reason to not show up. I've had Mondays where my husband and I are fighting, or the kids are fighting, or I'm fighting with the kids, I'm trying to get supper on the table for the six of us before I leave, making sure everyone has a ride to their sports activities, feeling guilty for leaving my crying child or I'm just plain tired. Sometimes I just have a heaviness I can't shake that's unexplainable or a real unspiritual attitude. Sore throats, headaches and nagging coughs have accompanied me when I'm preaching or teaching. I recognize it all as a way the enemy is trying to keep me from going. I had decided long ago to push through and I always come home so thankful I did.

I left a houseful of sick kids with my husband who just arrived home from work as I was flying out the door to make it on time to our Monday Night Evangelism Team time. I was preaching and I really needed to get going. After our team meeting, I drove downtown, focused on what I was going to preach about. Once parked, I slammed my car door shut only to realize I had locked my keys in the car. I smacked my forehead and went to tell a team member. She graciously called her AMA and dealt with it for me. The crowd was growing, became very large and it was time for me to stand in the box of the pick-up truck and preach. The Lord took over and projected my voice. When I was finished, I challenged the group and invited them to give their lives to the Lord. People began raising their hands and many surrendered their lives to the Lord! I thanked God for touching the people that were listening. I knew that it was the Lord who touched people through me. If He didn't show up, all my preparation would be in vain and I would just be spewing out empty words. It was incredible to watch the Holy Spirit working in so many as they responded. I was so thankful I was obedient and didn't cancel. I was given my keys back from AMA. I surrendered my kids' health to the Lord and went home spiritually refreshed and grateful.

Tonight was a big night and much preparation had gone into it. It was almost Christmas and we were going to be handing out gift bags on the streets. There would be lots of homeless and vulnerable people joining us. There would also be lots of friends and family coming to join our team who had never come out before, some of whom were not Christians. We had done this for many years and after the first year, I made sure I never preached because of all the logistics and the need to engage with others on this busy night. However, for the last two months as I took different people to the Lord to ask who should preach this particular night, He kept saying He wanted me to. I felt a huge responsibility for this specific message and had a desire to put a lot of prayer and preparation into it. There is a lot of suicide that happens this time of year with those who are lonely, hopeless and empty. I felt I needed to address it head on and passionately lay out the gospel. As I was driving to the church, I was worshipping and asking the Lord to anoint what I said, to place His truths into the hearts of the hearers and . . . should I put more Bible verses in it? As I worshipped and prayed I had a flash of Jesus' face bending towards me and His voice broke into my thoughts, "Val, even if nobody gets saved tonight, I still love you. I love who you are. I love your heart. I love what you're doing." It shook me out of my concerns. I choked up and thanked God for His presence. I stood humbled in the confidence of being His daughter. And I was glad not to bear the burden and responsibility of getting people saved or healed. Hearing His voice was like a fresh breath that lightened my load.

We packed bags, prayed and organized at the church. I ran to the bathroom before leaving. I happened to have a fire extinguisher in my bag which I had grabbed from home since we were setting up a fire pit on the street. I seemed to be carrying a hundred things in my hands (Okay maybe like six or seven) as I walked through the church. Everyone was waiting for me outside. Suddenly I heard the sound of air. No, it wasn't angel wings or the Holy Spirit's presence. I was very confused as it was coming from my bag. I opened it to look and whoosh!! The fire extinguisher had somehow discharged and the contents inside burst forth out of my bag as I gasped. A fine yellow powder sprayed all over me. I got it stopped but there was a yellow cloud settling all around me. I paused and thought, "Are you kidding me!!!???" I walked outside and my team members looked at me in

awe as I explained what happened. I was covered from head to toe. My good friend, Melinda, started wiping my hair and coat the best she could. I quickly dusted off my face and knew we needed to get going. I jumped in the motorhome. As I drove, my lips, throat and hands started to burn. I realized I should probably get the chemical off of me. When we arrived, I wiped my skin with some bacterial wipes. I had to laugh. Who does this happen to?! "Well, if the devil thought he'd put out your fire, he underestimated you, now didn't he!?", one team member joked.
We had amazing worship leaders singing. Right before I was going to preach a man came up to me and said, "Val, I can't stay but I went to the doctor today and I'm passing blood. They did a bunch of tests and I need you to pray for healing." I didn't recognize this man. I asked him if I could pray for him after the preaching and gift bags. He didn't have a coat or socks on and was cold. He just ran out there for me to pray for him. So I told the singers to sing another song and prayed for him.

With yellow powder residue on my hair and toque, I began to preach. There were so many conversations happening when I began that it was a bit noisy. I stopped my message and asked them all to give me their attention. I told them what I had to say was extremely important and that they would want to hear. I preached probably some of the most blunt, straight-forward preaching I have ever done. I preached about twice as long as I normally do and had complete silence. I was very real and gave the audience utmost respect, but also called them on some things and challenged them passionately. When I was done, I had arranged for the team and singers to sing over the crowd to bless and honour them, which is something we had never done before. The team members went to each individual, gave a hug or handshake and a Christmas bag to each person. I just stayed with the worship singers and worshipped over them while it went on. When everyone had a bag, I prayed over them. As I prayed, I felt the Holy Spirit urge me to step out in faith and pray for complete physical healing over the entire crowd and that the destinies God had created for each of them would be fulfilled. I did this as they began the pizza line. Then I walked through the entire line, looked them in the eye, shook each one of their hands and wished them a Merry Christmas. A few stopped me to comment on what I had preached about.

One man told me he was really struggling right now and he needed to hear the words I spoke, that they were life to him. Another told me he would "be there" after Christmas, indicating he wouldn't be committing suicide. I had several more incredible conversations that night and was able to pray with people.

That night I went home and had a miserably cold shower to wash off all the fine powder from the extinguisher to prevent it from going into my skin. My husband, out of concern and love for me, was not impressed that I had it all over me and helped me clean up the contents in my bag and my clothing. He did not have as much trouble as I did believing that something like that would happen to me. I was able to laugh about it that night but my husband needed a little more time.

The next time things around you are not going well and it seems completely chaotic, you may just need to stop and ask yourself: Does Jesus have plans? Recognize the enemy's distractions and harassment, pull on your armour from Ephesians 6 and stand firm through the battle.

CHAPTER 22

THE HOLY SPIRIT STILL SHOWS UP IN THE COLD -WHY DON'T WE?

"Don't be afraid of the radicalness of His demands… If He asks much of you it is because He knows you can give much."- Saint John Paul the Great

Tonight was -29 Celsius with a windchill of -34 Celsius. I just know that God still works in those cold temperatures and although it looks different, ministry still happens. We split into two teams, one that went to the mall and one that went near a homeless shelter. After multiple attempts, the motorhome just wouldn't start. In desperation I laid my hands on the dash and said, "In the Name of Jesus, motorhome, start!" I tried again and again and it still would not. "Lord, can you get this to start, please?!" I decided to grab some stuff from my vehicle and put it in the motorhome praying the whole time. I came back and tried to start it again, and it did! I let it run for twenty-five minutes as I went inside. Believe it or not, that night there were new people there to join our team! Crazy. If I was new, I'd wait for a warmer night. We had an amazing sixteen people show up! "Wow God, You are so good and amaze me! I give You all the glory." When I got into the motorhome to take it downtown I noticed something was wrong. No fan, no gas gauge, no signal lights. A fuse must not have been working because of the cold. I decided to drive it anyways and use arm signals. However, at my first two turns, I realized no one could see my arm out the window as it was too short and the motorhome sides were blocking the view for anyone behind. As I drove a bit more, suddenly everything started to work again. Thank You, Lord! When we arrived, I was very surprised to see a group of men, about thirty, waiting for us! In that cold! They knew we would come, and I'm so glad we did. We didn't preach, we didn't sing (it hurt the singer's lungs), we just gave pizza, hot chocolate, and the goodies we had. We accompanied it with short conversations, prayer and hugs.

On another night it was a windchill of -25 Celsius yet we had around thirty team members come out. Incredible warriors! I went near a homeless shelter, as we had no singers and the preacher cancelled. Since it was so cold, my plan was to run into the shelter and let the guys know that we were there and then I would just pray over them as a group on the mic as they got pizza. I ran into the shelter and invited them out. When I got back, I saw that there was a good size group of about forty men lined up. I decided to preach a short message. I shared with the men how I had gone to a funeral a few days earlier at a church. I told them how some of the things said at the service bothered me. I focused on two points.

1. The Reverend said that the lady who had passed had been baptized as a baby. At that time God made a promise to her that she would get to spend eternity with Him.

2. The Reverend said that before the funeral was done we had to pray for the deceased soul to be at rest, and then led the congregation in a prayer for her afterlife.

Of course, I found these two points to be very theologically inaccurate and I explained to the crowd why. They actually found it very interesting and stayed for the fifteen minutes that I spoke. Afterwards, I received many thoughtful comments and questions regarding it. It was a quick night as everyone was so cold but I know that seeds were planted.

During another incredibly cold night, everyone had come and gone but there was one group remaining in a corner consisting of two of our team members with a gentleman. They waved me over and said he wanted to meet me. As I met Jordon he thanked me over and over for having the team come there every week and for the impact it has had. I noticed he was dressed very well and was very, very clean, probably in his fifties. I asked a few questions since I had no idea what he and the others had been discussing all night and I found out he had been a Christian in a very charismatic group years ago. He asked me if I had ever heard the term "drunk in the spirit". I laughed, as I haven't heard that terminology for a while and told him yes. He shared that this had happened to him at one meeting and a woman had a vision over him. He had it typed out. That was years ago. He told me he had just spent nine years in a maximum security prison and was presently serving another four years under parole. I suspected that it was under probation at a halfway house. I figured he must have done something pretty bad in order to be serving a sentence like that. He got emotional as he shared how he saw terrible things in prison and the memories were tormenting him. He shared he had come back to God and had been so thankful for our team's encouragement for the last two weeks that he'd been out. I sat him down and grabbed another male team member. I introduced them and told the team member I really wanted to minister to Jordon and pray for him. Jordon was extremely cold and shaking so I took off my gloves and fished out the warm hot packs inside them, put them in his hands. I then explained to him I wanted to listen to the Lord and pray for him. As my team member prayed I waited on Jesus. The Lord gave me an image of Jordon before Jesus, humbled and broken, his hands spread out before him and he was on his knees, head bowed in shame. Then Jesus took a power saw and began making cuts on him. What???? I was kind of shocked and tried to understand. "What was encouraging about this, Jesus?" I thought. As He made cuts on Jordon, it was painful but necessary. In this vision, if Jordon did not hold still and stay in a position while Jesus worked, it would kill him. I did not know the "why", I just knew it was necessary. I saw how Jordon was voluntarily allowing it to be done. My team member had finished praying. Because I knew Jordon had a history in the charismatic church I knew I could use Christian terminology. I decided to tell him the vision straight out and not soften it. When I was done we sat in stillness as Jordon wept and wept. I pulled tissue out of my pocket and gave it to him as he sobbed. He struggled to get out the words, "I understand what this means." I told him Jesus was so delighted and proud of him when Jordon postured himself this way and allowed Jesus to do what He needed to do in him. I then prayed over him. When we were finished, I asked him if he had anyone in his life walking with him in his Christian journey, encouraging him and helping him heal, grow and deal with these things. He said no. He explained that after getting out of prison just a couple months ago adjusting to the outside world has been really difficult. He really had no friends, some family, but the relationships were distant. I told him that we would meet with him in the motorhome every week, pray for him, answer questions, go through the Bible with him and encourage him. He really wanted that and said he'd be coming next week. We gave him a big hug. Later in the motorhome I asked one of the team members some background of her conversation with him. She said he has nightmares and suffered from post traumatic stress syndrome from the trauma that happened in prison. We could see he was in need of deliverance and inner healing at some point but our helping him would depend on how committed he was to coming out and receiving discipleship.

Oh yes, it was -36 Celsius and we were heading out! I had five layers on the top of me and three on the bottom. I had offered team members chocolate treats if they came out. I was thrilled and let out a "Whoo Hoo!!!" as the motorhome started even though it hadn't been plugged in as it has no engine block heater. Down on the streets, I was amazed to see about twenty people gathered to see us. We ignited a propane fire pit and heater and handed out hot chocolate and pizza. We had no singer or preacher but quickly placed hot chocolate into hands as the crowd gathered around the heat. What was particularly interesting is that about four of those in the crowd all resided in their own private homes and yet all bundled up to come out and be with us. I asked one, "Why are you out here, Sam, in this cold!?" He said, "Because I knew you guys would come." This was their outing, their activity for the week, their community, and whether they knew it or not, their church. Which is pretty fantastic. I chatted with Sam a bit, encouraged him, told him we were praying for him and noticed that he came out every Monday night. Tears streamed down his face as I prayed for his knee and spine. I talked with Brian, who handed me a late Christmas present, a nice toque and card, which was ironic since we usually were the ones handing out toques. I had a couple of other very deep conversations about faith. That evening I looked around and I saw the team praying for others, I witnessed conversations and hugs. It was 9:30pm. We had been down there for over an hour and despite the cold, no one was leaving. I thanked God for cold nights like this one, for tough warriors of the Kingdom of God and for the Holy Spirit who still works in -36 Celsius weather.

The wind was bitterly cold and strong. We stayed out for one and a half hours as people streamed to us from all over: grabbing a snack bag with tracts in them off of our tables, going through our donated clothing, and conversing with six team members. The wind was extremely cold, and yet people wanted to stay and be there.

I talked to George. He told me right away that he read the first six chapters in John!! That was amazing after so many years of pleading with him to read his Bible. I was able to talk to him about some of the content. He shared with me that he lived with his sister and brother because they had disabilities and would have difficulties living on their own. I shared with him that my daughter had special needs and he was surprised. I was able to relate with him about the challenges in it. I prayed for him and gave him a banana bread loaf to take to his siblings.

I spoke with Craig, the guy who had just had surgery a few weeks ago. He became a Christian through Alcoholics Anonymous thirty years ago, but didn't go to church or have Christian community. I asked him if he had a Bible with him. He said not one that was available to him, so I grabbed him one and explained the importance of reading the Bible on a regular basis.

I got into a conversation with Aaron who was from Africa. We had a deep discussion on having a relationship with God and putting health ahead God in his life. He was dressed poorly and shaking from the cold, snot running down his nose. I challenged him further about some of his thoughts and perspectives, then prayed over him.

At the end of the night we were all frozen and said goodbye to our last few visitors. The five of our team who were left chatted about our night. So many who met us on the street had thanked us for coming out despite the weather. I again thought about how the consistency is just so, so needed. I was frozen and it took an hour to warm up at home with a hot water bottle but was so glad that I had gone out that evening.

I read this book, The Heavenly Man: The Story of Brother Yun. It was amazing. When I got to page 290 he talked about the training each missionary received before going out to share the gospel with Muslims, Hindus, Buddhists and Communists. The training included how to suffer and die for the Lord. They taught how to witness for the Lord under any circumstance, on trains or buses, or even in the back of a police van on their way to the execution ground. They also trained on how to escape for the Lord. They taught the missionaries skills such as how to get free from handcuffs, and how not to get injured when jumping from second-storey windows when escaping.

At this time in history, when I think of our western culture's excuses that keep believers from sharing Jesus with people, I have to soberly reflect. Is the cold or any kind of weather going to keep me curled up at home on my couch? What circumstance would keep me from seeking the lost? Cold? Weariness? Fines? Handcuffs? Prison? Death? Many would testify that the Holy Spirit always shows up in all these circumstances and more.

I was standing and listening to our team member preach. There was a woman standing beside me shivering and listening in the -30 Celsius weather. We smiled at each other and I quietly grabbed a blanket from our supplies. I gently put it around her as she listened, and she was very glad to receive it. The preaching was powerful. As I placed the blanket on the woman, I put my arms around her shoulders to help her stay warm. I began to silently pray over her, that she would be moved by the preaching and able to understand what she was hearing. I continued to intercede when suddenly she jolted, threw the blanket off to the ground, turned towards me and spoke in an indiscernible language with very angry, venomous tones. It was like she wasn't even there in her eyes. She was only two feet from my face. I found what was happening to be very interesting as the woman went on and on but was seemingly not present. A friend of mine came over and stood beside me. I calmly said, "I think this is demonic tongues." I had never heard demonic tongues before although I had heard it existed. The woman continued to speak in an angry, growling voice. I quietly spoke out loud, "In Jesus' Name, I rebuke you. You have no power over me." Within a minute, the woman stopped talking, turned away and went back to listening to the preaching. I stood there and silently prayed. When the preaching was done, the woman turned to me, completely friendly, with a totally different demeanor and said, "Wow, is it ever cold out here. I need to go to the YWCA tonight. Could you give me a ride?" I looked at my friend, uuuuhhhh, no I don't think that would be a good idea. Instead, I politely asked, "Could I arrange for you to get a ride?" She was happy for me to call a service that would pick her up and give her a ride. Since our hands and feet were hurting from the cold, I quickly asked her what her thoughts were about the preaching, handed her the blanket that she had thrown on the ground (which she seemed oblivious to being the one to have thrown it there) and gave her a hug before we parted.

Many Christians don't believe in heavenly, godly tongues let alone demonic ones. I was thankful for the opportunity to hear the difference and have that experience. Obviously, the demonic in her was reacting to the Holy Spirit working through me. How fascinating and awesome! I sure would hate it if the demonic didn't care that I was praying. I suppose it makes sense that if the Holy Spirit still shows up in -30 Celsius then so does the demonic. All the more reason to face the cold . . . and the rain . . . and the inconvenient times . . . and all the times we simply just don't feel like it.

CHAPTER 23

OTHER SPIRITUAL BELIEFS

"The Bible tells us to go out into all the world and preach the gospel. We are living in a time in history where the world has come to us!" - Valerie Hopman

At the transit station, I prayed for God to show me who to talk to and what to say. A man walked by us and the Lord showed me in his eyes that he really wanted to follow God and to do the right thing. I also saw a gentleness about him. He went into a little waiting booth so I motioned for my team member to come with me. We entered the booth. I smiled, told him I knew it sounded strange, but as he walked by, God showed me that he was a gentleman who really wanted to do the right things and was very interested in the things of God, pursuing Him and wanting to serve Him well. A smile broke over his face, defenses came down and he said, "That is very true. I am a Muslim". I knew that even though there were many differences between us, many who come from an Islamic background truly want the truth, and Jesus is revealing Himself to those of that religion. I try to find common ground and then ask them about their thoughts about the prophet Jesus, referred to in the Quran. I asked the man, "Why do Muslims follow Mohammad if the Quran mentions Jesus at least three times more?" I made sure that my tone was very sincere and gentle. I always try to smile a lot to take any tension out of the conversation. I like to ask people a lot about what they believe and why. They usually love to tell me. Then I usually get a chance to share what I believe. They often tell me, as did this man, that Islam and Christianity are basically the same. "Ahh, yes, there are similarities and it's great to discuss them," I responded, "but I've noticed one huge difference. Even though the Quran mentions Jesus a lot and it seems to have much respect for Him, it doesn't agree with the words Jesus spoke." I told how Jesus had a best friend who wrote down a bunch of things that He said and one of those things was, *"I am the Way, the Truth and the Life, no man comes to the Father (God), except through Me."* (John 14:6) I asked him why he thought Jesus said that. He told me, "It's because the Jews have changed the Bible into what they want it to say and it's false." I gave him a look that said "possibly" but then went on to say, "I know for sure that God loves us and is a loving God. He wants a relationship with us. God doesn't want us to go through life wondering if we have a relationship based on whether we followed all His rules perfectly. No matter how hard we try, we never measure up." When he responded, he seemed very firm on defending his beliefs. When I saw this tension starting to rise, I shut down the controversial side of the conversation. I was not interested nor had researched enough at this time to debate him. I said, "I am so glad that you want the truth, so do I! Obviously God sees your heart and wants to let you know He sees that you really do want to know Him and that is why He had me come talk to you. Can I pray to the God who created you and I as we search out the truth?" He gave me permission. So I put my hand on him and prayed to God for truth, for this man's life and everything the Holy Spirit put on my heart to pray. Then I ended it "In Jesus' Name". I shook his hand and gave him a gospel of John. I told him to read it and compare the words of Jesus with who the Quran said He was. It ended up being a very friendly, warm conversation and parting.

Aaden was a younger man, originally from Somalia, who moved to Toronto when he was eleven years old. He had recently moved to Calgary a few days ago and had heard about our team handing out food. Something really drew me to Aaden. As we chatted I found out that his dad died in Somalia and his mom had raised him. I asked him if he was of the Islam faith because of his upbringing. He was Muslim and yet had an openness to all religions. At one point he had looked into Catholicism and Christianity. He had even read parts of the Bible along with his Quran. He believed the two religions were all basically the same. I asked him who He thought Jesus was. He answered, as all Muslims do, "A good prophet." I shared with him that I believed

Jesus was the Son of God. He knew that about our faith. I went deeper and gave him a two minute version of what Jesus did for us. I shared with him that many faiths were continually having to do all sorts of good things to outweigh the bad things they did. When they died they never knew if they had done enough or where they were going. He agreed that was totally how he felt. I told him that I did not fear death. I knew without a doubt where I was going when I died. I explained how God did all the work of enabling me to have eternal life and a relationship with him. I had done my part, which was confessing that Jesus was Lord and believing that God raised Him from the dead. As we chatted, I looked at his eyes and asked the Lord, who was Aaden, really? I shared with Aaden that it was no coincidence that he came to Calgary, and in fact, the Lord had brought him to Canada from Somalia for a reason. I shared with him that I had a relationship with God where at times God spoke to me and showed me things about people. I could see he had kindness, compassion, wanting to defend the weak, and had a desire for integrity. He smiled and said that, yes, those things were in him and important to him. I shared with him about the gospel of John and how he was Jesus' best friend. John wrote about his experiences with Jesus and quoted what Jesus said. I asked Aaden if he would be willing to read it, to see what Jesus said about Himself, and then to compare it with the Quran. He said he would read it. So I gave him one. I asked him to come back next week and tell me what he thought of it. I then asked him if I could pray for him and he said yes. He actually put his arm around my shoulders when I prayed, which showed me he was not a serious Muslim. If he was, he would not have touched me. It also showed me he had a great potential of openness to the Truth.

I saw a young Muslim woman. The Lord shared with me the word "sweetness". I was not getting anything else and time is always of the essence on the public train platform. In faith I went over to her and intentionally used the word God instead of Jesus. I shared with her that God had drawn my attention to her and that He saw in her a sweetness which He had placed in her. She was very happy to hear that and was receptive to talk. I asked her a few questions. She was raised a Muslim but said she was not a very good one now. I love that answer. It opens up the door to share honestly. I shared with her that I was a Christian. I quickly outlined in a few sentences our different views of who Jesus was and how I, too, knew I was not good. It was only by the grace and love of God that anyone could gain eternal life. I asked her if I could pray for her. She said yes as she was in school for Early Childhood Education and needed prayer to pass her exams. I prayed for that and all sorts of other things about her spiritual understanding of Jesus. I ended my prayer "In Jesus' Name" and she got on her train.

Another night at the train platform it was a holiday and cold so there were not a lot of people, but there didn't have to be. I started off on my own. I walked up and down the platform slowly, praying as I watched people waiting and getting on the train. A lady caught my eye and I greeted her as I approached her. I found out she was originally from India and had been in Canada for a couple of years. I asked her if she went to the Sikh Temple in the city. She said she did and was surprised that I had gone there for a meal and tour. I told her I really respected the morals of her religion and I saw her soften a bit more. I told her I was a Christian and had similar morals to her. I explained that a big difference between our religions was Who Jesus was. It took me too long to get to that part of the conversation and her train came. So I quickly told her Jesus made it possible for us to have favour with God without having to follow a bunch of rules and that He loved us. It was all I could squeeze in before she thanked me and got on her train.

DO versus DONE

Every other religion of the world has come up with what a person has to DO to gain favour or reward from a deity or spiritual source. Christianity is the only belief system where it has been DONE.

Favour, love, salvation and merit cannot be gained through works. "*For by grace you have been saved through faith. And this is not your own doing; it is the gift of God, not a result of works, so that no one may boast.*" (Ephesians 2:8-9).There are books written on this subject; Bible commentaries, exegesis studies and sermons are dedicated to going through what the Bible says on this subject. Ultimately, the Bible makes it clear that works don't get us to heaven, nor bring us salvation. Neither do good deeds cause God to love us more. It is Jesus alone who saves, heals and delivers, having gone to

the cross and conquered death, out of love for us. It is not Jesus plus .... whatever else man has made up to require of us.
Every other religion leaves it's followers in a state of never knowing when they are good enough for reward or when they have achieved their desired goal spiritually until they die. I bring this up to them by asking questions such as, "When you die, what do you think will happen?" It's been very interesting and sad to hear time after time many do not know their status with God nor future with their belief system.

I was walking downtown and saw a man smoking outside of a fancy hotel. He was a nicely dressed Asian man. The Holy Spirit had given me a quick picture for him of a funnel around his neck and head. The meaning I understood was that he was intelligent and loved to take in information, logic and knowledge. That's all I had and I made the decision to approach him. As I explained that God had highlighted him to me and shared the message. He was very surprised. I received more understanding as I spoke, that the funnel blocked things from reaching his heart and had directed everything to go only to his mind. I found out he was from Japan and he was here on business. I welcomed him to Canada and asked him if he had spiritual beliefs. He was hesitant to talk but said his culture was Buddhist. He explained to me that people from Japan got married in a Christian church and buried in a Buddhist temple. I asked him who God was to him and what happened after he died. He gave me the Buddhist answer. Through good actions and ethical conduct, Buddhists hope to either gain enlightenment or to ensure a better future when reincarnated. Depending on the actions performed in previous lives, rebirth could be as a human or animal or even ghosts, demi-gods, or gods. Being born as a human is seen by Buddhists as a rare opportunity to work towards escaping this cycle. The escape from the reincarnation cycle is called Nirvana or enlightenment. I told him I was familiar with this and asked him if he knew anything about Jesus and what He did for all people throughout the world. He said he knew very little. I explained the whole gospel to him. At the end he said he had heard that story a little bit before. He looked at his phone and said he had to go. In the last few seconds I reminded him of the message that God had for him which I had spoken about at the beginning. I added, "I want to encourage you to read a Bible and find out more about Jesus!" He was polite and we parted ways. I just prayed that the Holy Spirit would take it from there.

I was out walking and saw a taxi cab driver with a turban on and moved towards him. I introduced myself and asked him if he was a Sikh. He said yes and I shared that I had been to their temple in the city and told him I respected the morals in his religion. I asked him if he knew who Jesus was according to The Book in his Sikh religion. He said he had heard the name but really didn't know anything about Jesus. I asked him if I could tell him who Jesus was and what He did. He said yes so I explained the gospel very quickly. I asked him if he knew what would happen to him when he died. He said he believed there was nothing and that the present was all there was. That surprised me because it was not what the Sikh religion believed, but I was discovering he did not know much about his religious beliefs. He asked me, "What is that place called that many believe in after death which is a good place to go?" "Heaven?" I responded. "Yes!" He believed heaven was right now here on earth. I thought for a moment and said, "Oh, but heaven is a place where there is no sadness or evil. Look at our world. There is much evil and sadness here. This can't be heaven." He thought for a moment and agreed that probably was true. As I explained more truths about God and how we cannot earn salvation, nor cleanse ourselves from our sin, he said, "This is a very deep concept. I would like to meet with you and talk to you more on this subject." His taxi cab line was continuing to move so I was slowly walking with him as I talked. I gave him my contact info. I could see his cab was just about at the corner where passengers were picked up so I told him about Jesus' best friend John who wrote down all about Jesus' life and quotes of what He said. I asked him if he would like to read it while he waited for passengers. He told me he would so I gave him a New Testament, folding the pages of the book of John for him to easily find .

A Catholic man, Herman, came back again from last week. He was not homeless, he just stumbled upon us one time when he was out walking. I actually wonder if he is quite well off. He immediately came over and said to me, "I did a lot of thinking this week but did not read what you told me to." After a bit of chit chat, he asked me why I wanted him to read the book of John. I told him there were many powerful verses in it and I wanted to find out what he thought about them. He said, "What's that verse they always put up at sports events, John 14:2 or something?" I laughed and said, "John 3:16?" "Yeah, that's the one. I suppose you know what it says, don't you." I quoted it for him and he said, "That's a difference I notice between Evangelicals and Catholics. You guys always know the references for verses and can quote them. Catholics don't, we just know the gist of the verses." I found his observation interesting and explained how the Bible says over 150 times that we are to memorize scripture and explained why. I shared how I was trying to do that so that I could measure everything up to its truth. He thought that was good and then said, "Sometimes when people spew off where it's found, like 'John 14:6' or 'Moses 2:4', it makes me feel like they're all smart and I can't converse with them." I nodded, amusingly smiled, paused and said, "Me too. I feel that way sometimes when people can do that because I just can't keep it all straight." Then he said, "We both believe that Jesus is Lord and there are just some small differences between us." I think my eyes gave my thoughts away because Herman laughed and said, "Okay, there are some catastrophic differences between us. Like the Eucharist for example." And here's how the conversation went.

Me: So you believe the bread becomes Jesus' literal body?

Herman: Yes. Jesus said, "Take, eat, this is my body."

Me: Yes, He did but don't you think He was showing how it was representing His body? I mean, He hadn't been tortured yet and was fully intact. It's not like the bread became His body right then.

Herman: Hey, I'm just quoting Jesus. He didn't say, "Take, eat, this <u>represents</u> my body."
We went back and forth and I didn't want to continue this debate that has gone on for years between many others.

Me: Why is this so important to <u>you</u>, Herman? Why does the bread have to turn into Jesus' flesh in order for it to have meaning to you?
Herman: Because when we swallow it, we have more of Jesus in us.

Me: Ahhh, so what does that do for you? (I knew that this was Herman's view and not necessarily the official belief of the Catholic church)

Herman: If there's more of Jesus in me then there is more good in me and I can be a good person.

Me: So if you regularly take the Eucharist, you believe you have more Jesus in you?

Herman: Yes.

Me: Well, what about the Holy Spirit? Why do you need bread to become Jesus when you already have a "piece" of God in you? When you give your life to the Lord, you are given the Holy Spirit. Is that not enough of God in you?

Herman: Well, yes, but this gives us even more so that we can be even more good.

Me: So, you want to please the Lord in your life, right? Where in the Bible does it say you can be more like Jesus and love Him by taking the Eucharist? It is not for this purpose according to Scriptures. It is to remember what He did for us. We are to be filled with the Holy Spirit and it is through the power of His Spirit that we are able to follow Him, be counselled and know how to live. We have access to God through His Holy Spirit. Access to Him enables us to follow Him when we belong to Him. Continuing to take the Eucharist doesn't increase more of Jesus in us, He's already there. However, Jesus did say, "If you love me, you will obey me." How will you know how to obey Him if you don't read His word? Taking some bread every week doesn't cause you to be better. Knowing what He says and doing it out of love for Him enables us to do good things. Yet, Herman, you won't even read the Bible!!!

Herman: Okay, okay, you need to talk to a priest and he'll answer you.

Me: I don't want to talk to a priest, I want to talk to you! You're the one who needs to know why you are doing what you're doing. It's between you and God. Herman, has there ever been a time in your life when you have felt close to God? Where you felt known by Him and perhaps even heard Him speak to you in some way?" He thought about it and said, "Yes, there have been a few times." I asked, "How long ago was that?" He hummed and seemed to not be able to think of when. He finally told me when he went through his divorce he was really upset with how the Catholic church handled it, the things that were said to him by the priest and how he was treated. When that happened, he had stepped away from the church and distanced himself from God. He knew God was there and ready if he called to him. He then said, "But hey, for some reason I keep coming out here whenever I'm in town, even when it's freezing." I nodded, "Yes you do, there's something that keeps drawing you." He agreed although he didn't know what it was. He said he prayed every day, "Lord Jesus, come into my heart today, make me a good person and use me to help others." I winced at the words "every day". I said, "Herman, you don't have to ask Jesus to come into your heart everyday. It's a one time choice and decision. But you can surrender to Him every day. He doesn't need you to be good; He wants you to be close to Him." He waved his hand and said, "Well, when I ask Him in my heart it's my way of saying I surrender." He went on into some other things and I said, "Herman, take away the Catholic church, or any church from your association with God. Who does God say you are? What if it was just you and God? You could just be with Him? Think of how close you'd be to Him. Do you miss Him?" He paused and said, "Well, I know He's always there." Then he quoted some sort of Latin chant about who he was in Jesus. I questioned him further, "Yes, that is who you are. But who does God say that you are, Herman? He knows you uniquely and your identity to Him is different than what anyone else says or thinks about you. What about the intimacy you have felt with Him in the past, to actually be really close to Him. Do you miss it?" He sort of mumbled things and said he'd have to process it. I shared with him that I was growing in hearing God's voice and would like to ask the Lord who He said Herman was. Herman thought this was very different and hadn't heard anything like that before but was open to it. I looked around to grab a team member to join me but there was none available. So we stood in silence as I brought him before Jesus. I immediately saw a gold chain around his neck. Then I saw him stand before Jesus holding a cross up before Jesus, but the bottom of the cross was in his hand and was actually a knife, cutting his hand. I saw that in the past Herman held an umbrella over his head. It was what Herman thought of as the protection of the church but then a wind came and wrecked the umbrella, turning it inside out. Herman was thinking the umbrella was useless but Jesus said He would still use it. As rain came down, the umbrella was used as a funnel to store up water for Herman to drink. I saw the word "resilient" placed upon Herman. I was feeling pressure as I knew time was ticking and we were both shivering. I sensed the meaning for the gold chain was representing something that it held a lot of value to Hermon. However, I wasn't sure of the cross in his hand. I began to tell Herman all of the images. He listened intently and when I was done he said he needed to take time to process it. I agreed that he should definitely take it to Jesus and pray about it. Then he said, "The gold chain is interesting, I had a gold chain and two weeks ago a guy literally came up to me and ripped it off my neck and ran away. It meant a lot to me and it did bring me much comfort." I prayed for Herman and he headed home.

There was a guy who was highlighted to me and was sitting all by himself. I grabbed another male team member and struck up a conversation, even though it was the end of the night of evangelistic outreach. His name was Tom. I got right to the point and asked him what his spiritual beliefs were. He said he was a Christian, well, a Catholic. So I asked him if he thought there was a difference. He said yes, and he was probably more a Catholic. I asked, "What do you think is the difference between the two? Like, what made you decide just now that you were a Catholic?" Tom faltered, "Uh, I'm not really sure actually. I was just raised in the Roman Catholic church." I asked, "Are you a practicing Catholic?" Tom replied, "I don't go to church but I sometimes talk to a priest, I pray every day and try to help others. I'm not a killer, a rapist or a suicide bomber so I think I'm good." I laughed, "Alright, well, I'm Christian. Can I sit down and explain to you some differences and then you can decide what you are or aren't?" He agreed and this began an awesome conversation. I explained to him why we as humans cannot have a relationship with

God because of sin and then what sin is. I explained the Catholic church had decided a person could have a relationship with God. It was Jesus + : Jesus + Mary, Jesus + sacraments, Jesus + rituals, Jesus + the Roman Catholic church. I told him many of those things were very good, such as the sacraments, and I respected their rich traditions that led them to be reminded of Biblical truths. However, the Bible never said we had to do anything apart from Jesus. I explained what Jesus dying and rising to life again really meant. I shared with him that Jesus was the final priest and that there was no need to go to a priest anymore to confess sins, unless of course, you wanted to. I explained that the Bible does say it is good to confess our sins to one another but that is only a requirement for salvation to confess and repent of your sins to God. Tom had felt that because he had been baptized as an infant and done some religious requirements from the Catholic church he was doing all that he could to gain acceptance from God. Tom shared with me he prayed and prayed but felt God never answered and that there was something missing. I told him he was missing a relationship with God because he was trying to have one differently than the way God had designed. I outlined to him what the Bible said about how to have a relationship with God through Jesus. I asked him if he could confess that Jesus was Lord, that God raised Him from the dead and if he knew that only Jesus could forgive his sins and take the guilt and shame. Tom said yes he believed all that. I wasn't expecting him to be so ready and open to receive the truths, so I dove in, "Tom, do you want to do what the Bible says and have a relationship with God, and having Him as the only God in your life?" Tom answered yes and so after explaining it one more time to make sure he really understood, he prayed on his own, out loud to God and biblically gave his life to the Lord! I followed up by explaining to him the spiritual exchange that had occurred, that he was now a son of the King, and that there was a party in heaven going on. He had an old little Gideon Bible. I explained to him about the gospel of John and told him to read Chapter 1 for next week. He seemed excited to come back and talk more. I welcomed himas my brother in Christ and gave him a hug. We prayed for him and when we were done, I noticed he did the Catholic sign of the cross. I kindly asked him. "Tom, do you know what that means when you do that?" Tom answered, "Yes, it's the Father, Son and Holy Spirit." I responded, "Yes, and it is what the Catholic church designed in order to demonstrate who a person is praying to and as a physical reminder. It's good and there is nothing wrong with it at all. However, I want you to know, it is not mentioned anywhere in the Bible, nor is it a requirement that you have to do that sign after a prayer. You can pray when you're driving, walking or anywhere and never have to do that sign. It is not disrespectful to the Lord. You can do that sign if you want, but you don't have to. It was a ritual made by man. It is not bad, I just want you to know it is not a requirement of God to get your prayers heard." Tom's eyes and mouth went big and he couldn't believe it. He thought that was amazing to know. Then he said something that was very interesting to me, "I have talked with so many priests over my whole life and I keep telling them I feel far from God. I pray and pray and never hear Him and just feel like something is missing. Never has anyone ever explained to me how to have a relationship with God the way you just did. They told me to just keep being kind to others, do good works and don't do anything wrong. And I tried but it never satisfied."

Perhaps you are wondering why I am including the Catholic faith in this chapter of different spiritual beliefs. Honestly, when I used to find out that someone was Catholic I assumed that they had salvation and understood the gospel. However, over the years I have researched and met many that are simply following a religion with many rules and regulations made up by man. Catholicism doesn't apply the grace of Jesus alone. Ephesians 2:8-9 states, *"For it is by grace you have been saved, through faith—and this is not from yourselves, it is the gift of God - not by works, so that no one can boast.* I am NOT labelling all Catholics as unsaved or having a lack of understanding. There are amazing, born again, on fire Catholic followers of Christ and I will enjoy being with them in eternity some day. When someone identifies as a Catholic, I certainly want to dive into conversation about what they are believing just as I would with someone claiming to be any type of Christian.

It's wise to uncover what a person's faith in any particular spiritual belief system is based on. Is it based on:

a) cultural identity?

b) exclusively on the act of attending church or a religious event one to two times a year?

Romans 10:9-10, *"that if you confess with your mouth Jesus as Lord, and believe in your heart that God raised Him from the dead, you will be saved; for with the heart a person believes, resulting in righteousness, and with the mouth he confesses, resulting in salvation."*

c) "Jesus/God plus" qualifications or requirements for eternity? Examples of what I mean are this: Jesus plus praying to Mary. Jesus plus the sacraments. Jesus plus praying to saints. Jesus plus works. Jesus plus traditions. God plus praying a certain amount of times a day. God plus extra-biblical religious requirements.

John 14:6, "Jesus answered, *'I am the way and the truth and the life. No one comes to the Father except through me'."*
Romans 5:1, *"Therefore, since we have been justified through faith, we have peace with God through our Lord Jesus Christ, through whom we have gained access by faith into this grace in which we now stand."*

d) someone adding or changing the gospel that claims salvation, forgiveness or relationship with God can be achieved apart from or in addition to Jesus Christ?

Acts 4:12, *"Salvation is found in no one else, for there is no other name under heaven given to mankind by which we must be saved."*

I was standing on the transit platform and within a minute, a lady dressed in a purple coat came near me. I told her I liked her coat and it looked warm on such a cold night. She was very friendly and I quickly got past the pleasantries. I found out she was from the Philippines and had been in Canada a short time. I had a pretty good idea that she was Catholic because that is the main religion of the Philippines. It was a great question to ask and a way to chase the conversation to the cross, so I asked her if she was indeed a Catholic. She was and I told her I was Christian. She said she knew there were differences, such as she prayed to statues and to Mary. I agreed and told her that we prayed only to Jesus. Her train was coming in one minute and I asked her if I could pray for her and she said yes. As I prayed for her, I just let the Holy Spirit lead me. When I was done, she opened up. Her heart was grieving as she told me her husband and two sons were back home and she needed to send money to them but she hadn't found work for a whole year. Though she had found a job recently, it was difficult. Her train pulled up. I quickly gave her a loving arm squeeze, encouraged her and told her to go straight to Jesus with all things. He was the only One with the power to answer her prayers.

I saw a waiting booth with three young women standing in it. One of the women had headphones in her ears and was standing by herself. The other two were young and full of laughter. I began to chat with those two. I found out they were friends and from the Philippines. I asked if they were Catholic. They said yes. Carla was in high school and the other girl in junior high. I chatted with them about the importance of having a relationship with Jesus and not just going to church or doing rituals in an attempt to be good Catholics. It was a friendly chat. Then I then got a bit more serious with them and told them that the most important thing for their whole lives was to know Jesus and to have a relationship with Him. I urged them to read the Bible for themselves and know what it says. They were very receptive and I asked them if I could pray for them. They looked at each other and I laughed, telling them I knew it was a weird question and a strange thing to do while waiting for the train. They laughed too and agreed. Then the younger girl asked for prayer for her family and the older girl got serious. She shared that she struggled with depression and wanted prayer. I really appreciated her honesty and began praying passionately for the girls. When I was done, their train had just pulled up. They began to leave and the older girl turned to me, gave me a hug, and off they went.

Spiritual beliefs such as Wicca, Satanism, Witchcraft, New Age, or Atheism I engage a little differently. I will ask people who engage in these practices why they joined that religion and then what they love about it. Many, if not all, are not raised in these spiritual beliefs and I like to hear the reasons for their perspectives. It helps me understand the root of what is important to them or where they've been hurt. When it comes to those who claim to be atheists, there's always a reason. Instead of debating if there is a God or not, I find out why they have decided there is no God. Usually it is because of a wound. I want to reveal that wound to them once it has been exposed. This enables them to see that perhaps their reasons for some of their beliefs are not "science or logic" but based on misconceptions or an issue that has tormented them. Again, I'm wanting to understand where they are coming from, to see if there's anything I can relate to, to find common ground, or perhaps uncover a root as to why they have chosen these beliefs and once revealed to me I lovingly expose it to them.

In conversations with these types of spiritual beliefs I remove all forms of "Christianese" out of my terminology. I've had to learn how to explain gospel truths without the churchy terminology so many Christians have become accustomed to.

I was standing in line at the grocery store and there was an older woman two customers ahead of me. She had a walker and cheerfully engaged with the cashier. I was drawn to her and the quietest prayer went up to the Lord as I asked Him if He wanted me to talk to her about Him and if so, what was it He wanted to show me. I watched her slowly shuffle away but I was stuck in line and had received nothing except that I could pray for healing for her. Still I wondered, so I prayed, "Lord, if you want me to talk to her, then have her in the parking lot by the time I get out." I got through the line and stopped at the inside coffee shop to get a coffee to go which took an extra ten minutes. When I stepped outside, I scanned the parking lot wondering if the Lord had somehow kept that lady from leaving so I could talk to her, nope . . . Oh, ha ha, there she was, going the exact direction that I had to. I happened to be walking, not driving, and so was she, pushing her walker. I caught up to her right at the crosswalk and the words were ready, "I see you are a lady of laughter and have chosen to be joyful." She looked at me, startled, and I said, "I was standing in the checkout line at the grocery store and I saw you there." She broke into a smile and without any prompting began to tell me about herself as we walked together for the next ten minutes. She had lost four inches off her height because of surgery on her spine. She had osteoporosis and a few vertebrates in her spine were disintegrating. She shared with me how this had begun at age seventy and at age seventy-one she had the surgery which had taken her a year and a half to recover. She was now seventy-four. At first she had been angry, but she had now decided to do all sorts of things she loved and live life to the fullest. This all sounded great but then she began to tell me her secret to getting through it all. It began with the planets, the power of the universe and many other New Age ideas. She told me how the Kundalini was within everyone and awoken at different times in a person's life. Hers had awoken when she was seventy years old and it was very powerful. She asked me if I was familiar with the Kundalini. I said, "Yes I am familiar with the Kundalini spirit." She was very fond of it and had a great desire for the Kundalini in her. All the while she talked I was praying silently, "Ooookaaay, Lord how do you want me to deal with this? How do I reveal You?" I said to her, "Well, I love Jesus and am very spiritual. He loves to speak to people in all sorts of ways, such as dreams and visions. Sometimes He speaks to me through pictures and highlights people to me. While I was in line at the store, He drew my attention to you and I really felt like He wanted me to pray for you for healing." She exclaimed, "Well now, isn't that interesting. Just yesterday I was having a massage. My massage therapist is a wonderful woman and she is a healer. She does all sorts of spiritual healing things on me and it is simply wonderful. But yesterday while she massaged me, Jesus appeared to me on my left shoulder!" I did not expect to hear her say this! Then I wondered, was it the real Jesus? She continued, "And then on my right side appeared the badger spirit." She went on to describe the badger spirit to me that it represented mischief, secrecy and negative energy. She said, "So Jesus was on one side of me and the badger spirit on the other. I concluded that I was glad I was balanced." I was a bit bewildered by the whole scenario and her reasoning but suddenly knew what to say. I realized Jesus really was arranging for me to talk to her. I said, "Hilda, I love that you have chosen to be joyful regardless of your circumstances and you love to have fun. You truly have chosen to rise above your circumstances with a good, positive attitude. I know that Jesus is trying to get your attention. It is not a coincidence that you had that experience during your massage and then the very next day Jesus tells me to come and pray for you. Jesus is the Healer and He is more powerful than any other spirit. You will not get healing from anyone else, neither a spirit, not even the kundalini spirit. Can I pray for you right now to Jesus for healing?" She carefully answered, "I don't really feel comfortable with that. I know Jesus is a Master and was a very great man here on earth. He taught good things and He is very powerful but I am not wanting you to pray to Him for me. I'm just not comfortable with that." I smiled and said, "Okay Hilda, that's totally fine. Could you try something? Go home tonight and ask Jesus, 'Jesus Christ who came in the flesh, why are you trying to get my attention?' and see what He says." She thought for a moment and said, "Yes, I will do that." We ended our conversation and went our separate ways. I prayed for her that night, and asked that all ungodly spirits would be silent, the veil lifted off her eyes to see and hear the true Jesus and His words. I was so thankful that I had taken the time to talk with her. In the busyness of life I often don't. I was thankful that I did not ignore the Spirit's prompting even though I didn't know the full "plan" of what to say. I loved that Jesus had an agenda that I got to discover. I wonder what He said to her . . . .

All religions have some sort of positive aspect and admirable morals, which is why the person chooses it.

I have intentionally learned the morals and some of the foundational teachings of different religions. I also like to ask whoever I'm in conversation with about their morals. I comment how I really respect those morals and how I too have similar morals. In this I'm bridging the gap. I'm not agreeing with them theologically, just on some of their heart convictions and beneficial behaviour. This opens conversation up to be respectful and honoring, and I'm truly not attacking them personally. I'm also appreciating their desire to live in a way that honors others. I sincerely believe that people in any of these religions actually want the truth.

I struck up a conversation with a man waiting in a line to get on a train. I asked him about his thoughts on some happenings in our world. Eventually I asked him where he was from and found out he moved here from Montreal looking for work but had not been able to find any yet. I asked him if he had family here and he said no, he didn't have anyone. I asked where he was originally from and he said India. I inquired, "Do you mind me asking, are you Sikh or Hindu?" He answered Sikh. I told him I had been to the Sikh temple in the city. He knew it as all Sikhs go there. I said, "I'm not Sikh, I am Christian, but I went there to understand what the Sikh religion believes."

He laughed, "I can see you are not Sikh." I laughed too, "I learned a lot, had a tour, was given a delicious meal and had some conversation." He nodded and said, "I am actually not a very good Sikh. As you can see I am not wearing a turban." I said, "Oh, how come? What makes you not a good Sikh?" He said, "Ahhh, I can't keep all the rules. In fact, you will not find many who can. There are very, very few serious Sikh's in the religion. I mean, I go out with my friends and then I drink, which of course is not acceptable." I said, "I see you are wearing the Sikh bracelet. Why do you do that? (The Kara bracelet is a constant reminder to always remember that whatever a person does with their hands has to be in keeping with the advice given by the Guru.) Is it because you follow that particular rule and want a reminder to keep your hands from doing evil or is it just because it's something you should have as a Sikh but it doesn't really affect your life?" He laughed and said, "Probably it is the second thing you said." I proposed, "Now correct me if I'm wrong but I remember being told that there are five main pillars of the religion." He nodded and I continued, "I really admire and respect some of the morals that the Sikh religion has. Our Bible has those morals in it too and so I respect those who try to live by them." He was really listening and responded, "Oh yes, thank you. Yes, that is good." I asked, "So if you are not a good Sikh, is it true that when you die you will then have to enter another cycle of reincarnation and probably come back as a lower form or in a lower position?" He answered, "Well yes, that's true. To be honest I try not to think about it, just live this life now." I nodded and said, "When I was at the temple I saw that you have a book that Sikhs believe is alive and they learn from the teachings in it. We also have a book. It's called the Bible but it's different in that we don't believe the book is alive but that the God Who it talks about is alive. It talks about Jesus." He said, "Oh yes, it's the same as the Muslims." I clarified, "Well, actually it's quite different. The Muslims believe Jesus was a man who was a prophet. Christians believe Jesus was the Son of God. He was deity, fully man and fully God. Have you heard much about Jesus or know what He did?" He said no. I knew I didn't have much time left before his train came so I gave a two minute summary of what Jesus did. Speaking so he could understand and relate, I ended with, "Jesus ends reincarnation. When a person dies he stands before God. It's just like you said, we are human. It's impossible to keep all the rules and good morals. We keep failing. God knew that, so Jesus took the penalty for our sins. All His righteousness can be put on us and all our sins get put on Him. There is an exchange that happens for those who believe in Him and make Him Lord of their life. So I do not fear death." His train pulled up and I said, "Is this your train?" He said yes and so I quickly said, "I encourage you to research Jesus and what He did for you." He thanked me and got on the train. Phew, talk about "fast food" gospel There was a lady that one of my team members began to talk with. She was super friendly and accepted prayer for her mother who had liver trouble. When my team member was done, she asked if she could give us a hug. We did and then I shared with her that while he was praying, God showed me a picture of a diamond representing her. A diamond was formed through pressure but is extremely strong and sparkled. She had a sparkle about her which everyone around her noticed. I asked her if she had spiritual beliefs. She told us she was raised Sikh. She believed some of it but believed more in positive energy and that when we died our souls went into babies and we lived in other bodies. It was a mix between Sikh religion and New Age beliefs. We discussed a few aspects with her. She was not deterred and it became a bit of a debate. We remained very gentle and kind. In the end, her train came and I asked, "Would you like to take a short book of the Bible called the book of John? This man was with Jesus and wrote down what Jesus said and did. You could take it and compare it to the books of the Sikh religion and at the very least gain some knowledge of who Jesus is." She said yes, took it and went on her way.

I've had many times where someone has told me they are a Christian and seemed to be, however, as the conversation goes on I realize their beliefs are not in alignment with scripture. It often can be difficult to correct and speak into the fallacy of their claims of following God.

Nigel arrived on his bike. Garry also came slowly around the corner, as he was recovering from surgery. I had my Bible with me ready for a spiritual conversation. I had hoped these two men would show up, as they had the week before at our weekly outreach. I said to them both, "Well, did either of you read your Bible this week?" Neither had so I opened up to John 5. I began reading to them verse 24. "Very truly I tell you, whoever hears my word and believes him who sent me has eternal life and will not be judged but has crossed over from death to life." I stopped, read the verse a second time and said, "The Greek word for "hear" is *akouo* - to hear and understand, to hear with the ear of the mind. So the more literal way to read it's meaning would be, 'whoever hears and understands and aligns himself with God has eternal life and will not be judged but has crossed over from death to life.' So many people say they believe in God or even are Christians but here Jesus is defining that a person must understand and align himself or come into agreement with God - what He says, who He is, what He declares is right and wrong. Only then will a person be in a true relationship with God and go to heaven. That is why it is so important to read this book, the Bible, so that you can know Who God is and what He says." Nigel and Garry took it all in and I continued. "The next verse says, 'Very truly I tell you a time is coming and has now come when the dead will hear the voice of the Son of God and those who hear will live.' Now I have a question for both of you. Who do you think is 'the dead' ?" They both shifted nervously and finally Nigel said, "Well, it's unbelievers." Garry added, "Yes, it's those who do not follow Jesus." I smiled, "YES! Look how smart you both are, ha ha! Jesus is saying that the spiritually dead, when they hear - remember that word means hear and understand, - when they hear the voice of Jesus they can become alive spiritually." Garry needed to sit down so as we walked over to a bench I read loudly, "What do you think about this one? It's down the page at verse 39: 'You study the Scriptures diligently because you think that in them you have eternal life. These are the very Scriptures that testify about me, yet you refuse to come to me to have life.' That word "life" is *zoe* in the Greek. Here's the definition of *zoe*: 'life, real genuine, a life active and vigorously devoted to God, blessed in the portion even in this world of those who put their trust in Christ, and to last forever.' Jesus is saying a few things here. He's saying: don't just pursue religious knowledge but leave out an experiential relationship with Jesus. Don't follow a bunch of rules and rituals and think you'll get to heaven by doing that." I then gave examples of other religions that do this. "Jesus goes on to say to go directly to Him, talk to Him, have a relationship with Him. Then you will have life in your spirit while here on earth." Garry said, "Now see, I have an issue with the Bible. It was written by men so I don't want to base my faith on men. I want to base it on my experience. One time, years ago, I was sitting on a park bench and I prayed, 'God, if you're real give me a sign.' Then a magpie came and stood right in front of me and gave a chirp as it looked directly at me. I knew it was God and I decided to believe in Him. He gave me a sign. A person's faith should be determined on their believing and experience of God." Oh, how these statements are difficult to respond to. I had to take a deep breath to start untangling the truth from opinion, from false information. "I agree, it's really awesome to have a 'sign' or an experience with the Lord. I love that, especially when I know He's communicating with me somehow. However, we have to take that experience and what we believe the Lord was communicating to us and test it. If it doesn't line up with scripture, then it would not be from God. Your magpie story obviously made you decide to follow God. That's great. There are others who have spiritual experiences and are involved in cults or have other spiritual beliefs that are not in alignment with the Bible. Let's take the extreme opposite of Christianity: Satanists. They have many experiences with the spiritual realm. There are angels and demons. They have experiences with demons and they often feel, at first, powerful and curious. However, they are not in alignment with God and therefore are spiritually dead and have not crossed from death to life. Or take Mormons, they claim to have spiritual experiences with God. But they believe Jesus and satan are brothers. They believe that they need to earn their after-life experiences and if they do well, they will become gods of their own planets. Just because they believe this and claim to have experiences does not mean they are following the truth. Garry, you are questioning the authenticity and credibility of the Bible being God's word, His thoughts and truths. Have you ever researched this?" Garry shook his head no and I gave some ways he could research it and told him about author and apologist Lee Strobel. Garry said, "I just think I need to believe and everyone else needs to believe based on their experience of who God is. I think people are not afraid to die, I think they are fighting to live. I think people are afraid to be born." I looked at him puzzled, "And on what do you base that opinion on?" He said, "Well, we are souls waiting to be born and then we choose our parents. The birth process is very painful and the soul is fearful to be born, wondering if it chose right and how life will be." I responded, "Whoa, you think our souls are already made and we are waiting to be born and consciously choose our parents? That is not in the Bible, where did you hear that?" Garry answered, "It says in the Bible that the amount of souls will run out and babies in the end will be born without a soul." I said, "Garry, that is not in the Bible." He said, "Yes it is, you must not know it well enough. Do you have a pastor you can talk to? Ask him, he'll tell you and show you where it is. I have talked to many priests, pastors, ministers and they all say the same thing and it's in the Bible." I didn't want to humiliate Garry nor insult his story but I had Nigel listening and so I wanted to correct him. I turned to Nigel and said, "Nigel, in your years of being raised a Catholic have you ever heard this?" Nigel said, "No, that is not logical at all, nor is it possible." Garry said, "God does not do things by logic." I jumped in, "Garry, if it will make you feel better, I will ask a pastor but I am sure, as I have studied the Bible for years. I absolutely don't know everything but I know that is not in the Bible. If I research it, you research it, even go and ask the chaplain at the Salvation Army. If we find out it's not in the Bible, would you be willing to let go of that belief?" Garry said, "No, I've believed it for so long, nothing can change my mind." I laughed and said, "Garry, let's go back to that verse, the one that says only if a person comes into alignment with what God says can a person be saved. Do either of you know what God said about Himself through the Scriptures? 'I Am Who I Am.' He said, 'I AM Who I AM.' Not who you want him to be. No one can change Him, or decide to accept some parts but not other parts of Him. He's not a god you can make up in your head. That's what I was saying that every other religion has done. The Muslims say Jesus was not God, the United church says Jesus was a way , and that God is he/she. The Jehovah Witnesses say God didn't make a hell for people. The Buddhists say god is everywhere and we are gods. Be careful not to do the same thing. Jesus clearly said we must come into agreement with how God says things are because He made it all, He knows." Garry had enough, he smiled and said, "Well, I should go in now." I smiled, "I know you don't like what I'm saying but I'm telling you because we have to be willing to be teachable and keep each other accountable to follow the One true God." Garry said, "Well, you are passionate, I'll give you that!" I said, "Well now, why would I say I am a Christian and settle for a shallow faith, never finding out what God really had in mind? No! I want to be all in. I want all Jesus died to set me free from. I want to live passionately for what I believe. If I can't, I would have to wonder, do I truly believe it?" They chuckled and Garry left. I turned to Nigel and said, "Nigel, that's why you need to read this Bible more. Garry is off on what he is saying. He does not know his Bible and he is easily deceived because of it." Nigel agreed and then said, "I have trouble reading it. I have trouble focusing on it. Not just reading but trouble even listening to music or watching tv. Doing anything really." I asked, "Why?" He got serious and nervous, then said, "Well I have depression and I'm on medication." I said, "Oh, do you think it's the medication?" Nigel said, "No, I've only been on it for four years but it's been like this for a long time." Through all my questions he shared with me that he has been depressed since he was a teenager. He went to university and studied politics. He was in that line of work but eventually had to stop working. He had a deep heaviness that had come upon him. It got really seriously depressed four years ago and he was almost hospitalized. That's when he went on medication. I asked, "Nigel, what happened as a teenager that started it?" He shrugged, "I don't know. I, uh, I remember my mom saying to me, 'Nigel, you've lost the light in your eyes.' I always remember that." I asked, "Well, did you lose the light in your eyes?" He answered, "Yes, I did." I asked, "Why? Were you hurt? Wounded? Was there a trauma? Did someone say something to you?" He shook his head, "No, I don't remember anything. I just know I was a happy kid, didn't care about anything and then, well, my mom said that and it really hurt, you know but I knew it was true." I asked, "Did it ever come back . . . . the light in your eyes, like in your 20's or 30's?" He said, "No, I've been depressed ever since. My dad died, but later, you know. That just added to it." Now Nigel is probably in his sixties so that was truly sad. I said, "Hmmm, thanks for sharing that with me, Nigel, now I know how to better pray for you. I wonder who the real Nigel is." He looked up at me for the first time, "What do you mean?" I said, "Well, the Nigel who doesn't have heaviness or depression, because that's not really you." He thought about that and said, "I don't know. I know who I was as a kid. I laughed and had fun." Very gently and thoughtfully I responded, "Yes. Jesus can free you from this, Nigel. This doesn't have to be the rest of your life." He laughed, "Gee, I don't even know why I talk about all this to you. You could be making $200/hr you know, for all the counselling you do. I shouldn't even put all that on you." I said, "It's an honour that you would trust me, Nigel. I'm going to pray for you." And I did. I prayed and rebuked the spirit of heaviness and depression. I asked God to cut off negative spiritual generational ties, to reveal the source where the enemy had gained access in Nigel's life. I then asked the Lord to free Nigel, to enable Nigel to be a man of laughter, a man of integrity and a man after God's heart. I asked the Holy Spirit to guard his mind when he read the Bible and that he would be able to focus and understand. I prayed many things and when I was done, Nigel didn't know what to say and chuckled, "I don't know how you have all that passion stored up inside of you. You should bottle it and sell it." I smiled, "Nigel, it's the Holy Spirit and you can have it too by saying yes to Jesus."

You don't need to be an expert on every religion or spiritual belief in the world. It's really great if you can learn a little bit about each one or even study one or two in depth. However, a lack of understanding and knowledge of another person's spirituality should not cause us to shrink back or avoid spiritual conversation. We know Jesus and Jesus is Who we can talk about. We ask questions about their beliefs and find out why they believe what they do but ultimately we want to find out who they think God is, who Jesus is in their belief system and then reveal who Jesus Christ, the Messiah, the Son of the living God is.

I like to leave people with truths that they may ponder or help them in the future as they process what we've discussed. For those involved with spiritual cults and beliefs, I may mention that Jesus has authority over all the spirits and that they are serving lesser spirits.

I may also mention that when they realize they no longer have power over the spirits but that the spirits have power over them, they will want to get free. I tell them to call out to Jesus Christ who has come in the flesh, as He is the only one who can help them.

For those who are part of other world religions, I want them to have the knowledge that Jesus loves them and wants a relationship with them. They do not have to earn His love, it is a free gift.

One of the most fun and effective ways is to ask the Holy Spirit what He wants to say to them. What does He love about them? And then share it with them. This is very powerful and ministers to them in a way that I can't. It brings an encounter with Jesus to them and they will never forget it and will hunger for more.

I often end my conversations with, "Hey, I can see that you want Truth and I want Truth. Can I pray to the Creator, Who created Heaven and Earth, created you and me, and ask Him to show us Truth?" Or I may say, "Would it be okay if I pray a blessing over you?" I pray sincerely and passionately over their life and always in Jesus' Name. It's powerful and effective.

CHAPTER 24

DEMONS

"Enemy-occupied territory-that is what this world is. Christianity is the story of how the rightful King has landed, you might say landed in disguise, and is calling us all to take part in a great campaign in sabotage." - C.S. Lewis

We know that demonic spirits have influence and impact. There are different words and viewpoints on how, such as the demonic can harass, demonize, possess or oppress people. Now don't get all nervous and judgy on me as you read this. There are many differing opinions in biblical theology regarding the role and influence of demonic spirits on both the unsaved and on the saved. I suggest you research this topic thoroughly and not simply depend on someone else telling you what to believe. However, I have also found that it is one thing to sit in a Bible study group discussing all sorts of opinions and interpretations and quite another to actually talk to a demon through a human and deal with a demonic manifestation. I have had the privilege of experiencing both. I have learned a great deal and have come to enjoy the hands-on training.

During one of the first times I went out on the street to participate in an evangelism ministry, I was standing casually in a line of people, listening and watching evangelism going on. A man with a long beard, very dirty, baggy clothes and looking like the stereotypical homeless man was watching me in a piercing way. I just sort of ignored him but then he crossed the area and came straight towards me. He looked me in the eyes and said, "Why are you here?" I thought that was a very blunt question and stammered in my reply, "Well, I want to share about Jesus Christ, what He's done in my life, the truth about who He is." He gave me a strange smile and said, "Now tell me why you're really here." I was a little confused and repeated what I had just said. I noticed he was snorting between his words at times. He began to tell me how on January 8, 2005 he was a regular construction worker when a piece of metal rebar fell and somehow pierced him right through the inside of his forearm. He promptly rolled up his sleeve and showed me a huge long scar to prove it. He lost so much blood that he legally died in the ambulance for seventeen minutes. He awoke to his own voice saying, "Give me another chance." From that moment on he knew Yiddish (I didn't realize it at the time but found out later it was the Jewish language), began to snort like a pig uncontrollably and now had a voice in his head that told him about his new purpose in life, which was to live on the streets. It also told him when he would die. Then he said, "I don't know why I'm telling you all this but 'it' told me to come talk to you." I asked him, "Who's 'it'? What's 'it's' name?" He said, "I can't tell you, 'it' told me not to tell you." I realized he was listening to a demon speak to him. "It" was a demon who knew that if I knew it's name I would have insight on how to deal with it by either stopping it from operating or casting it out. He said, "My time is short, 'it' told me, my life will be over soon." I said, "It doesn't have to be." I was new to evangelism and really didn't know how to handle this conversation. I fumbled my way through as he challenged my beliefs, snorting all the way through. He told me there was much I didn't understand in the spiritual realm and anything I thought according to Christianity was not true. Then he requested that tonight, when I laid on my bed, to ask "it" a question and "it" said it would answer me. I, of course, was not going to do anything of the sort to engage with this demonic spirit. Eventually the man left. I thought how creepy and sad that a demonic spirit(s) had come into him. What an abomination of the devil to combine the Yiddish and snorting like a pig in a manifestation of demonic possession. Later, the leader at that time came over and we discussed the interaction. He told me it sounded like a big distraction from the enemy to keep me from talking with others. In having people come to oppose me, the demonic is reacting to the Holy Spirit in me. Years later, I actually now get excited when things like that happen because I now know that the presence of the Holy Spirit in me is causing the spiritual realm to pay attention. How awesome is that!! It certainly has been a steep learning curve and an adventure I was fairly wide-eyed and new at evangelizing down on the streets. As we were talking, a guy came up to us shaking and completely out of it, acting weird. A team member went to lay hands on him and the guy bolted. He ran away, jumped over a fence and went into the train tunnel. We looked at each other, knowing the spiritual reaction that had taken place. Twenty minutes later he came back still shaking and so this time we all laid hands on him and prayed. He was wearing a tag that said his name was Ronald. One of our team said, "What is your name, spirit?" and he answered, "damon" (which I later learned meant son of the devil). They cast it out, prayed and prayed. Ronald calmed down and had a conversation with them about Jesus and the gospel. It certainly was a wild night for me as a newbie.

A few weeks later I was out and saw a big line-up of people standing on the sidewalk. I turned to a big, tall guy to strike up a conversation. I found out he was waiting for a bus that took people to a shelter in a different location. I asked him if I could pray for him and he asked if he could pray for me. Before responding to this question, I always want to find out who the person would be praying to before I accept prayer from a stranger. I asked, "What do you believe?" He had a lot of knowledge of the Bible and as we talked, I tried to discern whether he was a Christian or not. Sure enough, the truths began to twist. He said God talked to him all the time and taught him a lot. He assured me the time was short and that someone was coming who would be powerful, would replace Jesus, finally set things right; someone the world will follow and be enlightened by. "Sounds like the antichrist," I said. He didn't really acknowledge what I said and he told me that a new heaven and earth had already been made. "Well, that doesn't sound biblical." A verse popped into my head (thank You, Lord). "In Revelation it says the old earth and heaven passes away and then the new is made. (I later looked it up: Revelation 21:1)." "Trust me," he replied, "I know." I smiled and kindly said, "I don't trust man. I can't or I'll believe anything. I have to trust the Bible. Who are you listening to? You've got to be careful not to be deceived; spirits can talk too. Is it Jesus Christ you are following?" He laughed and said, "God tells me, the virgin Mary talks to me. She tells me lots." I asked him if he was Catholic and he said he was raised Catholic but now was not. "God teaches me everything. I don't need any church or person to teach me." We discussed that the Bible does not tell us to talk to the virgin Mary, but the conversation was going nowhere. "Oh! She is speaking to me right now!" he said. "What is she saying?" I asked. He answered, "She says, 'Defend me, defend me to her.' She is telling me what words to say to you." Oh great! How do I address this?! Do I try to talk to him or do I deal with the spirit speaking to him? He was so convinced and wanted to follow these spirits. I was not very experienced at this point and so after I tried to talk to him more about biblical truth I eventually decided it was time to end it. "Can you do me a favour?" I asked. "When you talk to God, ask Him to silence the voices that are not from Him, because you need to be very careful who you are listening to. Pray and ask Jesus Christ, the Son of God to reveal Himself to You. Let me pray for you." I quickly jumped to pray and asked God to reveal truth to him, to expose any deception. Then I moved on.

This happened very early on in my journey with evangelism. I have learned how to handle these types of conversations with demonic influence and voices more confidently and wisely, and have grown in knowing my identity and authority. It is important to know who we are in Christ, so we can know what we can do. Otherwise it leaves us fearful of the demonic realm and intimated when the enemy roars. Through many, many encounters the Lord has grown me greatly in this area.

One time the man I mentioned earlier in the chapter on healing, Jay Cooling, said, "We need not fear because we have Christ in us and He is greater than any other." In great humility but authority he explained that because of this truth he would not be afraid to lay his hands on anyone. "I would not fear if someday I get to lay my hands on a witch because 'He that is in me is greater than he that is in the world'." (1 John 4:4) I was shocked to hear him say that! I mean, I know that Bible verse and principle but, a witch? I thought, "Wow!

He is so spiritual. I hope I never run into or talk to a witch." Ha ha, fast forward three years . . . I was now leading the street ministry and there was a lady sitting on the ground swaying back and forth like a child in pain while our worship singer praised God with her voice. This woman had her hood up and kept reaching her hand out towards us, painfully saying, "Stop!!" I watched her behaviour out of the corner of my eye, as I was engaging many other conversations. We were packing up our stuff to leave and a male team member told me I should go with him to talk to her. We spoke to her and she revealed to us that she was a white witch. For a moment I freaked out silently. Through questions, I found out she had two children who had been taken away from her but she said she talked with their spirits everyday. She shared how she loved the power and things she could do as a witch, of course, all good things. I told her I followed Jesus and asked what she thought about Him. She said, "Oh, I know Jesus, He's very powerful. The spirits tell me not to talk to Him." I told her it was because they were afraid of Him. She said, "His power is very dangerous." As we were talking, she shared with me that the spirits were constantly talking to her. She was very proud of all this. Other people were waiting for us to go and I really didn't know how to engage this woman any further so I planned to wrap it up when my team member asked her, "Can Val pray with you?" I was stunned. I mean, is that even allowed, praying with a witch? Ha ha, I wanted to smack him. She turned to me and looked straight into my eyes, held out her hands to me and challengingly said, "Sure, let's pray." Instantly, the words of Jay from three years ago flashed into my mind, "I would not fear if I get to lay my hands on a witch because 'He that is in me is greater than he that is in the world'." I heard the Holy Spirit whisper, "Val, do you really believe 'greater is He that is in you than he that is in the world' or do you just say it?" This all happened in seconds and in that moment the authority of the power of God's Spirit rose up in me and I gave her my hands. It was really weird but she took my hands and placed them on her face. Our eyes locked for a few moments, then I closed mine and said, "I declare that Jesus Christ has all power and authority and is King and Lord. In Jesus' Name, I command every spirit contrary to Him to be silent." As I prayed, I felt like the Lord had taken over my tongue and the words just flowed. Out loud, I rebuked spirits that came to my mind. My spirit connected with the Holy Spirit while my mouth spoke and

I asked Jesus what He saw in this woman. In the spirit, He showed me beauty that had been broken, pain, suffering, betrayal and a desire to be strong so that she would not be hurt again. I began to speak these things over her, "This is what Jesus sees in you . . ." Tears began to flow down her cheeks and onto my hands that were pressed firmly on them. I prayed and prayed over her. When I was done, she let go of my hands and wiped her face. She had a totally different demeanor. We gave her a few moments to take it all in and speak. She stammered, "I . . . I . . . don't pray like that." Then my team member piped up, "Would you like to pray?" Again, my eyes went big as I looked at him. I quickly added, "He means, like, would you like to pray to Jesus." She laughed softly and said again, "Oh, I don't pray like you . . . but okay." I instructed, "All you have to say is 'Jesus, help me' and He will." She closed her eyes, cupped her hands together and held them out. "J . . . . Je . . . . Jes . . . . I can't, I can't say it." I had my eyes open and watched her struggle. I repeated to help her, "Just talk to Him. Just call out and say 'Jesus, help me!' " She adjusted herself, again cupped her hands and held them up and out, "Je . . . Jes . . . ." Suddenly, the look on her face changed. She got a lustful look on her face with a mocking smile and said, "Jesus, kiss me," Then she puckered her lips. I had my eyes open and had watched this ungodly change. I quickly interrupted, "Ooooookay, let's just stop there." She snapped out of it and was back to "normal". I said, "I want to encourage you that when , not if , but when you can no longer control the spirits that you speak to and you realize they are controlling you, remember to call out to Jesus for help, because He will be the only One able to save you." It was time to leave and we said goodbye. As my teammate and I were walking away, I began to pray for protection over us and rebuked any demonic spirit from harassing us. It was like taking a spiritual bath. We prayed over our sleep and our families. Guess what?! No harassing, no bad dreams, no sicknesses, nothing.

When I've told that story to people they've asked, "Did she get saved?" The first time I was asked that, I was a bit taken aback but realized the question was measuring the fruit of the interaction. My answer? "I don't know. But I don't think that was the point of all of it. I do know two things. First, It was training for me and boosted my faith. It definitely was a turning point in understanding my identity in Christ. It grew me and was a game changer. Fear has left me in this area. Second, I don't know if there is anyone else in this entire world interceding for that woman. I got to stir up a war in the spiritual realm over her soul!"

I received a text from a team member, Marc, who was scheduled to preach that night on the sidewalk to a group that had gathered. He told me that right before he got up to speak, he lit the fire pit on the street for people to stay warm. As he was feeding the fire, he accidentally threw in his preaching notes and realized it when they hit the fire. He had to preach without them. Ha ha, but it turned out great. Then he told me a man had come up to him after he had spoken and asked Marc if he was aware of the dark figure standing beside him, calling him names as he preached. Marc, of course, did not. This man was seeing a demon. What a great reminder that there is much happening in the spiritual realm that we are not aware of.

There was a man sitting on the sidewalk that no one was talking to. There were a lot of people around, coming and going and in conversation. It was like a big, busy party on the street with our team providing music, food, clothing and conversation. This man had black smudges on his face, black nail polish, pink socks, and many black and gold necklaces. I smiled and asked, "Hey, what's on your face?" He said, "Oh, I put on eye makeup earlier today and it must have smudged." I asked why, and he answered he was doing a kind of Goth look. Again, I asked why and he expanded that it was because he was trying to portray suffering and how to deal with it, as well as the evil and sadness of the world. I asked him to explain this to me more. As he did, I found out his name was Joe and he had lived at the homeless shelter for two to three years. He had quite a bit of biblical knowledge and said he was a Christian. While we talked though, I could sense his thoughts were tormenting him and I suspected he was hearing voices as he would wince over and over when I spoke. I asked him if he heard voices. He told me it wasn't voices but very loud thoughts, like he was being screamed and yelled at. I asked him what the thoughts were. He said they were tormenting and terrible thoughts, ones that were very inappropriate, laughing, mocking, and urging him to do things. However, he assured me he had never hurt anyone. I asked him if he knew where the thoughts were coming from, was it him or something else? We talked openly about demonic spirits. He knew all about them and all about the Christian spiritual perspective of them. He said he had been baptized and people had prayed over him in the church. I asked when it started. He said eighteen years ago. I asked him how old he was now and he said thirty-six years old. So it started when he was eighteen years of age. I asked him what was going on in his life during that time. He said nothing that he could think of. So I questioned further, "Were you involved with any kind of occult or dark practices at that time?" He said yes, he had gotten into black magic and the occult very heavily at that time. He was very curious about the dark spiritual world and wanted to see what it was. He knew now that it was powerful and it had overtaken him. He knew what it meant to be possessed and had felt the power of it within him throwing him down and being completely controlled by demons. He said after he became a Christian, he felt the possession had left but now the thoughts were back and he was harassed constantly. He explained that when he was possessed, the evil was inside of him and took over him. He was controlled and everything else in him became faded. I told him about the power of Jesus and he knew all about it. I asked him if he had repented of everything that he had been involved with. He paused and said, "Well, not everything. Most things, but not all." So I explained that until he did, he was giving access to the demonic to have a hold in him. He totally agreed. I asked him if he was having any evil thoughts while he was talking to me. He said yes and I asked him what. He told me just 'stuff' that was very inappropriate. A voice was also telling him to go jump off that bridge beside us. I asked him if he wanted to be free and he said yes. I asked him if I could pray for him, he said yes. I first asked, "Joe, can you say, 'Jesus is Lord. I surrender to Jesus alone.'?" He nodded, and repeated my words, truly believing what he was saying. He kept darting his eyes around and getting distracted. I told him to look at my eyes. Up until this time he had a hard time keeping eye contact and kept noticeably wincing. He did look in my eyes and I called his spirit to attention. I bound every demonic spirit, commanding them to be silent. I told Joe who he was in Jesus, that he was a child of God. I rebuked the demonic spirits and commanded them to cancel their assignment. I asked the Holy Spirit what spirits were active. The spirit of suicide, mocking spirit, lying spirit, spirit of deception, etc. I rebuked them and told them to cease. I asked the

Holy Spirit to hover over the wounds of Joe deep down. I asked that the helmet of Salvation be placed on his head, to protect his mind and proclaimed that as a child of God, he had the mind of Christ. I continued to pray that each piece of the armour of God would be on Joe. I prayed over his future and destiny and declared this was not going to be his reality in the future. When I prayed over his heart, he broke eye contact with me. I asked him to continue looking at me. He recovered and did. When I was done, I asked him how he felt. He said he felt calm, light and clear-minded. The voices had stopped. I asked him if he had a Bible and he said yes, so I told him to read it as much as possible, that it would clean and renew his mind. He got up and said thank you and left. I suddenly felt sick to my stomach and so did my team member. I saw the real Joe, saw into his spirit, when I called his spirit to attention. I saw fear, desperation, and . . . something beautiful. I saw him. It's hard to explain. My heart ached for him to be free. When I closed my eyes a day later, I could still see his eyes and all that was in them. My team member and I prayed, rebuked the demonic and declared that we were daughters of the King. We prayed the demonic would not dare attack nor hang around us, to leave us and not return. We also prayed for the Holy Spirit to just cleanse us from any demonic harassment. I looked down at my hands and I saw I had black make-up on them from Joe. He must have had it on his hands when he shook mine. I couldn't rub it off as there was so much and it just smeared. I tried super hard not to touch my face or eyes, and wouldn't you know it, I got a hair in my mouth and it was driving me crazy. I carefully used the cuff of my coat to remove it without letting my skin touch my mouth. I really need to carry my hand sanitizer!

The night was over and my team member and I processed what occurred as we walked back to regroup. That night and the next day my life went a bit crazy in a few areas. One being, that night we were notified our family credit card was compromised with over $10,000 of false charges. Also, my team member's car got broken into that night. I prayed for protection and threw my dependence, family, health, relationships and ministry completely on Jesus. Spiritual warfare is messy, but is my answer, "Yes Lord, if . . ." or just "Yes Lord."?

Our team had set up a booth offering spiritual ministry and prayer at a home show. A woman stopped by and told me her mom had died a year ago. Her mom was a very "bad lady" and was very mean to her. The woman had bad dreams about her mother every night since her death. It tormented her and caused her much pain. This woman looked in turmoil as she spoke. I told her the three of us listening to her were going to listen up to our Source. We pressed in and I received the words love and great value of her worth. I conveyed to her our source was Jesus. I also explained to her that her mom had passed from this life to the next and was not able to torment her from beyond. I carefully pointed out there could be some different reasons for the dreams/nightmares. Deep wounds and trauma from the past which were not healed could cause these dreams to occur as she replayed the hurt and messages over and over in her mind every night. I recommended that she consider counselling. I asked her if the dreams were repeating what her mom actually had said to her when she was alive. She thought about it and shared that although similar, it was not exact words nor did she think she was just replaying her experiences. The dreams content was fresh, condemning verbiage yet a continuation from past attitudes her mother had toward her. I suggested that it could be spirits who wanted to torment her. Through her unhealthy relationship with her mom, the damage that was done, the fact that our battle was not against flesh and blood but against bad spirits who come against us, I laid out that the reason for her nightmares could possibly be from these negative spirits. I described how I had made an agreement with Jesus. I acknowledged that He was all powerful, more than any other spirit, and that He had conquered death. I now had a relationship with Him and through Him He enabled me to have authority that He had over spirits, over dreams and over anything that was not good, right, pure and true (Luke 10:19). I continued to explain that I could pray for her healing, as well as against the spirits to stop. I made it clear that when her dreams stopped, she needed to acknowledge it was Jesus. As I spoke, I was battling my own fearful thoughts of: What if they don't stop? Will she think God is not for real? What if I'm praying wrong? What if she just needs counselling? I wanted to talk more and ask more questions. However, I knew I needed to be quick because the building we were in was closing and literally turning off the lights and locking the doors. I asked her if I could pray. I prayed for her healing from Jesus, I prayed against any ungodly spirits attacking her. Then we had to go. I gave this woman a hug. She was so shattered, insecure and beaten down it was like hugging a lifeless stone statue. Later, as I lay in bed, I remembered her and prayed, well, to be honest, I pleaded and begged the Lord to stop the dreams that night and reveal His power to her. The next day she came back to our booth. I was busy with someone else but she told another team member that she came back just to tell us that she did not have any bad dreams last night. She had slept peacefully and felt very refreshed for the first time since her mom died. She was very excited and so very grateful. Our team member had a further conversation with her. I was told this at the end of the day and rejoiced, thanking our good, good God.

Two men approached me after I had preached on the street. I had said in my preaching that Jesus was the only one who could deliver them from voices and torment and provide freedom, cleaning, and healing. One of the men I knew, the other I was introduced to, Roca. Both were indigenous men. The man that I knew was a Christian and a really great guy. I looked at Roca - he was not a homeless person. His hair was short, had highlights and was very stylish. He had tattoos all over. His nose had obviously been broken and it had a large scar. His eyes were very desperate as he quietly told me how he was being tormented by a demon. I asked him how he was being tormented and if he heard voices. He said he did and that the spirit always tricked him and confused him. I asked if he meant by "tricked" that the spirit mocked him. He said yes, by telling him he would leave but then it would mock him and say he would never be able to get rid of the spirit until his journey was done. I asked what his spiritual beliefs were. He said he believed in Christianity but also his Native cultural beliefs of the Creator. I probed deeper, acknowledging that yes, God was the Creator, Jesus was the Creator. The Bible said Jesus created all things and that through Him all things held together. (Colossians 1:17) Roca closed his eyes and grimaced. He said, "The spirit makes it so that I have trouble hearing and understanding things, like my mind goes unclear. When you were speaking there, I can't even remember what you said and I was having trouble hearing you." I said, "Okay, let me deal with it. I'm going to pray right now." I put my hand on his shoulder and said, "In the Name of Jesus Christ, I command you, deaf and dumb spirit, mocking spirit, confusing spirit and every ungodly spirit operating to be silent, to stop operating and I bind you. You must stop right now. Roca, I call your spirit to attention, to be alert and hear me." We talked for thirty minutes and he was able to focus and understand as I asked many questions. He had been mixing the two belief systems of Christianity and Native spirituality, which unfortunately were leading him into deeper bondage. He had done sweat lodges, many ceremonies, drumming, fasting (not in the biblical way), gone out to the mountains alone for days, offered tobacco sacrifices, etc. Nothing was working and the mocking spirit seemed to grow stronger. I asked him when the spirit had first come. He said it had started one year ago when he got "together" with his common law girlfriend. When he shared with her that he was hearing a demonic voice, she told him she had been struggling with the same voice for years. A couple of months ago she was admitted into the psych ward, and has gone completely crazy, constantly talking to herself, but actually to the spirits tormenting her. He was so desperate and tired, "I have just tried everything. I don't know what to do any more." He also told me that he used to do crystal meth and when he did that, the spirit always got much worse so he decided to stop. So many things to deal with. I began. I explained to him about soul ties through sexual relations and that the demonic spirit had gained access to him through his girlfriend. I shared with him that only Jesus could cut the soul tie. I explained to him how drugs lowered the gateway of the mind, giving the demonic access to a person. I carefully navigated the spiritual differences between Christianity and the Indigenous spirituality. I asked him, "Do you see any differences between Christianity and your Indigenous spirituality?" He said yes. I asked what they were. He said, "With my Native spirituality there is a need for a lot of suffering in order to get results. You constantly have to do difficult things to try and get cleansing or help. That is why I've been suffering so much by going to the mountains and spending nights there, fasting and doing difficult ceremonies. But in Christianity there is grace and no need for those things." I was so pleasantly surprised by what I was hearing and his recognition of this. I said, " You are right! I love your people, Roca, and the good things about your culture. Would you agree that many of the things in the Native spiritual beliefs are causing your people to be involved with demonic spirits rather than a God of grace and love?" He thought for a moment and said, "Yes, that is true." I explained to him how he was trying to get clean, trying to get freedom by engaging in Indigenous rituals, requirements and ceremonies. I asked, "Who is the only one that can clean and deliver you?" He answered, "Jesus". I said yes and asked him why he was trying to get free by doing things apart from Jesus. We chatted about Christian basics, which Roca said he believed and agreed with. I told him that Jesus had conquered all spirits, even the spirit of death. I gently but assuredly shared with him that the spirit tormenting him was a very serious matter that would destroy him. He knew this to be true. I told him that I had surrendered completely to Jesus and did not participate with any other rituals or spirits in order to make Jesus my only God and Lord. Because of that, through Jesus, I had the authority to kick the demon out but it would just come back if Roca continued with the Indigenous spirituality that did not agree with the Creator God of the Bible. I asked him if he wanted Jesus to be Lord of his life and serve Him only, knowing that only Jesus could save him. He said yes. I asked him if he had ever fully made that decision and he said he didn't know. I said, "Well, let's make it so that you do know. Would you like to declare that today?" He said yes and I prayed with him. He asked me to lead him. He fully committed his life to the Lord, then I had him confess, repent and renounce his involvement with rituals and sacrifices, cut off soul ties, and declare that he was a child of God and to command the spirit tormenting him to leave. I prayed over him as well. There was still much to be done but I knew it was too much and too overwhelming for him to do it all right then. I asked him if he had any Christian brothers or community that he was able to be with. He said before Covid he was going to two different churches but since they had closed due to the pandemic. He didn't know what to do because of that he went back to the Indigenous spirituality for help. I told him that we would stand with him as his brothers and sisters in Christ and fight with him for his freedom, but he needed to come back on Mondays, sit down with us and continue this journey. He agreed. I got a piece of paper and wrote down our email address, my name and team member's name. I also wrote down chapters of the Bible for him to read out loud when the spirit would attack him, as well as a prayer to say out loud if he couldn't think clearly.

A man who I had never seen before came over to me while our team was handing out food on the sidewalk. He asked what kind of Christians we were and if I understood the spiritual realm. He had overheard me preaching to the crowd and said it seemed like I knew what was going on. He then said, "Don't think I'm crazy but I'm being attacked by a demon. It's at night and it's horrible. I don't know what to do. I keep saying 'In Jesus' Name stop', but it doesn't stop." He then described to me the terrible ways the demonic spirit was attacking him. I have been hearing this more and more. I assured him that I believed him. I went deep into the need for Jesus to be Lord of his life, and I questioned him on when and how the demon had gained access to him. Jesus was not Lord of his life and I plainly but compassionately told him the demon would not stop until he chose Jesus fully. It was very late at night and my team was all needing to leave. He asked me to pray over him. I did and when I was done he said, "Do you have some way I can get teaching from you? You really know what you're talking about. It's refreshing. Most Christians have no clue about this stuff." I gave him our general email.

I tell this story because over and over I hear this phrase from unbelievers and believers, "Don't think I'm crazy but . . . ; but there's a presence that comes into my room and it's very dark; but one time a demon grabbed me by my neck, threw me against the wall and choked me; but I have negative thoughts that run through my head all day long telling me how worthless and stupid I am. People are scared to talk about it because we don't believe them. We don't believe them for various reasons: theology that demons today do not operate like that; we perceive they have mental health issues that need to be medicated or they need to receive counselling; it just plain makes us uncomfortable; we don't feel we are equipped to deal with it; and finally, many times we'd rather run away from the person because they are truly going to be a lot of work. If we don't give them answers and help as Christ followers, they will either get their answer from other sources which will lead them into deeper bondage or they will helplessly flounder with torment, trying to numb it in several ways. Jesus came to destroy the works of the devil. We have the answer for their freedom. Let's rise up!

Now I could hear someone talking a little ways away from me and saw this man who I recognized as a street guy, talking to himself. I went over, really friendly, and asked who he was talking to. He was jumbled and contradicted himself, telling me he was talking to Chris. I asked who Chris was. He very rudely told me, "Chris, Christ, Jesus Christ, who is a %&*@ . ." I said, "No, He's not. He has all authority, He is the King." The guy said Yeshua was who he talked to and that Jesus was a fake. As we talked longer, he told me he was controlled by Yeshua and that if he didn't listen to him, "Yeshua" would hit him in the head a few times and get mad. I told him it was a counterfeit spirit and said out loud, "In Jesus Name, I bind every ungodly spirit, every counterfeit spirit and command you to be silent." In a mocking tone he said, "You @**%, you (beep beep beep) you can't do that, you can't tell 'Yeshua' what to do." My team member was praying quietly beside me and I said, "Jesus' Christ has authority over all spirits and yes, in Jesus' Name, I command all demonic spirits to be silent and to not speak. Do you want to be free?" He again mocked and said, "I can't be free and I don't want to be free. I hate you people. I hate you Christians. I don't want to talk to you." He was getting pretty aggressive and he wouldn't tell me his real name so I said, "I call this man's real spirit to attention. If you want to be free you can call to Jesus and say, 'In Jesus' Name, I want to be free!'" He said, "What? My spirit? I talk to lots of spirits you don't even know about." He just kind of kept talking non stop and then suddenly he stopped and said, "Hey I'm sorry for calling you a *&%$ . . . but maybe you are one . . . . Who are you? What are you?" I just had a sense we were going nowhere and decided to go. I smiled and said, "I'm a daughter of the King." He freaked out and yelled, "A king? Do you mean King Jesus?" He was saying some other stuff but I spoke over him as I turned to go, "Just remember, when you want to be free, just say, 'In the Name of Jesus, I want to be free.' " We walked away and he started following us, yelling and pointing to me, "She's a daughter of the King! She's a daughter of King Jesus!" I could tell it was mainly the demonic talking. I had talked with him months before where he had a totally different personality. I felt like satan had sent a distraction to take up our time and that's why I decided to walk away. I was finding the whole thing very amusing and loved the insight I gained. It didn't scare me, nor hurt me. It just made me want to learn from it.Later, I texted my team member and asked him his thoughts. This is what he said:

"Yeah, it was really crazy. . . . I've never encountered anything like that before. He did calm down a little after we interacted with him and were praying, compared to how he was originally. What I saw was him holding onto that spirit, not the other way around. . . . He didn't want to be free because he thought there was nothing to be freed from . . . but I did feel that the spirit shut its mouth and it was just glaring in anger (at the end). So it might be just the influence and the confusion that was left. . . . I've never seen a person possessed like that; I just started praying. I wasn't afraid at the time but I didn't feel safe, not just for me but for you because you were standing so close to him and he had a needle in his hand and might have poked you with it."

That was good insight for me because I also sensed the man was not wanting to be free and that he backed off because of it. I saw the needle in his hand but the possibility of being poked by it didn't even cross my mind. Anyway, I hoped we would see him again and I would be ready.

I don't tell these stories to be creepy or dramatic. In fact, I have a lot more stories I could share but I don't want to instill fear or sensationalize the demonic. Call me for coffee and I'd love to share them with you. I'm not trying to convince the skeptics nor fan the flame of those who are freaked out with such things. However, I'm done sitting within the walls of a church debating whether these things exist. It's hard to listen to arguments of why the demonic doesn't manifest when I'm out literally speaking to the demons, getting a front row seat on how the demonic enslaves people and completely depending on the Holy Spirit with how to deal with it. I do have those woulda, coulda, shoulda moments but that's all part of the training. My Kingdom perspective has completely flipped since those earlier years. When the demonic in people sees me coming, instead of me fearing them, they better fear Who's in me, because they know what I know: I have been given authority to trample on snakes and scorpions and to overcome all the power of the enemy (Luke 10:19). It is not spiritual arrogance or ignorance, as I know all too well the attacks, the difficulties and the power of the demonic. Wisdom needs to be applied. Intimacy with the Lord must be cultivated. Scriptures need to be studied and applied. Chinks in your armour fixed up. Unforgiveness dealt with. But I will not let the fear of being "bloodied" or spiritually attacked cause me to shrink back or doubt my identity in Christ nor Jesus' power and authority. I'd rather believe the scriptures than be "safe" or intimidated and bullied.

Stephen was interesting. He had just arrived in the downtown area three days ago. He was a young man, probably in his thirties, was dressed in a suit and a leather jacket with his hair done. He looked fantastic, however, I could see a darkness in his eyes. I found out he got out of prison not that long ago and has been in and out of prison for years. He was raised by a family who he hadn't been in contact with for years. I asked him if they were a good family and he said it was debatable. He could not remember a lot about his childhood. I led the conversation, asking him about his spiritual beliefs. At first he told me I wouldn't believe him, all that he'd experienced, as most people didn't. When he shared, people just thought he was crazy. I assured him that I'm good to hear the crazy and most likely wouldn't be surprised. He began telling me strange things, things that didn't make sense the way he presented them. But what I gathered through my questions was that he had an experience with a crystal, it was powerful and the things he saw changed him forever. He shared how he watched things happen with his physical eyes that were confusing to him: creatures growing out of the smallest item, statues coming to life, the river bubbling like it was boiling, the buildings melting, people disappearing. I asked him if he saw all this with his actual physical eyes or just in his mind or perhaps when he was high from drugs. He said yes, he saw them with his physical eyes and he wasn't high or drunk. He said that God sent him an angel every single day. He opened his Bible often and got messages. I took in all that he was saying and asked, "Have you ever had any interactions with demons?" He nodded and said yes, that they were actually very helpful and kind to him. I told him that demons were great deceivers and could present themselves as angels who were very helpful but really wanted to control him. He chuckled and said, "No, demons are misunderstood and are always protecting me. They are actually very good and loving." I thought for a moment about his words and studied his eyes, then asked, "Have you ever made any agreements with the demons?" He paused and slowly nodded. I asked what the agreements were. In a quiet, low voice he said, "To stay alive, to not die and have protection." I gently asked, "Well, you must know satan. Have you made any agreements with him?" He looked up at me and then quietly nodded yes. I asked, "What agreement did you make with him? What did you had to give?" His voice was barely audible, "Everything . . . I've given him everything." I nodded. I was constantly praying and asking the Lord to show me what to say. I said, "satan wants to destroy you. He hates you. He has deceived you." Stephen shook his head and said, "No, no that's not true. He loves me. He died for me." I raised my eyebrows at this and then asked, "What do you think about Jesus?" He shrugged and said nothing. I said, "Jesus conquered death. He can free you from the agreements." He chuckled, "Noone can free me from the agreements, it's impossible. Noone can free me from the death agreement. I had to make the agreement, there was no other way." I said, "I want you to listen very closely and remember my words. You've made friends with satan and his demons. Right now it seems great, but they will turn on you. When you realize they are controlling you and destroying you, call out to Jesus. He's the only one who can free you." He defended that he never would need to. I said, "I get shown things too but it is God who shows me things. I can see that you have a dark heaviness deep within you. You are extremely lonely and tormented." He stopped, looked at me and then nodded yes. I asked, "Why haven't the demons and satan fixed this for you? They haven't, have they?" He said, "No, but I'm getting used to being alone. I've been married, I've had it all. I am getting used to the loneliness." I said, "I'm not talking about being lonely from not having a woman in your life, or even close friends. I'm talking about a deeper loneliness than that. A loneliness and darkness that taunts you, leaves you empty, very dark and tormented, especially at night." He raised his eyes to look at me, took in my words and nodded that what I spoke was correct. I said, "There's a truth that will free you through Jesus." He got adamant, "There is no truth. Truth is simply what you want it to be. Everyone gets to decide their own truth." I said, "That doesn't even make sense if you think about it. There's no truth? . . .There is truth and the truth will set you free, but it's not found in this world or in satan or demons.

Hey, can I pray for you?" He answered, "I'm okay." I pursued further, "You're okay? Well, then is it okay if I pray for you? I'd like to pray for you . . . to God. He said, "I pray to God every day but . . . if you want to then do what you feel you should do." I smiled, "I do want to!" I saw him look at the people in conversations beside us around the firepit we had set up and I offered, "If you want, we can pray here or we can walk over there and pray." He said he'd rather walk to another spot. We got up and walked. He was walking pretty briskly and said, "Do you ever go to that field just beyond these buildings?" He pointed ahead of us and I said, "No, I'm not familiar with that field." He said, "Well, we could walk over to it and pray there." Ha ha, my first thought was, "Wow, he's smooth. If he ever got me alone he'd probably kill me." The evil that I was sensing in him did not scare me, I was just very aware of it. I glanced back to see my "bodyguard" team member with his eyes on me watching where I was going and I said casually, "Oh, well, this is great right here." I stopped, put my hand on his shoulder and started praying before he could object. I prayed for this man, the real Stephen, for all sorts of things. When I was done, he said, "Well, it's nice to see some good for once. Thank you." I told him I was glad to meet him and hoped he'd come back for more conversation.

One night after a fantastic evening of evangelizing, a man came running out of the darkness towards my team member and I. He had a black hood over his head and we couldn't really even see much of his face. He turned his back towards us and kicked gravel at us, sort of like an animal would with it's back feet. He proclaimed a curse over us. It was very shocking. Without even discussing it or planning it, at the very same time, words flew out of my team member's and my mouth, "A curse undeserved will not land!" We said the sentence at the very same time. He turned and ran away into the night.

The spiritual realm is very real. The world is waking up to it. If we as the church do not have the answers or are afraid to engage, then our world will go for answers to other sources. Let's read the answers in scripture, know our identity in Christ, and allow the Kingdom of Heaven within us to invade the enemy's territory. Thank you, Lord, for Your power, dominion and authority that have equipped us. Let us not shrink back.

CHAPTER 25

HOLY SPIRIT LED VERSES THE FLESH

"What we need is not more learning, not more eloquence, not more persuasion, not more organization, but more power from the Holy Spirit." - John Stott

On a busy sidewalk, we prayed, watched and waited. A man was walking towards us and my team member felt led to speak to him so she stepped in front of him and began chatting with him asking him how he was doing. He looked confused and said, "Do I know you?" She laughed, "No, it's just that we are Christians and love Jesus. When you were walking towards us, I sensed God telling me that you had a question that we could answer." I was a bit surprised to hear this myself and wondered how he would respond. A big smile came across his face and he said, "That is so funny you say that. I just came from my sponsor's house just now. I have been in AA for drugs and alcohol for two months and they are really into spirituality. My sponsor has been telling me all about God. My question for you is this, do you ever doubt there is a God?" My team member told him no and thus began our conversation. He told us all about his journey of working for a large company, getting an injury, being put on morphine and becoming addicted. As he was talking the words that came to me from Holy Spirit were, "gentle and hard working". I sensed that the way he had been living his life was not reflecting who he truly wanted to be in character and convictions. He told us about how he got into street drugs, lost his job and isolated himself from family. He went to AA and had been clean for two months, reconnected with family and was now learning about God and Jesus. We encouraged him and I told him about the words I was receiving. He told us he used to think that he would feel "filled up" when everyone served him but now he was finding the more he poured into others, the better he felt. He just wanted to try to keep doing it so he always felt good. Right away I started telling him about Jesus and the woman at the well and how they talked about living water. Jesus said He could fill us up with water so that we would never thirst again. My team member got excited and pulled out a paper from her pocket which just happened to have the exact verse in John 4:13 &14: "Jesus answered, "Everyone who drinks this water will be thirsty again, but whoever drinks the water I give them will never thirst again. Indeed the water I give them will become in them a spring of water welling up to eternal life." We laughed at the amazing "coincidence". I explained to him if he tried to do it on his own he would get tired and give up, but if he turned to Jesus then strength, kindness, hope, joy and peace that would not run out. We had a great conversation with him and it was awesome knowing he had his sponsor discipling him. He said the sponsor had just asked him if he could think of any God-moments he had experienced where God made Himself really clear. He couldn't think of any except the one and only time was when he fell on his knees and cried and cried out to God in a prayer to help him get off drugs. Our talking to him at that moment was the second. We prayed for him and he thanked us. He said, "That was so great, awkward . . . but great." Ha ha, so funny and awesome.

Spirit to spirit ministry is a term I use to describe listening to the Holy Spirit and then sharing with a person what the Spirit reveals. I don't know if I've heard it before or if I just started using the term. Regardless, Jesus was the One who demonstrated it first. We are told to be led by the Spirit and not the flesh. (Romans 8:5,9,14 and Galatians 5:16) We want to always be operating by the Spirit and have Him speak through us. However, there is definitely the temptation and habit of evangelizing out of our flesh. We depend upon our knowledge, our social skills, perhaps our persuading or debating skills. We may use formulas and methods over and over. These can be effective but it is important to use them as tools when the Spirit leads. The Language in the Bible is very rich in describing the deep places the Spirit impacts, such as: "the eyes of your heart may be enlightened" (Ephesians 1:18) and "to know (Greek word: *ginosko* - to know experientially, allow, feel, understand, be sure) the love of Christ that surpasses knowledge (Greek word: *gnosis*-knowledge, perception, science, the act of knowing)" (Ephesians 3:19). Sometimes when I see that logic, reasoning or debating is not producing any positive fruit nor penetrating the person's heart, I will stop and realign myself to fully engage in listening to the Spirit and depend on His power to touch a person regardless of my strengths or weaknesses. If I win a debate but the person is still going to hell, what good is it? I've seen Spirit to spirit ministry occur when someone sits on a curb just listening to worship music being sung passionately on the street. Tears stream down their face and it touches them in the depths. No sermon needs to be preached. I've seen it happen when I've fumbled for intelligent words or explanations and it results in emotional reactions that are not from my lack of answers but from the presence of the Holy Spirit landing upon them. I've seen it when I've turned to the Holy Spirit and received a word, picture, verse or sense that is not based on logic or rationale but on the Holy Spirit's understanding of the depths of the person. I've been amazed to watch Him work. This is Spirit to spirit and it does not get to be formulated, regulated, or controlled. It is all God, working through His people, for those who dare to allow Him and have the faith to take risks. It does not depend upon knowledge, education, skills or abilities. This intentional approach causes the evangelist to be totally dependent upon the Holy Spirit so that only God can be given the credit. It is the type of ministry that enables people to have an encounter with God, to have a revelation of Jesus Christ, to intimately have their heart touched. It's incredible and fills me with awe.

There was a man who was carrying a backpack and shoes walking on the sidewalk. He seemed very agitated as he was walking around. I had asked the Lord if there was anything to say to him and I got a picture of mountains with snow gently falling, and stillness. I asked the Lord what it meant and I felt the Lord was saying He wanted this man to be still before Him. The Lord desired a deeper intimacy and was drawing the man to His heart. There was a sweet purity about it that would wash the man's heart. I tried to go talk to him but he left before I had the opportunity. I went about evangelizing with my team members and about an hour later we headed back as we were out of time. As we walked, all of a sudden there was that guy carrying the backpack and shoes. I quickly approached him and gave him a friendly hello. I told him I had seen him an hour before and explained quickly that I loved Jesus. He instantly said, "I am a Christian too." I went on to explain the above picture and message. He smiled and closed his eyes, truly enjoying what I was saying. He thanked us. I asked him if we could pray for him and he said yes, asking for prayer for his family. We prayed for him right there. It was so cool how God brought him back to us. I am convinced that if God gives us a picture/word/message, then it is to be stewarded and told.

On the street late at night the team had begun wrapping up with prayer in a big circle of about twenty five people. I joined in and during the prayer time a tall man walked by us who was very drunk. One of our team members brought him to our circle and when we said Amen, the team member announced that Cole wanted prayer. I looked at Cole and his eyes were wild; he appeared very unpredictable in his drunken state. He seemed upset with anyone touching him and I did not want this to become a "show". I could see the team freeze as we all eyed up the situation. I called two men from our team to come over to him, handed the keys for the motorhome to a team member and asked her to start it. I announced that everyone was free to go home or into the motorhome to stay warm. About half left and half stayed. I was going to let the men handle the situation, but as I turned toward the man, Cole, our eyes met. He pointed at me and loudly said, "I know you!" As he said it, I searched for something vaguely familiar about him. I didn't know from when but wondered if we had some sort of past conversation. I laughed and pointed back at him, "I know YOU!" He came toward me to hug me. Now this guy, I'm not exaggerating, was probably 6'7 and I was literally going to hug his belly button. I exclaimed, "And you are very tall!" He broke out into a huge grin and this eased everyone around us. Laughter followed at the sight of us hugging. I looked him straight in the eyes and said, "Cole, give me your hand. I'm going to pray for you." Like a child, he gave me his hand. I leaned into the Holy Spirit and said, "In the Name of Jesus, I bind all demonic spirits, every ungodly spirit I command you to be silent and you are not allowed to operate. Cole, I call your spirit to attention." I paused as I pressed into the Lord for my next words, "Cole, this is not who you are. You are gentle, you are a man who wants to do what is right. You have integrity and you don't wish to hurt others." Tears began to stream down his face and his eyes changed. I then rebuked the spirit of depression, addiction, victim spirit, and others that I sensed influencing him. I prayed that he would loathe alcohol and seek the Holy Spirit to minister to his deep wounds instead of using a counterfeit. When I was done he said, "I am a Catholic. I won't drink no more." I knew his mind was hindered because of the alcohol but could see his spirit had been touched by the Holy Spirit. He said, "Isaiah 18 - that's me, that's me!" This showed me he had been obviously raised with some sort of Bible training. We chatted for a bit but didn't get too deep because of his drunken state. The older team member gave him contact information to get together with him when he was sober. We told him Jesus loved him and to go to Jesus instead of alcohol. Later I looked up Isaiah 18 and found it interesting. I think I know the part Cole was referring to as he, himself, was a man from another country:

"At that time gifts will be brought to the Lord Almighty from a people tall and smooth-skinned, from a people feared far and wide, an aggressive nation of strange speech, whose land is divided by rivers - the gifts will be brought to Mount Zion, the place of the Name of the Lord Almighty." (Isaiah 18:7)

I wondered, as I drove home, of the words he said - "I know you!" His eyes had been so wild and then clear with recognition when he looked me in the eyes. Had I actually seen that man before? Or was a demonic spirit inside of him speaking? Or was it the Holy Spirit, deposited long ago, grieved no doubt, that spoke through him? . . . Just thoughts, just pondering. The tears that streamed down and the look of pain on his face when I spoke to his spirit remains burned in my memory. I agape that guy, Cole. I love, love, love the work of the Holy Spirit. He is so, so full of love and grace.

As we were at the Psychic fair, I saw him walking by and convinced him to come to the booth that we had set up at the fair where we were offering "spiritual blessings". He was attending a course in the building and was on his break. He only had ten minutes so I told him we would be done in less than ten minutes. Myself and two others asked the Holy Spirit what He loved about this gentleman. I saw in him a man who was strong, a man who was tender and compassionate, stood for what's right, defended those who could not defend themselves and had integrity. Another said they saw the word "Leader". One lady had a real gift of words of knowledge and she accurately saw that he loved being a hunter, there was an injury in his right leg and a bitterness towards his mother. He confirmed each thing that we spoke. She asked him if he wanted to let go of that bitterness towards his mother. He said yes. He was very surprised that everything we said was so accurate. We now had his attention. I then told him I saw him before Jesus. Jesus looked straight into his eyes and said, "If you truly knew Me, you would follow Me. Because the things you value are the things I have deposited in you." I told him, "I don't know your background or how you've heard about Jesus but I have a feeling it has been negative and appeared to you as an unattractive religion." He nodded his head that this was true. I continued, "The True Jesus is completely different. He had a best friend named John. John went around everywhere with Jesus and later recorded what they did and what Jesus actually said about Himself. John wrote it down sort of like a journal. Would you like to truly know who Jesus is? Would you be open to reading it?" Allan was moved by all that had been said and he agreed to read it. I gave him a gospel of John and he put it in his free bag from the fair. Time was up and he shook all our hands, thanked us and said he was really, really glad he came.

At the transit station I saw a very tall man get off the train and walk by us. I instantly knew he had a gentle spirit. So I rushed over to him and said hello. I told him that I loved Jesus and that He had shown me that this man had a gentleness in him, and that God loved that about him. He told me his English was okay but to speak slower so he could fully understand. So I repeated it slower. He smiled and asked very puzzled, "How did God speak to you? I ask because it is true what you said." I told him that I have a relationship with God through Jesus and that He shows me things about people through a sense, through a word, through a picture - all sorts of ways. Through questions, I found out he was from an African country I couldn't pronounce, nor did I know existed. He also had a very long name that I could not pronounce. He had only been here two and a half months. His friends who came to Canada went to Quebec as they all spoke

French, but he felt he should really come to Calgary even though he didn't know anyone. He was raised Christian but was not going to church at this point. I told him the Lord wanted to encourage him tonight and draw him into a deeper relationship with Him. I asked him if I could pray for him. I prayed slowly so he could understand. When I was finished he told me he thought God had sent an angle to him. I was confused and asked "an angle?". He pointed at me and repeated a few times. Then I realized he meant angel. His train came. We gave him a hug and encouraged him one last time.

I saw a gentleman in a booth waiting for his train. Something about him just drew me but I did not have anything yet from the Holy Spirit to say. I walked up to him and said "Hello! I know this sounds weird but I love Jesus and when I saw you, I really felt God just got my attention and wanted me to come pray for you. Is that okay?" He was surprised but said sure. So I prayed for him and as I prayed, I sensed from the Holy Spirit that he was gentle, humble and teachable. When I was done praying, I told him so. I asked him if he had any spiritual beliefs at all. He said no. He had gone to church as a very small child in a Catholic church but really didn't know anything about it. I quickly explained how we sin, how Jesus died and rose again, how He can forgive our sins, that He wants a relationship with us and how to have one. I asked him if he had ever heard that before, he said he had heard bits and pieces of that. I knew my time was running out so I told him that I believed God was trying to get his attention and reveal Himself to him. I encouraged him to ask God who He was and find out more about Him. As I turned to walk away, this quiet gentleman, who had hardly said a word stopped me and said, "Thank you, I'm sure that it is not an easy thing to come and tell me all that." I laughed and said, "It's not, but when God shows me something, I must listen to Him."

Look into people's eyes when you talk to them. It may seem weird or uncomfortable at first but as you continue to practice this, it will become easier. This is not just a word of advice for good communication but there's a purpose in it that I want you to understand. Not only does eye contact with someone indicate you are paying attention and actually listening to them, it increases retention of what is being said and it often promotes honesty. It actually produces a chemical in the brain and body called phenylethylamine that gives you heightened focus, attention and concentration. The gospels talk about eyes. Matthew 6:22: *"The eye is the lamp of the body; so then if your eye is clear, your whole body will be full of light. But if your eye is bad, your whole body will be full of darkness. If then the light that is in you is darkness* (vision, direction, reveals what the heart and mind are set on) *how great is that darkness."*

In many places the Bible talks about the eyes and the inner heart they reveal. Just search up the word "eyes" in the Bible and read what is said and described. I like that old saying, "The eyes are the window to your soul." My Grandma used to say that to me and it made me nervous as I wondered what depths she could see when she looked at me. If you've ever seen someone who has passed away and looked in their eyes you will see they are not there. That is because the physical eyeballs are just a part of the body. But when someone is alive, you see their soul, their character, their heart, their thoughts. Oh, as adults we get good at hiding all these things but as conversation happens (I'm going to talk about that specifically when it comes to evangelizing), the eyes can fill in the details of what is not being said with the mouth. This is something anybody can train themselves to do, to look in someone's eyes to gain a deeper understanding of that person. But what is even more powerful and effective is when you ask the Holy Spirit to show you what He sees, what He wants to reveal to you about the soul and spirit of that person. You will be amazed at how the Lord will give you discernment and a sense in your spirit, bypassing your logic and "head" knowledge when you look into someone's eyes and see with your physical and spiritual eyes the depths of the inner person. Countless times as a person talks, I have silently prayed to "see" as I look into the person's eyes. I see things like tenderness, compassion, depth, sorrow, fear, anger, desperation, loneliness, hurt, etc. - the list goes on. And when I speak it out loud to the person, many times it brings instant tears or has a significant impact because it was not revealed in their speech. The knowledge of being "seen" brings weight and value. I also steward this wisely as I never want someone to feel shame or condemnation. I ask the Lord why He's showing me this and what to do with it. This only has to take seconds and I will get a sense of whether to share it or speak into it. By speaking into it, I'm bringing clarity or inviting them to rise above it or encouraging them that Christ can bring healing and freedom.

All this is to say that the spirit can also be revealed through the eyes of a person. Through the eyes we can at times see the spirit of the person, any demonic spirits operating, or the Holy Spirit's presence. If we can see this in someone's eyes, they can also sometimes see it through our eyes, even if they are not consciously aware. The Holy Spirit in a believer is active and alive. Sometimes the mind is not registering what the spirit is picking up.

During an outreach I saw a man off to the side alone who was hungrily shovelling food into his mouth. I went over and began chatting with him, asking him how he was doing and where he was living. He was very receptive to conversation. I found out he was living outdoors because the weather had been so nice. He was very open and honest about his struggles. I sensed such a great heaviness on him. He told me he had been in for treatment years ago, came out, got married and had two kids. Then things went bad: they got divorced and he lost his kids. He had no contact with them. They were currently nine and eleven years old. His eyes welled up with tears. I asked him what he had been in treatment for and if he was still free from it. He shook his head no. He shared with me he was on crack and crystal meth. He said he took meth every day. I gently asked him why. He gave me the same answer everyone gives me. "I want to feel different. I just want to feel normal. I hate how I feel when I'm not on it." I looked in his eyes and said, "I can see you have a real strong heaviness on you." His eyes filled with tears and he said it was true, he had so much pain. I asked him if he was on meth right now during our conversation. He adamantly said no, that he had taken it much earlier that day and it had worn off. He was very straight and clear headed. He asked me if I had a tissue for him as the tears rolled down his face. I ran, got some napkins and more food for him. As I did, a newer team member asked if she could join me. Absolutely! So we came back to him. I shared with him my experience with deep heaviness. As I shared, it really resonated with him, he nodded his head and tears kept filling his eyes. I gently and passionately told him that getting treatment and counselling was good but it would never take away the pain. His drugs were destroying him and would only mask the pain for short periods but never take it away. He was in total agreement. I then told him, "I am going to tell you honestly and truthfully that the only One who can help you is Jesus. He is the only one who can heal your pain and change your life. Without Jesus there is no hope." I asked him his name, it was Ken. As he spoke, I was asking the Holy Spirit what He saw in him. I then said, "Ken, I sense you once were a man of laughter and it's been a long time since you've laughed. I also can see that you are a gentle and caring man. You have been a man of strength. This . . . ." I motioned my hand up and down in front of him, "is not who you are. This is a season. I believe God wants to restore to you laughter and joy." Tears poured down his face and he nodded that those things were true. He shared he had been wearing a mask for so long, hiding his pain and becoming someone he's not. He knew his life was ruined and felt like if he continued it would be over soon. I knew that the pain was deep - I could not minister deep enough but Jesus could. I asked him if he would like us to pray for him. I explained there were some of us on the team who had listened to God and we would love to sit down with him to take time to listen to whatever God had to say to him. He wanted that. I grabbed chairs and tried to put them under some shelter. I grabbed a blanket for Ken and wrapped it around him. He told me he was struggling with a chest cold and when the meth had worn off he often felt cold and shaky. I grabbed two other team members to come, listen to the Holy Spirit with me and had the newer team member continue to join us. I explained to Ken we were just going to talk to God and ask Him what He wanted to say to him. There would be some silence as we focused on praying and that we would share when we were ready. So we began. After a few moments my one team member shared that she saw Ken as a man who was full of laughter in the past! That he had not laughed for a long time but in the future, God wanted to restore his laughter. Ken and I looked at each other and smiled. He said, "That's exactly what you said tonight!" I laughed with delight, "God's confirming to you this truth. He's speaking to you!" The team member went on to tell him she had a song that came to her. In it were the words "Mighty Warrior" and she encouraged him that God was calling him to rise up and be a mighty warrior with the Lord, to fight this battle. It was my turn to speak. I looked directly in his eyes. I shared with him that God often gave me pictures and the pictures had meaning. I told him that I was growing in this, as we all were. I began to explain the picture the Lord was giving me for him. I saw him with a necklace of pearls around his neck. They were big and beautiful. I could see he understood how valuable and precious they were. He was thankful to have them. Out of the corner of my eye in the vision, I saw that he had purposefully stuck his hand into mud. It was strange because the pearls were so beautiful and valuable and yet the mud was so dirty and gross. I told him I knew that the pearls were truths from God about Who He was, God's Kingdom and the way to have a relationship with Him. The mud was things he had chosen to do that were . . . He chimed in, "things that are bad". I laughed, and said yes. He had been raised Catholic so he knew what sin was. I continued, "As I was looking at you I saw that the pearl necklace was ripped off of you and broken. It was like a tearing and it devastated you. You knew what you had lost and you were upset about it. I waited for Jesus and He showed me He had the pearls and wanted to place them back on you but He was waiting for you, Ken, to take your hand out of the mud." Ken told me that made a lot of sense to him. At this time I was battling with myself as Jesus had shown me a tattoo on Ken's arm in the vision. Since Ken was wearing long sleeves that night, I could not see if he actually had any tattoos or not. It was like Jesus was looking at the tattoo, drawing my attention to it. As I studied it in the vision, it seemed vague and I couldn't understand why it was being shown to me. All I could see was that it had triangles, which of course didn't make sense to me. Who tattoos triangles on themselves? I thought maybe it was a star or something else, but no, I kept seeing triangles. I felt like Jesus was not happy with the tattoo, that it represented some sort of labelling or mark of an identity on Ken that was false. I did not know if this tattoo thing was real or some sort of spiritual symbolism. When I had pressed in, I was really questioning myself if it was me or God coming up with the tattoo thing. I was wrestling with sharing it because . . . well, to be quite honest, I didn't know what it's significance was, maybe it wouldn't mean anything, what if I was wrong and . . . ha ha, what if I looked foolish?! It felt like a risk. But I decided I'd rather look like a fool than not risk, so I went for it. After I explained it to him, describing the triangles, I openly confessed I didn't know if he had any tattoos, if this was just a figurative symbol or if it meant anything to him. He sat there silent for what seemed like a long time. He said, "I do have a tattoo." I waited but when he didn't say more, I feared it could be personal or in an inappropriate place so I quickly said, "You don't have to tell me what it is or where, maybe it's just for you to know." He ignored me and said, "I only have one tattoo, only one on my body and it's on my arm." Trying to hold back my cautious excitement, I said, "Can I see it?" He rolled up his sleeve. He explained that he used to drive a truck and at that time he "got a stupid tattoo" of a "dangerous goods" sign. When I saw it, I smiled at the Lord. There was a right side up triangle and then an upside down triangle underneath. The words "dangerous goods" were between them. (I have pondered and found it interesting that in my vision, I saw the tattoo very vague and fuzzy. I just knew there were triangles. It was not like I got to see it clearly as the dangerous goods warning sign nor recognize it as such. I just saw triangles but it was so hard to make out. It was like Jesus wanted me to trust Him and take a step of faith in sharing about it, so that I could be delighted when I found out Ken actually had a tattoo with triangles. It was like Jesus wanted to make sure He gave me a distinct "clue" or confirmation that the tattoo did hold meaning, and that this was actually from Jesus by having me see triangles and then seeing in the physical the actual triangles in the tattoo, yet He did not give me the exact tattoo vision.) I looked at my other team member and she said the Lord was telling her what the tattoo represented. The reason Jesus was pointing it out was because, like I had sensed, it was showing Ken the lie of how he was identifying himself. He wore a mask because his feelings and pain were too "dangerous". His past was too "dangerous" to deal with. The enemy, satan, wanted him to believe that Ken was "dangerous goods" that could hurt others or himself and could not be handled. She felt like the two triangles were like a reflection or mirror of each other. He was reflecting the wounds and hurt. She then spoke hope into him. "God wants you to have a relationship with Him. You are not too dangerous for Him and He can handle all the pain. He wants to have you reflect His character, His love, His joy, His peace and you will become dangerous for God against the enemy." We further encouraged him and then I asked him if he understood what choice he had to make, what salvation really was and how to have a relationship with Jesus. He said he thought so. I asked him to explain it and he had a lot of difficulty doing so. So I rescued his attempt and was about to explain it but decided this would be a great opportunity to sharpen and mentor. I asked a different team member to explain it clearly to him. When she was done, I asked him if he wanted to surrender his life to God tonight. He told us he knew this was the only way but was feeling a bit overwhelmed and needed time to think about it. I let him know there was no pressure. In fact, the Bible says it is good to count the cost of following Jesus and explained to him the meaning of Luke 14:25-34. We all prayed over him. When we were done he was crying again and we all gave him a hug. When the others went off into conversation and other directions he leaned over to me and said, "When you were all praying for me I could feel energy coming on me, like a positive energy, it's hard to explain." I smiled and told him it was the Holy Spirit of God that was touching him. He told me he wasn't a hug person but really appreciated that the team members had hugged him tonight. I told him to keep the blanket and to come back next week and let us know his thoughts of what we talked about.

Another time, it was time to leave the train station and as we were walking I was still intentionally being spiritually aware. We passed several people, and then I was drawn to a man we went by. I stopped, took a second and asked the Lord, "Him? What about him?" The word "wanted" came to me. I asked for more but no more came. We turned around and went back to him. I began, "Excuse me, sir, my name is Val and I love Jesus. As I walked by you, God just drew my attention to you and spoke the word 'wanted' to me. You are wanted by God. He wants to have relationship with you." I didn't feel really satisfied with my interpretation with the word and felt there was more to it. Then the man said, "I am a Christian. I love Jesus and I have a relationship with Him." Instantly I understood in my spirit what the word meant. "Oh, that is wonderful! I now understand that the sense I'm getting is that Jesus wants you to come spend time with Him, to have intimate time together, to be still in His presence. You are 'wanted' to engage with Him at a deep level." Ahh, that was it and my spirit had peace. He smiled and said, "I understand," he paused. "I would love that actually. I will do that, thank you, that means a lot." His train came and as he boarded, we said goodbye.

There was a tall, large man who looked very serious and stern waiting for his train on the train platform. I paused and listened to the Holy Spirit. The words didn't seem to match the steel look on his face. I went over to him and said, "Excuse me, sir, I love Jesus and He showed me that you are a man of discernment, you are given wisdom in situations, you have maturity and integrity. That is how God sees you. Do you have any spiritual beliefs?" The corner of the one side of his mouth went up into a smile and he said in a thick accent, "I am a Christian. What you have said is God speaking to me. I know what it means and why God has said this through you." Then his train came and he stepped on.

The preaching happened outside on the street and the tall man who I talked to last week in the pizza line was there. He had been highlighted to me for weeks now. I asked the Holy Spirit if there was something about him He wanted to show me. When the preaching was done and he got his pizza I chased him down. His name was Brian. He was not a typical street person. He was more like a cool, well off, popular tough guy. He was clean and dressed nicely. I greeted him and told him that the Lord had highlighted him to me for many weeks. This surprised him and he was eager to hear more. Then I shared with him the pictures I had received for him. I saw him in front of Jesus. There were several thin metal bands that had been put around his left wrist. I ask Jesus what they were for and what they meant. Through waiting on the Lord I got the understanding that the bands were bondage that had been placed on him through relationships, I didn't know if it was broken relationships or ones that had caused damage or what but the result was he had baggage like bonds around him. As I said it, he began nodding his head and saying that's exactly what has happened and how it felt. I told him that in my vision the Holy Spirit came along, had wire cutters and showed me it was so easy to cut the bands because they were thin, however, if he did not deal with it, more and more bands would come and form into thick bands that would become shackles and be so much harder to break him free from. He really appreciated this. He opened up and I found out he had been in an addiction program for the last three months and had now finished it. He was ready to go back to work. I asked him if the program worked; he hesitantly hoped so. He had had a drug problem for twenty years and it had nearly killed him. He got a bit emotional and shared that if he went back to drugs, it would kill him. He said just before he went into the program, he had witnessed his best friend die from drugs. He wanted to now have God because he had nothing else that could help him. I asked many questions and he told me he was raised Christian, but when he was ten years old his brother died and his parents stopped going to church. That's all he remembers. He told me he was so desperate, exhausted and desired a change in his life. I asked him if he had ever made a decision to have a relationship with God through Jesus. He said, "I think so. I mean, I hope so. I want to." I gently and kindly asked Brian, "Do you understand, Brian, what exactly Jesus did on the cross? Has anyone ever explained to you how to have a relationship with God?" He honestly said, "No, I don't really know." I began explaining the answers to those two questions. I told him the definition of sin - to miss the mark and what that meant. I told him the exchange that took place when we received the gift that Jesus died to give us. When I was done, I asked Brian if he believed the things that I explained, and I asked if he wanted to choose Jesus as his Lord. He said yes! I smiled at Brian and he inquired, "Like is it something I should just do tonight by myself?" I answered, "You definitely can or you can talk to God right now, and choose to surrender to Him. I can help you if you'd like or you can just pray on your own. You are acknowledging that Jesus is Lord, you believe that He died and God raised Him from the dead. Ask him for forgiveness for doing things your own way. Tell him you want to have a relationship with Him." In raw words, he prayed and gave his life fully to the Lord! I put my hand on his shoulder and said, "Brian, tonight you have become my brother in Christ, and I am your sister. You are a son of God. I want to pray for you." As I prayed, the Lord showed me things about Brian that I spoke into him, declared over him and blessed him with. Tears streamed down his face. When we were done I told him I was a hugger and reached out to give him one .

As I was sharing about how the Lord had "highlighted" someone to me, one of my team members stopped me and said, "What do you mean God 'highlighted' a person to you. Like, what is that like, does a light literally go around them? Do they just like, light up?" He was completely serious and I had to laugh. But what a great question! I am sure someone, somewhere, may have had an experience like that from God, but that is not how I experience it. When I say someone is "highlighted" to me, I am conveying that as I intentionally ask the Lord, "Who do You want me to talk to?", I scan the people around me. It's like as my eyes look around, the people are obscure, but when my eye lands on someone, I "see" them. I notice them. I often don't know why, they just stick out to me. There is usually nothing physical that causes me to notice them. Then I ask the Lord, "Him?" or "Her?" Sometimes it's the faintest sense of yes, or a sense that I can't walk away from them or a gnawing feeling to be obedient. Sometimes, it's blank and I look at the people around them and someone else right near them is actually the one who stands strongly out to me. Then I ask the Holy Spirit, "What? . . . What do You want to say to them? What do You love about them? What is it that they need to hear from You?" Then I wait for whatever way the Lord wants to speak to me; through a picture, a strong sense, through a single word, through a verse, or maybe through a message. Then I ask the Lord, "What does that mean?", if I don't know the meaning. Sometimes I know right away, sometimes I have to be obedient first and start the conversation, speak what I know and the interpretation comes instantly as I say it, sometimes I just have to deliver the picture or word and leave the interpretation to them, knowing the Holy Spirit will take it from there.

As we were walking to the car there was a young woman walking in front of us who the Lord was highlighting to me. I told my team member to ask the Lord if there was anything He wanted us to say to her. Once the crowds had dispersed a bit and I had received from the Lord, I called out to her. "Excuse me! Hi! I know this sounds really weird but we love Jesus and He has just been highlighting you to us and has shown us a few things He'd like to say to you." She was surprised but said okay. I introduced myself and found out her name was Shelly. "The Lord has shown me you have a gentleness and sweetness about you. There are things about yourself that you do not like but He absolutely loves them about you." This lit up her face and she said, "Wow, thank you, that just really made my night!" Then my team member said, "The Lord showed me an ocean and in the ocean was a clam and in it was a pearl. That pearl was you and He sees you as precious, valuable and beautiful." Shelly's eyes filled with tears and I gave her a big hug. She didn't know how to handle what we were saying and stammered, "Thank you very much. I hope you have a really great night. You have all just made my night, thank you." I shared with her Jesus wants to have a relationship with her and that He loved her very much. Then a truck drove by and beeped at her. She jumped and said that was her ride. She wiped her tears, thanked us again and ran to her ride.

Two men on the streets who were believers discussed with myself and a team member who God was and what He wanted our relationship with Him to be like. Jerry shared a bit with us about how he had seen God work in so many ways in the past. After our conversation last week he had spent some time with God and dealt with some things. Instantly and amazingly, his circumstances began to change. He thought it was pretty awesome. I celebrated with him but then spoke to both of them about how we sometimes go to God in our crisis but then do our own thing when everything was fine. I shared with them about how the battle in our inner being needed to be fought before the battle outside could be fought and won. I explained how everything came out of our intimacy with God and if we made time to cultivate and grow in that relationship, then no matter what happened with our outer circumstances we were still ok. We needed to take our eyes off everything going on around us and fix our eyes on Jesus, rather than the other way around. We talked about how it was hard to do and stay in that posture. How it took perseverance and an act of the will despite powerful emotions. It was a really good discussion and a different perspective for both of them which they hadn't known. I invited two team members into the conversation. After introductions, I explained to Jerry and Sheldon that the three of us were growing in hearing from God and we would love to "practice" on them. Would that be okay? Both were intrigued and thought it was interesting so I explained to them we would take a few minutes to ask the Holy Spirit what He loved about them and what He wanted to say to them. We stood in silence and began when we were ready. We did Jerry first. One team member said she saw a picture of a top hat that was half white and half black. It was on Jerry's head. She saw a top hat in his hands which was all black. The white and black hat represented two opposite ways of thinking, two opposite decisions, and Jesus did not want him wearing that hat nor living in that duplicity. The black hat in his hand was the right hat, because it was all one colour, united, proper and firm. My other team member saw a stream of living water for Jerry to drink from. I saw Jerry before Jesus with a long sparkler that was lit and he was spinning it in a circle. It made a ring of sparks and fire. He was having fun with it and very confidently threw it in the air, then grabbed another and did the same. The fire and sparks were the power of the Holy Spirit. Jerry knew how to be engaged and if he would engage, he would display God's mighty works for all to see. I then saw Jesus ask for him to take off his belt. It was a fancy studded belt that was laid before Jesus. I looked at it and pressed into the meaning. It was this: the belt's looks and studs had no purpose except to look good, for show, but was useless. Jesus gave him a more practical belt that had places to put tools. I was praying in the Spirit for more understanding and continued asking Jesus questions: Is it the belt of truth, mmmm, no. Is it connected with his past, mmmm, no. What is the belt you want to give him, is it a tool belt, mmmm, no. I felt like I was to focus more on the fancy studded belt and the need to lay it down and exchange it. I wasn't getting anything else and hesitated in saying it but when it came to my turn I told him. When we were done, I gave him an opportunity to respond. He said it all was very accurate. The hat described how he was living his life. The water described what he wanted. And the belt . . . he lifted up his jacket and surprised us all by revealing a black and pink fancy studded belt!!! We gasped! I clapped my hands and laughed. We did not expect that as it didn't even match his outfit. God certainly got his attention and the analogy meant a lot to him as to how he was living and what he was doing with his faith. Sheldon was shocked. It completely gave credibility to both of them of the Holy Spirit speaking to them and Jerry took the words to heart. So we prayed over Jerry.

Then it was Sheldon's turn. We again took some time to listen. There was now an excitement and expectancy from both of them. My team member began. She saw Sheldon as a boxer, in the corner of the ring getting prepared to fight. He had a coach who was preparing him by putting stuff on his forehead. The coach was God. What she noticed was that Sheldon had no head gear on and God was tending to his head. God wanted him to know his identity in Christ so that he would walk in it before going back into the ring. I didn't catch all she was saying because I was having a vertical conversation with God at the same time. Then Sheldon looked straight at me with a huge grin and I tried to figure out why. As she explained the images, she was stumbling through trying to name and tell him what she was saying as she didn't know the correct boxing terms. When she finished, I had to ask him why he was smiling. He said, "You don't know this about me, but I am a three-time Champion in boxing. Then he named the Championships he had won. This was clearly a picture from God speaking to him in a way he would understand. We gasped again and laughed. Myself and the other team member shared the rest of our pictures and messages with Sheldon. He totally received each word and was delighted and moved by each. He said it was all so fitting for him and meant a lot to him. We then prayed over him and said goodbye.

It is truly exhilarating and life-giving to allow the Holy Spirit to minister through you. It is impossible for someone to come to Jesus unless the Father draws them (John 6:44, Luke 24:48-49, 1 Thessalonians 1:5, John 16:7-11). If we minister out of the flesh, we might as well just go home. We often worry about saying the right thing to someone. God knows exactly where a person is at, what they need to hear from Him and how they need to hear it. As we commit our ways to the Lord, inquire of Him what to say and how, asking the Holy Spirit to speak through us, listening for His voice and obeying, it changes evangelism into an exciting adventure that will ignite your passion, love and intimacy with God. You will find you won't "have to" evangelize, you'll "get to".

CHAPTER 26

WILL THEY THINK I'M CRAZY? A FANATIC?

"Christians are like manure: spread them out and they help everything grow better." - Francis Chan

Olu and I got some pizza from the street evangelism team and sat down to chat. Olu was raised a Jehovah Witness and now doesn't have any spiritual beliefs. He was adamant that Jesus was not God because the Jehovah Witness belief system had convinced him of that. I asked him why he "stopped religion". He said because it didn't make any sense to him. I asked him what didn't make sense. He said it was so confusing. I asked him what was confusing. He stared at me for a moment with a funny look on his face and then he slowly said, "Well, I don't know. I haven't thought about it that much." I laughed and said, "So you're going to base your whole view of God, the One Who created the whole universe including you, base your whole eternity on something you haven't thought much about?" He laughed and saw the humour in it. We began to get into a deep, very logical discussion. We discussed the definition of Hell, sin, religion vs relationship, the authenticity of the Bible, the Jehovah Witness Bible, other religious beliefs in regards to what "works" they have to perform in order to gain merit, reward and favour. We went over different religions; Mormonism, Jehovah Witness, Islam, Catholicism, Christianity and the differences between them. Then he said, "Ever since I quit religion, I feel so free now. I don't have to worry about some angry God up there watching me and keeping track about whether I've done good or bad." I loved that statement. I told him I agreed with him. Religion was like that, but God was not. He told me he was a good person. I shared with him the Ten Commandments and their purpose as a mirror. I shared with him the analogy of being in a courtroom where he had committed a crime. That the judge was not going to care if he was good most of the time but that the judge would look at his crime and give him a penalty. Olu thought that was a bit harsh because he thought he should get points for being good in other areas. Still, he was willing to go along with my story. I asked him, "What would you think if someone came into the courtroom and said, 'Your Honor, I know Olu did the crime. I know that he does deserve the punishment, but I'm going to take his penalty so he can go free.'" Olu said, "Well no one would ever do that. It wouldn't make sense." I kept going, "But what if someone did?" He responded, "Why would someone do that?" I smiled, "Because He loves you, Olu. Jesus did this for you. He loves you." Olu said, "No, He doesn't. I don't even believe in Him or follow Him." "Exactly," I said, "God said that while you were still a sinner, Jesus died for you." (Romans 5:8) Olu fired back, "Why would He do that?" I said, "Because He made you, He loves you and He knows the amazing plans He has for your life. He will never force you. He gives you free will to choose whether you want a relationship with Him or not. If you choose not to, then He honors your choice and allows you to have separation from Him on this earth and into eternity." Olu then told me that hell was earth. I told him hell was separation from God. God was everything good, and all good things came from God. I explained it a bit more. He disagreed with me and didn't believe that there was any good on the earth. Then he said, "There is no one in this world who does anything without the motive that it will benefit them. Everything that is good is done with a selfish, greedy motive so that there would be a benefit for that person." I told him he was right when considering human nature. However, when a person gave their life to God, He poured His nature into them, which brought good into the world without selfish motivation. He responded, "Okay, say you don't have God in your life. Take God completely out of all of this," and he swept his hand over our team, tables, food, "if you didn't have God, you'd still do this, because it makes you feel good to help others." I knew what he was getting at because it was true when speaking of human organizations that do good works. I leaned in and said with conviction, "Olu, let me tell you what I would do if I didn't have God. I would not be here. Over the years of doing this, I have been told countless times to f-off, I've been pushed, I've been accused, I've been freezing, I've been sick, I've been rejected and I've been spit on. I have a lot of other options to "feel good about myself". I come down here because God loves you. He loves the people here so much and because I follow Him, He has poured His love into me and I can't help but love people. I might see a person all messy and their life is terrible, but then God shows me what He sees in them, the good He has deposited in them, maybe even some reasons why He created them, who they could be if they follow Him, and who He created them to be. I do not come here to get some reward. I come here to love you, only because God loves you." I was so intense when I said this that he just looked at me for a few moments. Then Olu responded with the most perfect African-American mannerism, "Val, I don't mean to be rude but if I didn't know better, I'd look at you and I'd say - You are CRAZY! That's the craziest thing I've ever heard!" I didn't know if it was the way he said it or that I was so not expecting that response, but for whatever reason, I threw my head back and broke into the biggest, deep-down belly laugh that I've had for a long time. I laughed and laughed as Olu confusingly laughed with me. I laughed because no one had said that to me before, and I laughed because I love hearing people outside the church, unbelievers, comment on the things of the Kingdom. Of course it was crazy from a natural humanistic viewpoint and it does not make sense. When I recovered, I smiled and said, "You're right, Olu. It does sound crazy because it's not man-made. It's Who God is and who we as humans naturally are not." Olu went on, "Okay, so what if people in all those other religions never hear about Jesus being God? Then how can God send them to hell?" I explained that God was love and God was just. He would reveal Himself and judge according to what people were exposed to and the condition of their hearts. Before I could finish, he jumped in and said, "So you're saying that if I don't say that Jesus is God then I don't get to go to heaven. I'm choosing to go to hell?" I responded, "Well, yes, the Bible says: 'If you confess with your mouth Jesus is Lord and believe in your heart that God raised him from the dead you will be saved.' It's not just words . . ." Again, before I could finish, he started to get concerned in a half-funny, half-serious way and exclaimed, "Wait, so you're saying that because you just told me all that you told me tonight, I'm now accountable with it and God is going to judge me?" I tried to answer, “Well, I’m trying to explain to you that . . .” Olu stood up and started to pace, “This is a bad conversation. This is just bad, bad, bad! Now I’m responsible with this information.” I wasn’t sure if he was joking, serious, or just wanted to be done with the conversation. I stood up and calmly said, “Olu, I only tell you because I care about your soul, who you are, and for your life. You were responsible before I talked to you because you have the ability to think, to research and find truth. I’m just helping you see that.” He then told me that he should probably go as he had an early morning start. I asked him if I could pray for him and he said no. I asked him if he would take a book to read about some of the things we discussed. He said no. So I shook his hand. He then turned back and called to me, “I will come back though and talk to you more about this.”

As I was waiting for some friends to come I noticed a man walking by. I began to listen up to the Holy Spirit but it took me a little bit longer and by the time I was ready to talk to him, he was already across the street, across the train track and down the sidewalk. It’s in those seconds that I have to make a decision. Do I just leave it and not talk to him or do I run after the man like a crazy woman? So I said to a few of my friends who had arrived, “I have to go talk to that man,” and ran after him. When I caught up to him I was out of breath and began to introduce myself. After a minute or so he held his hand up and said in broken English, “I want to know what you are saying but I speak little English. Can you speak into my phone?” He spoke Spanish and pointed to Google translate. I laughed as I had to start over all that I had spoken. So I began again, this time speaking into his phone. “My name is Val and I love Jesus. As you were walking by me, God showed me some things about you. He showed me you have a calling on your life into authority - it is for the future. You are a man with strength and confidence. If you surrender and submit yourself to God, He will enable you to have authority, spiritual authority in your life. Do you have a spiritual belief?” He read through and then said yes he was Catholic. Through simple questions and talking into his google translate, I found out he definitely believed in God. He wanted what I talked about and he had a Bible. He was not going to church at that time. He was very intrigued and was glad to talk. We chatted through google translate. It was disjointed and difficult to get points across but he was eager. I encouraged him to read the book of

John about Jesus. I asked him if I could pray over him and he said yes. I slowly prayed many things over him, into his phone so he could follow. When I was done he thanked me for stopping him.

Another time, I was listening to Holy Spirit and talking to a team member as we were simply out walking. As we passed by a gentleman, I felt like the Holy Spirit was flagging him to me. I stopped and told my team member to just wait a minute while I took thirty seconds to hear clearly. I got the words from the Lord "hard worker, sensitive to others needs and kind". So I turned to my team member and said, "I have to run after that man. You can catch up to me if you'd like," and I turned and ran after him. I caught up to the man and while out of breath, I explained to him that I knew it was weird but when he walked by, God drew my attention to him. Then I shared what the Lord showed me about him. The man told me what I had shared was true about him and said, "God told you that?" I confirmed it to him and asked him if he had any spiritual beliefs. He said he had been raised Catholic but was not at all following it although he knew there was a God. I urged him to look to Jesus and read his Bible. I asked him if I could pray for him. His name was Sergio and he said yes. So I prayed over him, gave him a hug and let him on his way. He thanked me for coming after him and telling him these things.

I approached a man that I had been talking to for months about the Lord down on the streets during our weekly outreaches. I had just finished preaching on the street to a crowd. I asked him if he had heard what I said when I preached. He said, "Do you know what everyone is thinking when you preach, Val? I can tell!" I said, "What, Ryan, are they thinking?" He said, "They think, 'Shut the #@*! Up!' " I chuckled and said, "Well, why do they think that?" (I wasn't intimidated or upset that he said that; I recognized it's not true. It was just what he was thinking.) Ryan held out his hand and pinched his thumb and pointer finger together, "Because you are the only one who comes out here and speaks the truth right on, exactly the way it is and that bothers everyone!" I gasped in laughter and then said, "Well . . . thank you!" (I know that I'm not the only one who speaks the truth. Others do too. However, perhaps I'm one of the more straightforward, blunt ones.) This was perhaps one of my favorite comments and one I deeply appreciate. If it were a little more acceptable I'd frame the quote. Peculiar? Well, yes. I don't think most people would appreciate that comment as much as I did. It truly encouraged me.

I was thrilled to see him during our evangelistic outreach, and I caught up on what was happening with him. I hadn't seen him for a year. He was living at a homeless shelter. I began to ask deeper questions about where he was with the Lord right now. I knew he was a Catholic man and had been married with kids. After his wife died his life began to drastically change. He experienced chronic, pain physically while he was in pain emotionally and he began doing drugs. Eventually he ended up living on the streets. He was actually a very kind elderly man with old school manners. He told me he was still praying to God but he was "not a fanatic". With an amused smile on my face, I asked, "Do you think I'm a fanatic?" He hesitantly said in his thick Italian accent, "Well, yes, you are. I don't go around talking to people about God like you." I laughed and said, "How would you describe a person who is a fanatic about God?" He squirmed and said, "Well, I don't know." I said, "Do you think anyone can have too much of God in their life?" He agreed that no, they couldn't. I laughed and told him I thought it was a compliment that he thought I was a fanatic. I hoped he would become one too. I asked him if he was reading his Bible and he said not really. I challenged and encouraged him. I asked him if he had ever read 1 John. He said he had read John but not 1 John. I grabbed a Bible and showed him where it was. I told him it was a great book to read and I would be curious to know what he thought of it. He shared with me how his kids hated him and although they lived close, they would not let him see his grandkids if he had done drugs that day. I told him I thought that was wise of them. I asked him why he took the drugs. He answered it was for the physical pain. I commented that it was not just for his physical pain but it was for internal pain as well. He listened but did not acknowledge it. I asked him what would happen if he didn't take the drugs. He said he would kill himself. I asked him why and he said because he couldn't stand the turmoil and regret from his past, and also was overwhelmed dealing with the present problems and pain. I talked with him about how the drugs were a counterfeit "healing" and numbing of the pain. Jesus was the one who could actually free him from those things. He said he prayed every day, begging Jesus to help him, but He never did. I told him that he also needed to participate in the process by surrendering his life fully to Jesus and then acting upon it. I prayed over him and we parted.

In the New Living Translation of the Bible, 2 Corinthians 5:13 says: *"If it seems we are crazy, it is to bring glory to God. And if we are in our right minds, it is for your benefit."*
This verse always brings a smile to my face as I wonder about what others may think of me when I speak to them about Jesus, share what I believe He is saying to me about them, or tell my testimony. Will the world think we are crazy? Maybe. Or maybe they will be refreshed by seeing passion, stirred by hearing truth, renewed by sensing hope, impacted deeply by experiencing godly love and Jesus will be revealed to them, and the one true God glorified.

May I never lose my "fanatic" status. What's your status?

CHAPTER 27

FIND THOSE BLEEDING BELIEVERS

"God is able to take the mess of our past and turn it into a message. He takes the trials and tests and turns them into a testimony."- Christine Caine

Ricky is still untainted by the street life and would fit into any crowd that you or I would. As we chatted near a homeless shelter he was staying at, I asked him If he was raised with any spiritual beliefs. He told me he went to church as a kid and then at seventeen he went to a camp. He had good and bad experiences. He now has his own beliefs. As I enquired further for a more detailed explanation, I found out he had been in a Pentecostal denomination where, in his particular experience, there was a lot of prosperity gospel being preached. He gave his life to the Lord at the camp, however, he was also very pressured to give money to the church and that became a huge focus as they discipled him. In later years, he and an older gentleman got into racing cars. They attended a Pentecostal church in Canada and were told that if they raced cars and were involved in that culture, they could no longer attend their church. The older gentleman was very well off from the racing lifestyle and could donate large amounts to the church. This led to the church reversing their decision once they found that out. It left Ricky with a bad taste for church and he had faded out of that church. He believed in God now but he didn't want anything to do with any church. I seem to have this conversation over and over. Someone gets really hurt by people in the church and they either drop God all together or live a lukewarm life, acknowledging there is a God, but not wanting anything to do with His ways or His people. I went on to speak to him about how his experience was anything but God. It was classic religion, rules and regulations made up by man, and it was never God's ideas or intentions. I explained to Ricky how Jesus spoke harshest to the church leaders and hung out with the sinners. He and I discussed what Truth was, and how we must seek after a relationship with God, not getting distracted by other people's sins. He agreed politely with me in everything I said but I could tell some of my statements were catching his attention and making him ponder, perhaps making him feel a bit uncomfortable. He stuck out his hand and shook mine, announced he was getting really cold but would come out next week.

Siblings sure can be a pain sometimes, can't they! They rub us the wrong way, know our weaknesses, mock us, and keep us real. They sniff out our failures a mile away. It's the same with our spiritual brothers and sisters, especially when they have gone astray from their relationship with the Lord. Oh, how it causes us to weep and oh, how it can cause us frustration in conversation. They knew the truth but have turned to other things of this world. I often have to wonder, did they ever taste the sweet intimacy of the Lord or were they shoved religious rules and behavior? Was their spirit crushed and their supposed spiritual family avoiding the mess, too busy, ill equipped, or too fearful to help them heal? Perhaps it was just plain rebellion. Whatever the reason, satan laughs at the situation as he rides in to cause destruction and incredible sorrow to a bleeding believer. Many times there are others in the lives of those who have lost their faith who continue to try to help, but their influence is no longer welcomed for whatever reason. They are praying for someone, "some you" or "some me" to truly see their loved one who has fallen away from the faith and intentionally engage them, speaking to them truth and life about Jesus. Will we wade through the crap (sorry, I did look for another word but none was quite as accurate or appropriate as this one), and go after those bleeding believers? With the Spirit working through us, will we pour water on the wound and apply fresh ointment to help stop the bleeding?

We went to the transit station. As we walked, the platform was really busy with people. We were being sensitive to the Spirit and we walked by one young gentleman in a brown coat. I stopped and said to my teammate, "I'm listening to the Holy Spirit for that guy in the brown coat." She smiled, "I am too!" We stopped and watched as he and his friend walked towards the train, then stopped and stood there. We leaned against the back wall and listened to the Lord. We must have been looking at him or he sensed something because he slowly walked over and stood beside us. Then he leaned over to me and said, "Are you doing a survey or something?" I laughed, "No, why?" He said, "You look like you want to do a survey or sell me something," I laughed and said, "No, not at all." He asked, "What are you doing?" I said, "Well, when we were walking by, God got our attention and highlighted you to us." He raised his eyebrows. We shared what the Lord was showing us. Mickey shared with us that he was raised Catholic. When he was in prison he was given a Bible. His roommate led him to the Lord and he grew in his Christian faith. When he got out of prison he became very involved in a church and was on fire for the Lord. He felt called to move to this city in order to reconnect with his wife and kids. He did so, but after two years of battling an addiction, his wife kicked him out of the house and now he couldn't see them at all. He spoke very softly as he shared this and we had to strain to hear. His friend, Jonny, was listening to parts of our conversation and then going and looking for free train tickets. They were both homeless, living in shelters and on the streets, feeding their addictions. There was such heaviness on Mickey. I asked him, "Mickey, do you miss Him? Do you miss Jesus?" Mickey was still for a moment and nodded yes. He emotionally shared how he felt he could not return to Jesus the way it had been, as he used to be so close to him, but now because of the things he had done and was doing it could no longer be. I told him obviously that was not true, as God had just got the attention of two complete strangers to come and speak to him. We shared about the characters in the Bible who messed up and yet when they repented, God loved to welcome them back into intimate relationship with Him. I asked both Jonny and Mickey if we could pray for them. I felt very strongly to speak over Jonny as well. We gave prophetic words over both of them and prayed deeply over their lives. They both affirmed what we said was true. We urged them to confess their sins, repent and run back to Jesus. We gave hugs as they thanked us for sharing - their whole demeanour had changed. We walked away, thrilled to have been able to have a clearly divine-led conversation but wanted to cry at the spiritual and physical predicament of our young brothers in Christ.

I met a man named Lenny. Lenny told me his very interesting story. His parents were not Christians, and his dad was very abusive to him growing up. His father had hit him and broke his nose when he was ten years old. When Lenny was eleven or so, his dad got hit by a semi truck. He went flying in the air and although he survived, he had major back and neck injuries. His dad would crawl around on the floor at home or would get around in a wheelchair. Lenny said those were the best years at that point because his dad couldn't hit him or do anything abusive. Then Lenny asked me, "Have you ever heard of Benny Hinn?" I smiled, "Yes, yes I have." He went on to tell me that Benny Hinn had come to his town one day and that everyone told his dad to go to the meeting. His dad went and was completely healed, then gave his life to the Lord. Lenny said it was a complete miracle and he saw it with his own eyes. However, his life became a different struggle after that. As his parents learned and grew in their Christianity, they became very strict religiously. He asked me, "Have you ever heard of the PTL ministry by Jimmy Baker?" I smiled again and said yes. He told me that one day, after his whole family were Christians, they all packed into the car and drove a few days to go see the famous Jimmy Baker and go to a revival meeting. Everyone was very excited and it was very important to his dad and mom. They finally arrived in the city and got to the motel. They turned on the TV as they were getting settled and there on the TV was breaking news of the scandal Jimmy Baker was caught in. He said his dad was so mad that he zipped up the suitcases and told them they were leaving. It was a huge blow to their whole family. I was able to mention to Lenny that Jimmy Baker was out of prison and wrote a book called, I Was Wrong. He had a ministry today but I was not all that familiar with it and couldn't say what I thought about it. I asked Lenny where he personally was with the Lord now. He said he believed in God but didn't go to church. He was the black sheep of the family. I asked Lenny if I could pray over him. He said he should get going, so I told him I would walk with him and pray. We got a little ways away and he stopped for me to continue praying. I realized he was embarrassed with the crowd around him and needed to just be taken out of ear shot of those on the streets. I sensed such a tenderness about him and as I prayed, my praying turned into prophesying and speaking to him from God's heart. The words came to me with passion and authority. The message of it was: "Lenny, even though you were the black sheep with your family, to Me, you were set apart. I like that you are different, in fact, I made you that way. I have deposited into you the ability to have compassion, kindness and tenderness in a way that others don't have. You are adopted into My family, you are My son and nothing can separate you from Me."

It was really cool and by the end, I sensed God's deep love for Lenny. The Lord will often pour His love into us and allow it to flow out of us to others, even when they are strangers. The Holy Spirit will let us see a person the way God sees them and we get to understand His love for them which enables us to love them the way God does. We just need to be intentional with allowing our spiritual eyes to see and not just our physical ones.

I had known him for a couple years from times I had gone out evangelizing, having had in depth talks on the streets probably five times. Tonight we talked about brokenness and how life can really suck. He said it had been so much easier since he gave up going to church and following God. I asked him why he left his church. He was doing so well. Then he said something that stuck with me. "Every time I think of the church I want to puke!" "Wow," I said, "What about church makes you want to puke?" He thought and then said very strongly, "People in the church don't get the real %#@ world! Sorry, I didn't mean to swear." I listened as he shared he just couldn't fit into the young adult group, the services, the Bible studies or the Christian expectations. Now, I had no doubt that Fred was as much to blame as the other side. I know he was responsible for his issues and his relationship with the church. However, there was also something very true about what he was saying. So I sighed and said, "Fred, you're right. A lot of people in the church don't interact with the culture and don't experience it, nor do they want to. They sit in their safe pews, form a church bubble and don't know what to do with the mess of the world. . . . but there are some who do understand. Yes, there are hypocrites and religious people but that is not Jesus. I am the church, Fred. It's not a building. You are the church. So be different." He said, "But it's easy for people in the church. They don't have a bunch of stuff to deal with like me." I laughed, "Maybe for some, but I can tell you everyone eventually has stuff. Everyone gets hurt and broken, and if they're going through a season that is easy, give them grace because it won't last forever." I shared with him some things in my life that have broken me and he was very surprised. "I thought you had everything all together in your life - that's why you're happy." I laughed and then got serious. "Can I be straight-forward and blunt with you, Fred?" "Yeah, for sure. I don't ever feel judged by you. I can talk to you and it's totally different from the people I know that are Christians." "Okay," I said. "You're mad at God because you're not getting what you want in life. Simple as that. You've been hurt by all sorts of things and yes, they're big, but things like that happen to everyone. Everyone gets broken, everyone has stuff. We all have to decide what to do with it. Are we going to go around depressed for the rest of our lives? Angry? Resentful? Broken? For everything you've experienced, someone has it ten times worse. I've been broken in many areas of my life but I had to make a decision. It doesn't matter what happens to me, I know the Truth. I know there is a God, and I will serve Him whether I have everything perfect in my life or whether it is terrible. It's not about whether I get everything I want, it's about Who I am going to live for: myself, the world or God. You and I both know there is a God. I have decided to serve Him."

I said many other such things very passionately, and then Fred asked, "How did you get to that point?" I thought, laughed, took a deep breath and thought some more. "I suppose from going through a lot of hard stuff that forced me to choose that I'm not going to give up and die inside. I accepted that the only One who could help me was Jesus. I had to choose and so do you. I had to choose not to be controlled by emotions. I had to choose not to be controlled by situations. I had to grieve, forgive, pray, pour out my heart to God. One time I actually laid my hand on my heart and said, 'It's time. . . it's time, heart, to be healed. You are not broken anymore. I'm done being broken.' And then I just acted and spoke on that decision and chose to lead my heart and emotions, refusing to go back to that spot as I kept surrendering to Jesus." He sat there, thought and then said, "I just don't know anymore. It's just been so easy to not worry about God. Man, I seriously haven't talked to a Christian in like, over a year. You are the first. It's, like, so weird to be talking about this stuff again." "Well, you came over and found me. The Lord has His hand on you, Fred. You're my brother and I want to pray for you. I'm going to fight for you." He laughed, "I knew you would." I prayed fervently for my brother and we said goodbye.

Russ was not a "street" person. He simply arrived two days ago to a local homeless shelter and needed a quick place to stay before heading up North to work in the oil and gas industry. He had just spent the winter in a warmer country but was originally from Canada. He told me he had been married thirty years and had three children, but five years ago they were divorced and it had been a nightmare ever since. He had been spending a lot of his time and money in the warmer country with a young woman in her twenties (he was almost sixty). He had come to the conclusion that this lifestyle had brought emptiness. He said he was an alcoholic but had been sober for fourteen years. I told him he was no longer an alcoholic then. He said that once an alcoholic, always an alcoholic. Of course, I know this is in the AA book and a mantra spoken to keep people from falling back into that addiction. However, I liked to look at it from a Kingdom of God perspective, of not needing to continue to identify with that addiction once you are free from it. I told him with a smile, "I could debate that statement with you." We had a huge, full conversation for the next hour. I will share some tidbits. He told me he had been praying and praying and all his prayers had been answered. I asked him what he had been asking for and how have they been answered? He shared about his financial, emotional and relational issues. I asked him about his spiritual beliefs. He told me he was not religious, although he had been raised in an Anglican church. It had been years since he'd ever been to church. He was spiritual but definitely not religious. He wasn't really sure if there was a God. I had to laugh at all the contradictions. I began the process of asking questions and drawing out conclusions. I pointed out to him that he had said earlier that he had "prayed and prayed and all his prayers had been answered". So who was he praying to? Russ responded, "Well, God, of course." I pressed further, "And if your prayers were answered, then who answered them if you aren't sure there is a God?" He paused, smiled and laughed, "I guess I did say that. I don't know." I asked, "Well, what's the point of God listening to you and answering you if you are not going to acknowledge His existence?" Ryan pondered, "Hmmm, good point." I said, "And I am glad you are not 'religious'. Neither am I."

I love saying that as it's always met by a puzzled look and gets the listener's attention. I told Russ how religion often was a bunch of rules and regulations made up by man. But what I had was a relationship with God through Jesus. We talked about how church didn't save you, neither did a particular denomination. Then Russ said, "Well, when I die, I'm going to have a lot of questions for God!" I questioned, "Oh yeah? What are you going to ask?" Russ confidently blasted, "Why are we here? What is the meaning of life and what is my purpose? Why did God make us?" I answered with a question to him, "What if He has already told us and the answer has already been given to us while we are still on the earth?" Again, he was intrigued. I explained what the Bible said about our purpose and why God created us. We are to make a choice on this earth whether we want a relationship with God or not and that choice would be made before eternity. I explained if a person is lukewarm in their faith, neither hot or cold, God said He would vomit him out. Russ laughed in realization and said, "That's me! But I am a good person!" Again, I love it when people say this. Ray Comfort has an excellent way to respond to this in his method called, "The Way of the Master". Search it up. I explained the purpose of the Ten Commandments and how they were a mirror to show us our goodness. After going through a few, I asked him if he now thought he was good compared to God's standards. He said no. I shared with him about works compared to the free gift of salvation. We talked about other religions compared to Christianity. I asked him if he really understood the cross and what Jesus did. He said, "No, I don't think so." I then completely presented the gospel.

Russ began looking at his life and said he had so many regrets. He was trying to live life to the fullest and have fun on this earth. He was hoping to choose God at the end so that his fun wouldn't be ruined. I laughed. Isn't it strange how we think God wants to ruin our fun? We try to live these "fun" lives but the fun never lasts and we end up feeling empty. I told him my life motto: If I'm going to live for something, it better be truth. If I'm going to live by that truth, I want to be so sure of it that I would be willing to die for it. If I'm willing to die for it, it better be truth! I find whenever I say that to people, a light bulb goes on. They start contemplating what they are living for and pose the question, is it worth it?

I shared with Russ that if God created him, then He knows exactly what will bring him joy, peace and contentment. God had a plan for him to experience an amazing adventure that would bring him these things. Russ said he had never thought of it that way before. He wistfully said that now he wished he would not have divorced his wife, but instead had worked harder on his marriage. He wished he would not have been with all those young women just for the sex; it wasted his time and money. He wished he had a good woman and believed that would really help. He felt so lonely. I smiled at him and gently shared with him that I understood marriage was hard. However, I had also come to understand that no matter how terrible or wonderful a person was, whether it was a parent, friend or spouse, we could not get our value or identity from them because they would always come up short and we will always feel empty in the long run. I said, “I think what you're wanting is not actually a good woman because you know deep down that after the “honeymoon”, relationships get hard. What you're really wanting is to be known deep down, and still loved and accepted.” He thought for a moment and said, “I think you're right.” I quickly jumped in, “The only One who can give you that is God, because He loves you and is perfect.” Russ responded, “I think I’m in the last part of my life and I think I need to maybe give all this a try. Maybe I need to go to God.”

We chatted a bit more and then he abruptly stuck out his hand and said, “You have given me a lot to think about. I’m not sure if I will still be here next week, I hope not, but if I am, I’ll come talk with you again.” I shook his hand and he turned and left.

Rarely, do I get to go into that many different subjects and lay out the gospel with so much scripture that clearly .

I wanted to talk to the woman, I just felt drawn to her. I was passing out food on a sidewalk with a team. I went over to her. Her name was Melissa and she right away told me she was a pastor’s daughter. I found out through my questions that she was adopted at a young age by a pastor and his wife who were pastoring a church. She also had a relationship with her biological family who were bikers in a rough crowd. She went wayward for a while, was a drug dealer and did drugs but seven years ago rededicated her life to Christ and was baptized. She eventually fell back into drugs and alcohol but now she has been clean for eighteen months. She was living at a homeless shelter but wanted to get into some courses that would enable her to counsel and help those in addiction as she was currently helping many others around her. She was a very clear thinker and had depth of understanding. I asked her questions about how she helped others, what had she learned, and I asked how she resists temptation? She said she had clung to scripture verses to give her strength. She told me most people just want someone to listen to them and to care. Her boyfriend was there and I turned and chatted with him. He was raised in a Lutheran church. He had been to Bible school and many different types of churches. He believed Christianity was about Jesus and not the denomination. Ha ha, love it! As we chatted, I could definitely see they loved Jesus and were Christ followers. I could also see they were a bit dirty, lacking personal hygiene for sure and not shiny at all. Obviously, they were still working through things since they were living at the homeless shelter but I loved who they were. I asked them if I could pray for them as I was their sister in Christ. They said yes, so I prayed over them individually and together. As I prayed, the Holy Spirit gave me insight on how to pray. It was cool to pray like that. I was getting insight so slightly and prayed accordingly: that Melissa had fearlessness inside her, that the Lord delighted in her yet she needed to be bold, and that she could impact hundreds. For him, I sensed the need to know his identity so that he had confidence when he stepped into a room, when he faced different atmospheres, that when he read the Bible God would give him more revelation to understand it and to have a hunger to dive into it. I prayed over their relationship. It was pretty cool and I gave them both a hug when they left .

He was a social worker, believe it or not. He also was a born again Christian, active in his faith, helping people who were struggling, ministering to those who needed it. His marriage started to go sideways. They separated and then divorced. He came home one day and found his son; he had committed suicide by hanging himself. There was no note, no warning. Richard broke. As he began drinking, friends and family turned from him. He told me he just couldn't stop crying. He was currently in counselling. He came to me after I had open-air preached on the street. He had listened to the points I had brought up and he wanted to talk about brokenness. I spent the next five months talking with him on and off, praying for him and encouraging him to pursue the journey of healing. Then one day he came out carrying a box and gave it to me. It was a model-size cabin that he had made out of wood which he had taken from trees around the city's river. He had finally saved enough money and was going to go back east to build that dream cabin. He had the plans all written down but he wanted me to have the model cabin. He told me he had received a lot of religious advice but the true love of Jesus had been displayed in the team and myself over the last few months. Because of that, his heart had softened towards the Lord again, his faith restored in believers. He had been nurtured, encouraged and he would never forget his time with us. Richard impacted me so much, probably as much as I impacted him. When I prayed for him that one last time and watched him walk away, I prayed silently I would see him again in heaven. I turned and scanned the crowd, full of men and women from the streets, young and old. The Holy Spirit spoke very clearly to me that night, "Val, these are sons, daughters, fathers, uncles. They are the lost." My heart caught fire that night.

I stood on a picnic table and began to preach to a group of approximately one hundred people who had gathered in a public community space. As they sipped on ice tea, I spoke with all the volume I could muster for my voice. I asked, "Who here has ever been hurt by the church? Who has had a bad experience with a church or a Christian?" Many people nodded, some raised their hands, most eyed me warily wondering if I was worth listening to. I began a story and related it to how the church as a whole had failed many times to be who Jesus intended it to be to the world. I finished by saying, "On behalf of the church, on behalf of all Christians, I want to apologize to you for the wounds you have received. It was never God. It was us people not following the ways of the God we follow. Sometimes, the church has held back the truth and held back the love it was told to give away to this world . . . and to you specifically. I ask for your forgiveness even though we don't deserve it. We are sorry we ever represented God to you in hurtful ways. Jesus came to heal you, never to hurt you." There was silence and then one man started to clap, then another, then another and then the whole crowd joined in. It was a powerful moment when the bleeding in those listeners stopped.

My heart breaks when I come across people who once believed in the Lord and have either backslidden or turned against their God. I know there is always a reason that often involves being wounded or disappointed, followed by anger or indifference. It amazes me how the behaviour of a person(s) will cause someone else to turn away from God. It is as if they expected that God should've been controlling that person's decisions and behaviour, or that that person should be perfect like God if they claim to follow God. This is a very common reason people turn away from the Lord. I always try to make the distinction that we are to follow God, not people. If we truly are following God, why would we turn away from Him because of people and their brokenness? It's sobering and should cause us as believers to examine our own life and conduct as we are ambassadors for Christ. You and I also have been given a responsibility. We are ministers of the Lord; we carry truth and our tongues have the power of life and death. We can speak the truth to a fallen comrade. We can bring revelation and clarity. We can sift through the deception and expose lies. We can stir, lovingly rebuke, encourage, call them back, bring healing through the Spirit working in us, bind up the broken-hearted, help the captives and prisoners go free. (Isaiah 61) We can run into the fires of believers lives and point them to the way out. We can remind them of their worth, the identity they've walked away from, the true character of God, how God sees them, how much they are loved. May we humble ourselves, have compassion on our bleeding brothers and sisters in Christ. Because we are free, may we freely give, freely be unoffended, freely love the *hell* out of them.

CHAPTER 28

WHAT IF THEY JUST DON'T WANT TO TALK ABOUT IT?

"You can get in anywhere if you go to serve." - Brother Andrew, God's Smuggler

People don't always want to have spiritual conversations and sometimes they make it very obvious. I think about when I'm approached by people who want to sell me something or strike up conversation. Sometimes it's not the right timing because I'm in a hurry or I'm with someone and it's a huge interruption. Sometimes I'm just really skeptical of getting scammed. Sometimes, I'm not interested but because of the person's kindness and respect toward me, I take the time to listen. Sometimes I am interested but because of the person's forceful manner, I am turned off. When it comes down to it, I really want to be respected and honored, whether I know them or not. Likewise, when it comes to talking to people about Jesus it's important the heart posture we have toward them.

In the scriptures we have been forewarned:
"For we are to God the sweet aroma of Christ among those who are being saved and those who are perishing. To the one, *we are an odor of death and demise; to the other, a fragrance that brings life. And who is qualified for such a task? For we are not like so many others, who peddle the word of God for profit. On the contrary, in Christ we speak before God with sincerity, as men sent from God." (2 Corinthians 2:15-17)*

I think every situation is different. We definitely need to be sensitive to the leading of the Holy Spirit and to be socially aware. There are times when we can pursue and times when we need to release the person we are trying to engage with . Sometimes we are too timid, we shrink back instead of confidently pursuing the conversation. More often than not, we need to kindly leave the door open for them and let the Holy Spirit work through what was said. We are certainly not perfect and won't always get it right but we can always choose to treat someone as we would want to be treated, to love the person whether we've known them all our life or we've only just met. That's the power of God's love flowing through us.

On the streets I chatted with a man named Art. He had a lung condition and was sharing with me that in order to get disability funding so he wouldn't have to work, he was going to cheat the test next time he saw the doctor. I listened for a while as he justified this to me and then I said, "Art, would you like to not have this condition?" He said it would be impossible not to have it. I told him Jesus could heal him and he said, "No, not even Jesus could heal me. Nobody ever, ever gets better from this once they have it." I had a choice. I could walk away and encourage myself that even Jesus walked away. I could quote the verse in my head about not throwing your pearls before swine (Matthew 7:6). I could change the direction of the conversation to mere logistics and avoid the subject. I could kindly continue. I smiled and said, "So the God who created this world and created you, cannot heal you?" He stammered, "Well, I guess He could . . . ." I pointedly asked, "Can I ask Him to? Do you want to be healed from it?" He paused and said, "Well, yes . . . ." I decided to have him own it a little more and told him, "I will pray as long as you will give God all the credit for your healing." He swore, "Oh god, yeah, I would!" I had to chuckle as I went into my prayer for him. I'm glad that Jesus said on the cross, "Forgive them Father, for they know not what they do." (Luke 23:34) This helps me to plow forward in these situations without getting distracted by messy language and ignorance. When I was done I went and got Art some pizza. As I was walking away, Art called to me, "Hey thanks for that over there. It means a lot," and he pointed to the spot where I had prayed for him. Well, I can't say he said the "sinner's prayer" but I can say he went from not wanting prayer to being thankful for prayer.

I saw a younger woman going through all the garbage cans on the train platform, so I approached her and asked her if I could pray for her. She eyed me warily, with defensiveness. She slowly said yes. I asked if there was anything specific and she sharply answered, "To make it to the end of the month." I could see the jaded look in her eye and the hurt that had turned to bitterness. She was in a hurry and did not want to stay and chat so I quickly prayed for her before she kept going. Simple and short. When I was done she nodded and went on.

Prayer is an avenue to reveal volumes about the Lord and can be the most effective evangelism action which touches people more than any debate or explanation you can utter.

We walked a short ways on the sidewalk and I saw two moms pushing strollers with babies in them. The Lord showed me that the one would have strong influence on her daughter and she would need to be wise in how to direct her. The other mom would be the one to fill the home with laughter and her daughter would look to her for joy. I stopped them and shared this with both the moms.
They were a bit freaked out but thanked me. I could tell they did not want to talk any more and their body language indicated they wanted to get going. So I freed them by not pushing further. I gave them both a hug and let them go on their way.

A message from the Lord is very powerful and effective. It's too bad many Christians are too afraid to learn to hear the Lord's voice in fear that they will cooperate with something counterfeit. I get it - there are many false prophets and false doctrine out there. There are many saying, "Thus saith the Lord . . . " and it is clearly not the Lord. I know. It's always been there. satan always counterfeits what God has created. However, just because there's a counterfeit doesn't mean I run from the real thing. It's truly beautiful to speak the Lord's words to someone. It bypasses their worldly logic and goes straight to their soul, landing on their heart. It gets people's attention in ways like no other. It will be on their minds as they lay in bed that night and the Holy Spirit will remind them of it as He draws them to the Father. You may not see the power of it in their initial reaction. I have seen many people needing to process what is being said. On the occasions where I get to hear from them days, weeks, or months, later I often learn that the words held impact and influence.

Two of us approached a young woman and man outside a local festival. The man totally didn't engage but the woman was very polite. I asked her a lot of questions and found out she was raised in a Catholic church and continued to attend because of her parents. She was in her third year of University. She was very guarded and said she was figuring out her beliefs about God and did not want prayer. She was polite in saying she was glad we had our own faith and it was working for us. I knew my team member was formerly Catholic so I mentioned that and invited her to speak to her about her experience. She shared with her and the woman politely listened. I said, "Well, the most important difference between other religions and Christianity is . . . ." and then the man got up and said, "We gotta go right now. Our ride is here!" She stood up, said thankyou and they quickly left. My team member and I looked at each other and groaned. We were just getting to the meat of our conversation. It had taken so long to get there. So we straightened our crowns and kept going.

Maybe they really don't want to talk about it. We can always leave the fragrance of Christ . . . either that or a "pebble in their shoe". Whatever their mindset is at the beginning of the conversation, the Holy Spirit can always work. We need to learn how to be unoffendable, meaning to not take offence when others reject us. We can shake off fear, rejection and whatever else negatively comes our way. We need to be confident that He who began a good work will continue it on to completion. (Philippians 1:6)

I saw an older gentleman walking slowly with a cane on a sidewalk. He was very short and his face weathered. I asked, "Excuse me, sir. What happened to your leg?" He responded, "It was hurt." I said, "It was hurt? For how long has it been hurt?" He answered it had been three months. I asked for more details and although he was a bit vague, he stated he was a victim. I continued to question, "Did people hurt your leg?" He said yes and that it was complicated. His answers were short and did not invite more conversation. I paused, sympathetically smiled at him and said, "I believe in a God who heals. Could I pray for your leg to heal?" He looked me in the eye and studied me.

He said, “No, God will not heal me.” I kindly asked, “Do you believe there is a God?” He nodded and said, “I believe there is a God but satan is winning in my life.” I studied him, noticing he was perhaps a bit dirty, perhaps had some signs of alcoholism and then smiled understandingly, “Well, God is more powerful than satan. satan cannot win in your life if you cry out to God and fully follow Him.” He smiled at me and patted my arm, “I know.” I asked, “Can I pray for your leg?” He kindly said, “No . . . it's complicated.” I nodded and smiled at him. He turned and walked away.

I was going through the grocery store cashier line up. As soon as the cashier saw me she said, “It's you! Every time I see you I feel bad because I haven't read my Bible.” I laughed and said, “Well, maybe you should read it and then you won't feel bad!” We both laughed and then she surprised me by saying, “I actually read the book of John you told me about three times. I even looked up videos that explained it because I had no idea what it meant. The Bible is so confusing!” I was amazed and said, “Well, maybe you can teach me something about it. Let me know when you want to have coffee to discuss it!” She still hasn't called.

We greeted people as the singing and preaching happened. I could see there were so many new faces. I saw a man had gotten pizza and was standing off away from everyone. When I went over to him, he was crying as he listened to the music. I knew he was being ministered to Spirit to spirit. He was so choked up he couldn't even talk and so I put my hand on his shoulder as we stood in silence. Then he said, “I don't want to talk about it”. I smiled, said that was okay and waited. More tears continued to fall. He looked up at me and I held my arms out to hug him. He sobbed on my shoulder and he didn't let go. He sobbed and sobbed. To tell you the truth I was starting to feel a bit conscientious that others would be looking in disdain as I remained in this position, but then, within a few seconds, decided I didn't care; God knows. When he let go, we sat down and I asked if I could just pray for him. He said yes, so I did. When I was done he shared he was raised as a Christian and believed in God but he felt like God was silent. As we talked, I saw deep wounds and he confirmed that. He was in so much anguish that God was not answering his prayers and not speaking to him. He finished by saying, “Like I said, I don't want to talk about it." I smiled, nodded and encouraged him that God had spoken to him through the music. He abruptly got up and said goodbye before I could say much of anything else.

There are many, many times I've had strangers, family, friends and acquaintances shut down spiritual conversations. We should not get discouraged or be surprised. We are leaving the fragrance of Jesus, we are sowing seeds and we are loving them. We respect them and have discernment about when to speak, when to listen, when to be silent and when to move on to other topics. Above all we get to choose how to respond to their rejection. Let's respond with love, grace, patience, kindness and self control.

Sometimes, I simply trust that the Lord is doing something. I just don't understand it and that's okay.

CHAPTER 29

GET RID OF THOSE FORMULAS!!

"There is much room for humility when it comes to evangelism. We need to acknowledge that God is sovereign and can do as he wills to bring people to himself. There is no formula that dictates how God must work in evangelism. And though we may disagree with the evangelistic practices of individuals, ministries, or churches, we must also recognize that when people develop good-hearted commitments to evangelism, God can produce true fruit. I, for one, will take people practicing evangelism as best they can over those who forgo evangelism until they have the perfect practice."
- J. Mack Stiles

We approached two Asian people in a booth where they were waiting for the train to come. I told our team member I was only going to observe him talking to them. He began the same way he had with the other two previous conversations and went into a very long talk about sin, the Trinity and their need for Jesus. It was all very good but very rehearsed; even I was feeling a bit overwhelmed by all the information. So I began to press into Holy Spirit, asking what He saw about this woman. When my team member took a breath, the young woman said she would need time to think about it all and seemed very cornered. I decided to jump in. To my team member's surprise I very warmly told her I did not want her to make any decision and it was very important to think about all this information. I asked her if she had any religious beliefs. The young man said he was a Buddhist and the young woman said her culture was Buddhism but she was not practicing it at all nor had any firm beliefs in it. The young man kept busy on his phone and seemed very disinterested, so I asked her if she had ever heard of Jesus or anything that my team member had just said. She said she hadn't really. Her name was Lucy. I told her that I loved Jesus and that sometimes God would give me pictures about people of how He looked at them, felt about them and that He had given me one for her. She smiled and was curious. I shared with her that I saw a beautiful, perfect purple flower that was full of life and very delicate. It was the way God saw her, beautiful, full of life and delicate. He wanted to have a relationship with her and for her to know Who He truly was .She was very happy to hear that and softened to hear more. We discussed some aspects of Christianity and who Jesus was as deity and not just a good man. I asked her if I could pray for her and she said yes. I prayed for her and then her train came. After we walked away, my team member turned to me and said, "So that's how you do it. I wondered when you have taught about how you minister but I couldn't picture how it would work. Now I understand. People don't let me pray for them but they let you. That is so cool." We walked and discussed how his way was good and full of good truth but perhaps needed to be presented a bit differently, less rehearsed, to be more effective. I was glad I was able to have that time with this team member and it showed me the need to be doing this more with other Christians. I love that everyone has different styles, strengths, and personalities and we get to sharpen each other.

We often love formulas, however, there never is one method or rigid formula with how God works, only tools. We must always lean on the Holy Spirit for every person and situation.

I came across Jack during a time when we were doing an evangelistic outreach. Jack wasn't interested in the pizza but just wanted to talk. So we moved beside a heater that we had set up and began talking. He would've loved to just visit but I always drive the conversation to a spiritual one. I reminded him of our conversation from two months ago and that he was going to think about being all in for Christ and not just lukewarm. He said he had thought about it and decided- to be all in and felt like he was doing good. I asked him what he was doing differently than before. He didn't have an answer. I knew nothing was really different except perhaps his choice but I wanted to make sure. So I explained, “Well, God says in the Bible that if we love him, we will do the things He tells us to do. That also shows who’s all in and who’s not.” Jack asked, “Like what things? I pray everyday, all the time and I always try to be very generous.” I said, “That’s very good. Tell me, when’s the last time you read your Bible?” He smiled and shrugged, “I haven’t for a very long time.” He did have one and he was having trouble understanding. He wondered why he should read it if he had already read it through once. I explained the power of scripture and the reasons to understand it fully but I wasn’t convincing him. I asked him if he would commit to reading it at least once this week. He hummed and said he would think about it. I kept digging and he said that if he was going to do something then he would want to commit and do it fully so he would wait until he was ready to do that. He told me he maybe would on Sunday since that was the Sabbath. I said, “Yeah, but aren’t you leaving on the weekend for BC? Then you will be distracted and forget. Why don’t you just read it tomorrow morning?” He chuckled and had no answer for why not but didn’t want to commit. I thought for a moment and tried another way, “Jack, have you ever been in love?” He was surprised and said, “Lately?” I said, “No, like ever, in the past, whenever.” He smiled and I saw a pleasant memory in his eyes as he thought back to the past. “Yes, I have. It was a long time ago.” I continued, “I want you to think of that woman, how you felt about her, how she made you smile.” He was puzzled and said, “Okay . . . .” I continued, “What if that woman had said to you during that time, ‘Jack, I really love you and I just want to be with you. Would you meet me tomorrow morning when you wake up? I just want to hear your thoughts and I want to share my heart with you.’ Would you do it?” Jack got a big smile on his face, totally wrapped up in the story, and said eagerly, “I would be there!” I said, “What would stop you?” He said, “Nothing! I would move mountains to be there. I would not let anything get in the way!” I continued, “Would you ever say to her: I’m not sure; I’ll think about it; maybe next week?” He looked at me with a frown, “No way!” I smiled and looked him straight in the eye, “Jack, Jesus loves you deeper and more real than any romantic love. He got whipped, spit on, tortured and killed so that He could have a relationship with you. He wrote you a book full of truths, a love letter, telling you who He is; His heart for you. You can meet with Him tomorrow, read His letter to you, talk to Him, have Him hear your thoughts and heart, but you don't know if you really want to because you can't decide if you want to commit to fifteen to twenty minutes? Are you all in or are you not?" Jack looked down and with a gentle smile said, "I promise. I will read the Bible tomorrow." I immediately said, "Oh, don't be promising unless you're going to doit! I take promises very seriously!" He said, "So do I. I am promising you. I give you my word." I said, "Don't be doing this for me! You do it . . . ." He interrupted, "I'm doing this for myself, and for Him." and he pointed up. I crossed my arms and looked at him skeptically. He again said he would. After a moment we laughed and I asked him if I could pray for him. I did and when I opened my eyes, he was wiping away tears. I said goodbye, if he came back, he knew where he could find me.

This definitely was not a formula written in books about how to evangelize or explain the gospel. When we look at Jesus, He used real, everyday examples to explain spiritual truths so that people could understand. It's important to discern your audience and how to convey truths to them in a way they can relate and gain insight. This was not the end of the story though with my unformulated conversation with Jack . . .

Well, Jack came back and you guessed it. I asked him if he had read his Bible. He said he would be honest, he hadn't. I asked him why and he said he had just been busy. I said, "Wow, you get up at 7 am and you don't have fifteen minutes to read that Bible because you don't have enough time in the next fifteen hours to get everything done that you need to get done?! You must be super busy!" I smiled with my sarcasm and he did too. I took him over to the side of the motorhome where I had written on it during my teaching from last summer when I had street preached on lies and stronghold's to a crowd. I began to explain to Jack how something can happen in our life causing us to believe a lie, which leads to a foothold, stronghold and then to bondage. To get free there is a need to expose the lie and the root cause of where it came in. As I was explaining this to him, another gentleman came up and heard the last part. He said, "Hey, you're explaining it backwards. You're supposed to start over here." He pointed to a different part of the motorhome where I had the beginning of my teaching. I was surprised, "You're right! I did already explain it . . . but hey, you remember the teaching I did on this?" He nodded, "I sure do!" and then he commented on how it flowed. I thought it was awesome that nine months ago I had taught on it and he still remembered and could explain it back to me. We fist bumped and he left. Jack told me he understood what I was saying but it didn't apply to him because every day he prayed to God, had let go of all his hurts, forgave people and was at peace. This sounded great and yet I knew the fruit in his life and the words he spoke about the Christian life did not align with scriptures. I tried a few more times and then I said, "Okay, okay, I know how to show you what I'm getting at. Let's start backwards. You have told me that you have not made a decision to be all in for God, right!? There's just something holding you back and you don't know why or what is holding you back. You just can't commit. It's a mystery. It's like you're stuck. Is that correct?" Jack nodded. I continued, "That's a stronghold. There is something between you and a full-on relationship with God. The words you keep saying to me are, 'I don't have time to read the Bible.' That's a lie you are believing. You do have time. What you are actually saying is, 'I'm good. I don't need to read the Bible, nor do I need to do the things that God has told me to do in the Bible in order to have a relationship with Him. I'm a good person and I'll approach God on my terms.' My question is: what is this?" I pointed to the diagram that listed causes/roots. "What is the cause for this lie and thinking? Because until you figure that out, you won't want to read the Bible, nor decide to go all in for Jesus. Remember what I said to you a few weeks ago? The Bible says: If you are not hot, only lukewarm, the Lord will spit you out of his mouth, you are not in a right relationship with Him. Stop saying you pray and love the Lord if you're not going to do what He says." As I spoke, Jack's face changed to understanding how I was applying the words on the motorhome to him and he said, "Ohhhh, I get it, I see now. Hmmm, I'm going to have to think about that. . . . I have a question for you first though. There's a man behind you and I think he's waiting for you to talk to him. How about I go over and get some food while you talk to him." I turned and saw indeed there was someone waiting. I sighed as I had just made a big point to Jack and he avoided responding to what I had just said. I prayed that night that the Holy Spirit would wrestle with him all week about the conversation and the truths that were spoken would bother him.

Every individual is different and truths need to be explained in ways they can relate. Otherwise there is no understanding, nor a change of mind or heart. Jack's story is not over. I am looking forward to what happens when he dives all into his relationship with God.

Jesus spoke in parables. He used everyday examples of the culture and the circumstances of the people so that they would understand the truths. When revelation came, it brought a crossroad of decisions to either walk away or to act upon what was revealed by applying it to their lives. Some followed Jesus, some walked away. We should not think it will be any different for us when we present truths.

I guarantee that if you have been depending on a formula to bring people to Jesus, where if you say a+b should equal c, you will be disappointed again and again and carry a heavy burden of trying to fit people's responses into your formula.

I approached two men who were sitting on some grass eating lunch near a local festival. I asked them how they were enjoying the day and if they had gone to the festival yet. After some friendly conversation, I told them I was out praying for people and wondered if I could pray for them. They said yes and so I asked them if there was anything specific. They said they would like me to pray for world peace. It wasn't exactly a request with too much depth. I closed my eyes and wondered how to make my prayer mean something without just offering a shallow prayer. As I began, I can truly say the Holy Spirit took over my words. "Lord Jesus, I thank you for these men who care about the people you've made and the world you've created. I thank you that they desire peace and see how the world desperately needs this. But Lord, You said there will never be peacefully on this earth until You return and set up your Kingdom. You said You will bring justice to the nations and judgement to all who do evil. Lord, I can't wait until that day. I pray that these two men will be in that train of Your followers, knowing the truth and declaring you as Lord and Saviour. In Jesus' Name, Amen." The men were staring at me when I opened my eyes. I smiled and wished them a good night.

As I was out with my mother in law, I saw a woman sitting on the bus bench so we started walking towards her. I went to sit beside her but the bench was wet so she actually gave up her seat for us. I gave my mother in law the seat and thanked the lady. I asked her where she worked as she was wearing a uniform. She said she drove the bus for the city and was waiting to start her shift when the bus arrived. I made all sorts of small talk about her job and then I asked her where she was from. She told me from Punjab but she had been in Canada for thirty two years. I asked, "It is my understanding that in India most people are either of the Hindu or Sikh religion. Are you from either of those belief systems?" She said she was raised Sikh so we started the whole conversation about their temple in our city and that I had visited it once. I told her I really respected their moral standards. She surprised me by saying she went to all kinds of churches because she believed they were all the same and believed the same things. When I asked a few more questions I still wasn't clear if she had ever been in a Christian church. I told her we loved Jesus and asked her what she knew about Him. She said her husband, like her, drove the bus for the city and one time a man had given him a very nice Bible. They had it at home and she wanted to read it but hadn't had the time yet. I briefly explained how the Bible was set up with the Old and New Testament. We chatted a bit more and I was aware that her bus was coming soon for her to start her shift. I asked if I could pray for her. She was surprised and said yes. I asked her if there was anything specific. She stumbled around with her answer, not knowing what to say and finally said "health and family". I began to pray. As I was praying, I felt the faintest breath of the Spirit showing me her heart was beautiful and that God was delighted with her desire to serve Him. It was one of those feelings/thoughts where I could have dismissed it or acted upon it. I chose to speak it and as I did the tears began to run down her face as the Holy Spirit ministered to her spirit. I love that. When I was done, she couldn't stop crying. She assured us they were happy tears. We gave her hugs. She told us nobody had ever prayed for her before. I told her God knew her and wanted a relationship with her through Jesus. She needed to go and as she was walking away, wiping tears, she stopped and said, "I will never forget you two as long as I live. I will always remember you and this conversation. I'm going to read that Bible we have." Wow, that was pretty amazing . . . amazing that in thirty two years of living in Canada no Christian had ever prayed for her . . . amazing to watch the Holy Spirit touch her so powerfully.

CHAPTER 30

LAYING IT DOWN

"Some knowledge is too heavy...you cannot bear it...your Father will carry it until you are able. If you look at the world, you'll be distressed. If you look within, you'll be depressed. But if you look at Christ, you'll be at rest."
-Corrie Ten Boom

Journal Entry:

"Sometimes after evangelizing, people's faces and eyes are burned into my mind and my heart aches over them. This was one of those times. For the last few days I keep seeing the older gentleman's pain filled eyes, the cashier's look on his face when I had gone back, the woman's lost and blind eyes, and Tony's brokenness all over his face, heavy eyes, heaviness covering his shoulders . . . what a blessing to take them before the throne and feel the Father's heart for them."

When ministering to people, it's important to know how to lay it down. Many people leave ministry because it throws their hearts and minds into chaos. It is easy to take the heaviness of someone's life and carry it on your heart. I have done this many times. At the very beginning of my evangelism journey, I would come home on a spiritual high from all the amazing spiritual conversations and couldn't sleep all night. Then I would be consumed with turmoil and grief over the conditions of each life I had come in contact with for days, if not weeks. I would suffer a lot from all that I had heard, sensed spiritually or taken spiritual authority over. I learned that I could not continue doing this. Unfortunately, many Christians decide to back off and stop because of these ramifications. I told the Lord, "Lord, if you told me to obey You by loving people the way You love them and engaging the way You engaged, I need You to lift these burdens from me. I need You to protect me - teach me how." I began taking each person and all the "stuff" I had heard, seen and spiritually sensed before the Lord. I would picture laying them down at His feet, pouring out my heart in prayer for them, telling Him all I desired for them. Then I would imagine standing up, acknowledging that He loved them more than me and I would walk away, leaving them in His care. I rebuke any spiritual attack or demonic harassment. I declare who I am as a Child of God and go to sleep peacefully. Oh, now don't get me wrong, there are times I forget or wrestle through it. Here are a few of my journal entries from the past and present.

"I didn't sleep well at night, tossing and turning. I prayed through the night as I felt so restless and awake from the time of ministry. Not sure why. Was my soul just still reeling from being poured out deeply for these people, or was it some sort of spiritual ramification from taking authority? I will have to be more vigilant in praying after ministering."

"As I drove home, my heart was grieving over the people I talked with. I went to bed and tossed and turned all night. I wrestled in prayer, I interceded, and prayed off the enemy. Others came to my mind as I ached for their salvation or healing from wounds. I could not get the turmoil to lift off my heart and I groaned in my spirit for God to intervene. I haven't had that for a long time. It used to happen all the time for the first two years I began the street ministry and then moments of burden-bearing sprinkled throughout the years but I have learned how to lay people before the Lord, unload the burdens and move on peacefully. I don't know why this night was different. I think I fell asleep around 4:30am."

"I did not think the people I had talked to affected me much and it didn't at all phase me as they told me their stories. I hear a lot and nothing surprises me. However, the next day, my mind wandered

to processing the conversations. My whole body jolted as I was suddenly envisioning what had happened to the people who had described their disturbing pasts to me. I startled myself and then wondered why I just did that. Images of their descriptive accounts of trauma in their life had flashed in my mind. I realized the details of their stories had affected me at some level. A couple hours later I was driving in my car and again my mind wandered to them. Suddenly my eyes filled with tears and I sobbed. I grieved their stories and the evil of this world. My heart went out for them, when they were just young children that satan traumatized. I guess my mind had been able to listen and deal with it the night before but now my heart had to catch up. I hate the evil that is done to people. I want Jesus to return soon to end all this . . . but then all these broken people would not have a chance to turn to God and be saved from an eternity of hell. I think the Lord tarries out of mercy so that not as many will perish."

It's very, very important to take each person who you have been ministering to straight to Jesus. We are not made to carry the crisis and trauma of another. Jesus is the One who takes on people's burdens and offers freedom and healing. There are many ways to process these things; and to guard your heart and mind in Jesus. Here are a few I have found effective.

- Have a few people who you can trust to tell and process with.

- Have others praying for you. I know this sounds straightforward but it's actually difficult to find people who will consistently pray for you on a continuous basis, warring on your behalf. It's more precious than gold.

- Journal. Personally, I keep a prayer journal where I can pour out my heart to the Lord and "vomit" on the page if need be.

- Recognize the source of the evil and acknowledge the truth of Who God is. For example, the horrendous act of rape over a person occurs from the devil wanting to destroy the person. God is the God Who Restores, He alone Redeems, He heals. He desires each person's wholeness and hates injustice.

- Take the time to pray over the person in depth. Place them at Jesus' feet and then leave them there for Jesus to take over the care of.

- Command any ungodly spirits who are involved in that person's life to be cut off from any access or ties that would try to attach to you.

- Worship. Throw the spirit of heaviness off.

If you can apply this wisdom, it will affect your longevity and ability to persevere. Our souls were not meant to carry the heaviness of sin in this world. We were meant to carry the burdens of others straight to Jesus.

CHAPTER 31

I WANT TO SEE THE FRUIT OR I GIVE UP

"It is clear you don't like my way of doing evangelism. You raise some good points. Frankly, I sometimes do not like my way of doing evangelism. But I like my way of doing it better than your way of not doing it." - Dwight L. Moody

His name was Ken. He was a teacher but did not currently have a job. He came down from another city three months ago to look for work. His mom had been diagnosed with a lung issue and was dying so he was going to get a bus ticket back. Through our conversation out on the street, I found out he was raised a Seventh Day Adventist. His dad had been a pastor. Ken had been struggling with his faith for a while now. He didn't believe God existed but prayed to Him every day in case He did. I asked him if he struggled with negative thoughts and voices. He said he did, really badly. It had caused depression and anxiety. He tried medication and it didn't work. He was not on drugs nor was he drinking. I asked him if he knew the spiritual principles for silencing the voices. He said no but wanted to find out. So I carefully explained the possible roots of the thoughts/voices. I went through the roots of unconfessed sin with him, unforgiveness, unhealed trauma or wounds, and generational bondages passed down. As I explained each of these he revealed that depression was huge in his family. He also shared he used to be into pornography very badly and it had really destroyed his life. He was able to get free from it by sheer willpower and out of the hatred of what it had done to him but he had never actually asked God for forgiveness from it, nor renounced it, nor dealt with the ramifications that it had left in his life.

He said he had turned to smoking and that he now found smoking gave him temporary relief from his anxiety. Through our conversation he had the revelation that pornography and smoking were ways he was "medicating" himself I suggested there was a root cause that made him seek relief in these two things and he agreed. I understood that Jesus was not Lord of his life. I addressed his need for that to be decided before he could deal with the root and get freedom from the voices. He told me he was highly educated and that basically disabled him from fully embracing Christianity. I told him education did not impress me nor God. Truth did however, and that there are many highly educated people who followed God and the Bible. I ended up giving him Lee Strobel's book, The Case for Faith. He eventually wanted to get going and I could tell he was getting uncomfortable with the subjects of having to deal with his sin, unforgiveness, and addictions. I asked him if I could pray for him and he accepted. I must have gone a little long as he interrupted me and said he needed to go . . . but he didn't really. I knew that the way I was praying and what I was praying for over him was making him uncomfortable and uneasy. I suppose when I said, "Lord, breakoff this addiction to smoking and may Ken puke every time he goes to smoke . . .." was perhaps a bit more of a bolder prayer than he was ready for. He left abruptly and I saw no fruit from our conversation. Did I just waste my breath and all that time? Only God knows.

Don't we all act like children sometimes? I mean, none of us wants to be known as immature. Especially as Christians, we don't want to be known as one still consuming spiritual "milk". (1 Corinthians 3:2) However, sometimes we act like two year olds when it comes to evangelism. We demand results within five minutes and if *we* don't see any fruit then we rationalize, justify and play the blame game. We chalk it up to error on the evangelist's part: "I'm just no good at this evangelizing thing." or "If the person was truly operating in the Spirit, the person would have gotten saved." Another common perspective is that perhaps an error on the lack of structure or program a church has is the problem: "If there was proper discipleship, then there would be more fruit"; "If there were better written tracts, people would turn to God"; "If we had better resources . . ."; "If the church had better teaching . . . ." We also turn to finding error in the person being evangelized to: "If he would have had more faith, he would have received revelation"; "If she would just say the prayer (see chapter 7), then her eyes would be opened". Although all of these problems could truly be a hindrance to one's salvation, to be blunt, we are acting like spiritual infants if we think we get to choose the measuring stick of how effective we are in a spiritual conversation and use it as a deciding factor weather we should continue evangelizing. We must stop basing our evangelism obedience and validity on the immediate results that we get to see.

I have hundreds of stories where I never know the results, and certainly not the end of the story. I can't wait until heaven for many reasons, but one is to be able to talk to all the people who I've spoken with in this life who will say something like, "Hey, remember me!? I was the one who got really mad at you and walked away, but the words you spoke kept coming back to me over and over and five years later I gave my life to Christ." or "Hey, it's me, the one who you felt like you never got anywhere with spiritually. I never told you, but I wrestled with our conversations and fifteen years later through many more links in the chain that God orchestrated, I repented and realized my need for Jesus. Thank you for not giving up even when I was rude and uninterested." This all comes down to the question: Do we feel like we need to save the soul of a person or do we actually trust that the Holy Spirit will work, whenever and however He sees fit? I often pray, "Lord, don't let that person find peace in anything in this world because it will only be a counterfeit. Remind them at night in the silence of any words that You spoke through me. May it resound over and over in their mind and heart. Wrestle with him/her and may their soul not be relieved of any turmoil until they turn to You for true peace and life because I know that is the only way they will ever be free."

I would love for every person to get saved, healed and delivered after talking to me. There's so many reasons that would not be good, ha ha. Pride would creep in and I may start depending on myself. Perhaps people would turn to me instead of God. I have had to learn to let go of each person, lay them at Jesus' feet and trust He loves them more. He will carry on the work He began.

There was a man who caught my eye in a crowd during a time when we were handing out food and I started talking to him. His name was Chris. I found out he went to church until the age of twelve and then his parents bought a farm and stopped going to church and focused on the farm work. Over the years he ended up becoming an alcoholic and drug addict. Eventually he overcame those vices only to become a gambling addict. Chris said he went to an AA meeting where a Catholic man "shoved his beliefs onto me" and from that point on he felt nothing of God, or for God. I asked him where he was now with his beliefs towards God. He thought carefully and said he was on the fence but he did not feel Him. I was trying to get a sense from the Holy Spirit of where to go in the conversation. We talked about the difference between other religions and Christianity. We talked about sin and relationship with God. I felt led to share with him that I haven't always felt God either. At times when I cried out to God, there was silence, and I did not feel Him. However, I knew there was a God, and no matter how difficult each situation was, I decided to follow the Truth. I realized life was not about having constant happiness but rather a decision whether to have a relationship with God or not. I have decided to have a relationship with Him. God has kept me from being destroyed through life's difficult situations. Sometimes I did feel God, but when I didn't, my belief was not going to be dependent on my feelings. I told him I wanted to live my life intentionally and since I knew there was a God, and I had a relationship with Him, no matter what happened, I would choose to follow Him and love Him, because He loved me. He asked me how I came to that place. I told him it was through a lot of research, through pursuing the true God, then making decisions which led to a deep relationship with God through Jesus, and I know that what He says is true. I once again shared that I wanted to live by a Truth that I would be willing to die for and if I am willing to die for it, it better be Truth. I no longer questioned the existence of God, nor if He was good, but instead I questioned my feelings and if they were true. I shared with him a verse from Isaiah 61 where it said that Jesus came to bind up the broken-hearted. Chris asked me what that meant. I told him the Hebrew word for "Bind" gave a picture of putting pressure on a wound to stop the bleeding. Jesus came to stop the bleeding which happened from painful wounds in our lives. The word "Bind'" also meant to govern and rule over. The words "broken-hearted" was the crushing, incredible destruction, breaking and tearing of the most inner part of a person. Jesus had come to stop the bleeding and to heal the wound deep down. No program, no method, no drug or no person can ever heal that. Time does not heal. "I've seen those in their eighties weep over unhealed pain in their childhood," I shared. Chris nodded and said he agreed, time did not get rid of pain. As I spoke, I could see in his eyes that he was really connecting to what I was saying. I sensed he had traumatic wounds in his life. I asked him what he thought about all this. He said, "I think you are very well researched in the Bible." Ha ha, so I asked the question a different way, "How does this verse about Jesus make you think about God? Does it make you want to know a God like that?" He answered, "Of course I do. Everyone does." I told him he could know Him and God made a way for that to happen. I shared with him about Jesus, what He did, and then the choice set before him. He took it all in. I asked him if he had wounds from the past. He stumbled a bit and said, "Yes, of course. Everyone does." I asked him if they were still pretty painful and he said yes. He didn't offer any other information and I sensed not to push. I asked him if he'd like to be free from gambling. He said he absolutely did. I asked him if I could pray for him and he said yes. As I prayed he stared at me and hung onto every word. I prayed into his wounds and over his addiction. When I was done he shook my hand and thanked me. Then a lady from our team, who had only been out once before, started talking to him. I found out later that she actually had seen and talked with him at length back a few months ago, the first and only time she had been out. Chris hadn't been out since and she had been praying for him that whole time. Tonight, right before she came, she prayed that she would see him again. He just "happened" to be there. She had spent time with him before I had. We gave him a gospel of John and he said he would read it for next week.

I saw an older man walking toward us on a sidewalk. I could immediately sense in the Spirit that he was burdened and weighed down; he had a spirit of heaviness on him. As he got closer, I joined him and walked with him as my team member trailed behind us. I said, "Hey, how are you tonight?" He was a bit surprised and he politely answered he wasn't having a great night so I told him I loved Jesus and asked if I could pray for him. He told me I could but not right then. I don't know why, but I said, "Well, you look like you could use a hug." He said, "No! I don't hug. I don't like to be touched." Again, I don't know why but I put my hand on his shoulder anyway as we walked and said, "Oh that is too bad. Hugs are amazing. How about you just shake my hand?" He stopped and stared at me. He slowly took my hand which was held out. I looked him in the eyes and said, "You are a man who once had compassion and kindness and cared very deeply." He looked right back at me and said, "You're right but people have taken that and stripped it from me." I said, "Then fight for it back! But you need Jesus to do that!" He started to walk away and said over his shoulder, "My fight is almost gone." He had gone too far into the crowd for me to shout anything else. Do I know the outcome or purpose of that conversation? Not at all, but do I need to?

I was at the mall and an elderly lady with half of her head shaved was standing at the door waiting. I approached her and said, "Hello, how are you? I love Jesus and I'm out here praying for people. I was wondering if I could pray for you for anything?" She said no, so I asked a different way, "Is there anything physical that you need healing for?" She answered there was nothing that she can't handle and so I said, "Do you have any spiritual beliefs?" She said, "I am not religious." I said, "No? Were you raised with any type of spiritual beliefs?" She said, "No, I was raised with ethics instead. I was raised with right and wrong but no religion. Ethics are the most important." I said, "That's really interesting. Where do you get the ethics from? How do you know what is right and wrong?" She told me ethics were the same in every culture and religion. I asked her if she believed there was a God at all and she said she didn't know but that there probably was. This surprised me. I asked, "Well, what do you think happens when you die?" She answered, "There is a heaven and a hell to go to." Shocked, I said, "That surprises me that you would say that. Where do you think you would go?" She answered, "Heaven, I hope." I asked, "Well, why would you get to?" She said she was a good person. I asked, "Who decides you're a good person?" She shrugged, smiled and said, "Maybe God? I don't know, but I have to go soon when my ride comes." I respectfully said, "Okay, no problem. Let me quickly explain to you what the God of the Bible says. He says that every person will die. At that time each person will stand before Him. . . ." I quickly explained heaven and hell, the Ten Commandments, what Christ did to enable us to have a relationship with God and why our good deeds don't earn us a way to heaven. I smiled and asked her what she thought. She smiled and said, "I still believe it's all about ethics." Then she said she had to go and went out to the train station. I stood there baffled at her answers. I prayed for her silently and turned to find the next person the Lord would have me speak to.

One night while driving home I got to thinking, "Man, I don't feel like I evangelized or did anything meaningful." I actually thought I wouldn't write on this night, but when I sat down to write this, I realized the false condemnation. I had mentored one-on-one at 4:30pm, I taught at 6:30pm, I preached at 8:00pm and then had three conversations during the evening spurring on and encouraging three street believers who don't have great support or community. Then once back at the church I spoke separately with two team members who needed advice and encouragement and then I spoke with one other leader to discuss the Monday Night Evangelism ministry and got home at 12:20am. So why in the world would I feel like it was an unproductive evangelistic night? Because the enemy loves to attack our minds, our feelings and identity. I remember a few years ago having someone pray over me before I went to preach. He prayed, "Lord, protect Val tonight and *when* the spirit of discouragement and condemnation comes this week, and we know it will come, make Val aware of it and speak Your truth to her." This was a very wise prayer I have come to appreciate and pray it over others.

Discouragement is a very effective way to make a Christian ineffective. We must throw it off by means of the truth, we must throw it off by spending time in the secret place of the presence of God so that we can listen to what His perspectives are and align ourselves with His. We can keep on keeping on with passion and love for the Father because we know it is not about us, nor our feelings, nor what is seen in the natural realm. We love God by obeying what Jesus told us to do and leave the results and measurement of "success" to Jesus.

He introduced himself as Donald and as a believer in Christ. He was staying at a nearby homeless shelter and told me he had been coming out to our gathering for a while now. He had watched myself and the team minister to others. He wanted to encourage us by saying that our team had a huge impact on the guys at the homeless shelter. He got to hear all the conversation and comments among them after we packed up and left. He then told me he had listened to me preach many times and wanted to especially tell me what had happened last week when I preached on suicide. When the guys all returned to the homeless shelter at the end of the night, the conversations went wild. It stirred up the men. Many had opinions and many were touched in deep places. There was a huge discussion of the things I had talked about and it had incredible impact. He told me I was known by everyone as a “fireball”, ha ha. He shared that for months he had been watching me in conversations, interceding in prayer during them, sometimes overhearing, and appreciating how I engaged. He prayed for us while we preached. I told him how thankful I was for his prayers and the encouragement. He knew we didn't often see or hear the results of our being there, and he just had to come and share with me how hugely it stirred up the people that came out.

How incredible that God would set up a prayer warrior from the streets to cover me when I didn’t even know it! How amazing heaven will be when we get to hear all that happened as a result of our obedience to Christ.

CHAPTER 32

RELATIONAL EVANGELISM

"So relational evangelism? Go for it, as long as it turns into real evangelism. You hanging out having a beer with your buddy so he can see that Christians are cool is not what we're called to do. You're eventually going to have to open up your mouth and share the gospel. When the pure gospel is shared, people respond." -Matt Chandler

Okay, I know that most stories in this book have focused on evangelism to strangers. I do understand that there is a desperate need to share the gospel with people within our influence, community and everyday interactions whether it is neighbours, co-workers, the hairdresser you've had for ten years and the hardest of all . . . family members. I guess I have a bit of a pet peeve when evangelism teaching focuses only on this demographic of people in our lives and we dismiss the spontaneous opportunities around us. I also would like to make a case that one can share the gospel with someone who we do not have a relationship with and be very effective. However, because I know that evangelism to people who we are in relationship with is vitally important, I will dedicate one chapter completely to relationship evangelism.

We need to be incredibly more equipped in this area. Let me explain what I mean in using the term "relationship evangelism". There are people in our lives who we have relationships with due to our blood lines (family), our jobs, our residence, our hobbies, etc. I want to ask you to think of these relationships in your life right now. When was the last time you've had a spiritual conversation with them? No, I don't mean the pushy, awkward, condemning, "you're a pagan and going to hell" conversation. I don't mean giving them disapproving looks every time they do something worldly or speak inappropriately, hoping they will feel ashamed. Nor do I mean the, "Well, I hope they know I'm a Christian by my lifestyle", approach. Now, don't get upset. I'm not saying there is never a place for those styles and I know God can use anything. I'm asking: when have you intentionally revealed Jesus to someone you know and are going to see again and again in your life?

It's hard, isn't it!? People can get very emotional or take offense very easily nowadays. When it comes to family, did Jesus ever nail it when He said, *"Only in his home town and in his own house is a prophet without honour."* (Matthew 13:54-57). It takes on a whole new meaning of fear of rejection. You may have many or all members of the family who do not follow Jesus and are even hostile towards you because of your faith. I know people personally who have been disowned by their families because of their decision to follow Jesus.

I like to practically equip, so here's some tips for relational evangelism.

1. Be humble, be humble, be humble. Clothe yourself with humility and honor others above yourself. (Philippians 2:3, Romans 12:10) This doesn't mean to shrink back or be timid. It means to position your heart to have no judgemental, arrogant or prideful attitude. If you do, keep your mouth closed until you go to Jesus and get free from it.

I am fully aware I am not giving these in a fluffy, gentle way. That's because there's an urgency here to rise up because our people, your people, are desperately needing Jesus. Okay, let's keep going.

2. Pray, pray, pray. If you haven't prayed for them and asked the Lord how He wants you to reveal His truths, then again, it's probably good to just keep your mouth shut until you

have. It's just not worth doing in the flesh . . . you know what I mean.

Furthermore, when we go to the Lord in prayer for them, let's be intentional and on target with our prayers, remembering what scripture tells us:

- They are blind. (2 Corinthians 4:4)
- They have strongholds. (2 Corinthians 10:4-5)
- They need to be dragged, by the Lord, but not by us. (In John 6:44 the Greek word translated "draw" is *helkuo*, which means "to drag" -literally or figuratively.)
- They are captives. (Isaiah 61:1)
- They are precious to the Lord. (Luke 15:1-7)

3. Testimony. This is very powerful! Revelation 12:11 says " And they overcame him because of the blood of the Lamb and because of the word of their testimony, and they did not love their life even when faced with death."

   Don't tell people how to live if you're not applying it yourself. Your testimony is not valid when you live like this. There's the old saying, "Do what I say and not what I do." If you haven't found freedom from the things you are urging others to do or not to do then be careful. Get counsel, healing, and freedom. It would be wiser to wait for the struggle to actually become a testimony to the power and work of God.

4. Pray with them. Actually pray with them in person. As I mentioned in earlier chapters this is incredibly important. It models to them what relationship with the Father looks like, it enables you to pour out your heart to the Lord for

them as they watch, and they experience the presence of the Holy Spirit.

5. Be wisely vulnerable. Appropriately share your struggles, your hurts, your questions. Then share the way you are dealing with them. People can't relate to someone who has it all together, never struggles and whose life is perfect. Besides, that's not the truth about anyone's life. It's important to be real. This gives permission for others to be real with you. The more guarded and polished you are, the less people will open up to you.

   In saying this, I will give an important caution: Don't be vulnerable to the point that you regret sharing personal things that could be very uncomfortable for you or others involved. For example, if your mom is alive and you share to your family friend that your mother was verbally abusive and drank when you were a child. This could slander and shame your mom. Instead of your intention to be vulnerable, it could provide gossip for the person listening and be very hurtful to your mom. A wiser way to share openly may be in conveying that there were difficult things that you experienced as a child which you needed healing from when you got older. Then talk about how Jesus healed you.

   Of course, there are times to provide full disclosure of events which took place in your life. Be wise about who you are trusting and why you are sharing it: out of bitterness or out of a place of healing? Out of a desire to encourage the listener or to receive sympathy? Know why you are giving the information you choose and what details are necessary.

The Lord created us for relationship. Relationships form a level of trust and affinity. We also have relationships that we don't necessarily control. There are just people in your life, good or bad, and they are not going away. Your kindness and life communicate much. If you truly love God then allow the Holy Spirit in you to bring people in your life an encounter with Jesus. Honor and love them as you love yourself.

CHAPTER 33

I DON'T KNOW HOW TO START

"Sharing the Gospel message should be a conversation, not a presentation." - Mark Cahill

There are so many ways to start a conversation. What's important is to lean on the Holy Spirit and let Him lead. At this point, you have realized that I do not like formulas or making people projects. How do we chase a conversation to the cross and open it up to get into spiritual conversations? Once you have asked Jesus who to talk to, whether that be a stranger, your neighbour, your co-worker or family member, here are <u>some</u> questions and ways that can lead into a spiritual conversation:

- What do you treasure? (Then tell what you treasure)
- What are you passionate about? (Tell them what you are passionate about.)
- Have you ever had any spiritual experiences? Tell me about them. (Tell them yours.)
- Were you raised with a certain spiritual belief? Where are you now with that belief? Why?
- Tell me what your tattoos mean.
- Do you mind me asking how you were injured?
- If you could ask God anything, what would you ask Him?
- I see you're wearing a cross. Why do you wear it?
- I want to pray for you with that situation you're facing. (And then do it, right then.)

- Tell your testimony.
- If you had a week to live, what would you do?
- How do you deal with hurt and disappointment?
- Where, would you say, you get your identity from? How would you define your identity?
- What would you say is the meaning to life?
- Text them after praying for them. Let them know that you prayed for them today and ask how they are doing.

I had given my twelve year old son and niece $20. I told them to pray and ask the Lord who to give it to and some instruction on how. The night before, my niece had had a dream that a woman walked up to her and that my niece was supposed to tell her about Jesus. They went on their way. I was thrilled to later hear how my son prayed as they walked and as they were walking one way, he felt they should turn and go the other way. When they did, a woman came walking straight toward them. My son approached her and said, "Hi. We love Jesus and while we were walking by you, God highlighted you to us (I loved the language he used as I realized he'd been listening to my stories, ha.) and we feel He wants you to have this $20." The woman looked at them and said, "Don't give it to me, what would I use it for?" He said, "Whatever God wants you to use it for." She said, "Well, why don't you keep it and add it to your collection." My son persisted, "No, really think you need to take this $20." She finally said okay and when she went to walk away, there were tears in her eyes. The kids noticed she had a hospital tag around her neck and it looked to them like she was a patient going on a walk, not a worker. I was so proud of them. Later my niece remembered her dream and we processed that.

If only all believers would take the risk and do what Jesus commands us to do, but sadly, so many have not been equipped.

Take any conversation and drive it to the cross. Of course, ask the Holy Spirit to lead. Don't get caught up in superficial things when you know the Lord is nudging you to speak about Him.

One man, Steve, wanted to chat about his life. He lived in housing nearby and was on his bike. He shared with me how his parents divorced because his mom drank and his dad was an alcoholic and started beating his mom. He said he loved his dad but really hated it when he did that. He could've gone on forever telling me details about his life. I was interested but knew this might be the only time I saw him as it was a random conversation on the street. I asked him what his spiritual beliefs were. He told me he was Irish and Scottish. He chuckled that he was doomed because of it. He began to tell me all about the differences between the Irish and the Scottish. I waited for a pause and said, "So, that is your heritage but that does not tell me your spiritual beliefs." He told me he went to church as a kid, went to mass and expanded on details that were irrelevant to the question. Again, I turned the conversation back, "So you were raised Catholic?" He said yes and went on about other things. When there was another pause I asked him if he had ever read the Bible. He said he had read it through once a long time ago. I asked him if he remembered much from it. He didn't really. I told him he could never stop learning from the Bible and that he should study it more in depth. I quickly shared my experience from reading the Bible. I asked him if he had one and he did. I told him to read the book of John. He looked at me surprised, "Right now?!" I laughed and told him no, to read it over the week and come back to discuss it with me. He said he would and we finished the conversation in a friendly manner.

I haven't always known how to start a spiritual conversation. I had to start somewhere. Here is yet another raw and real prayer journal entry I made near the beginning of my journey in evangelism:

"Oh Lord, I fail and make so many mistakes, forgive me. How I want to be on fire for You and walk in Your Spirit. Lord, I hear and see the boldness of others who pray for healing. Have You given me this gift? Should I pray for people in this way? If so, Lord, then You have to show up. Lord, I hear how people share about You and explain Your truths. I really want to do that better. I know I am slow and have fear. Drive out my fear and do not give up teaching me. My heart's desire is to do Your will. Lord, I surrender to You today."

Ha ha, I know, far from a perfect prayer but you can see where I began.

Here are some evangelism tips.

1. Ask questions. A wise man once said to me, "Don't put into someone's ear what you can pull out of their mouth." I don't want to tell people everything and have them feel like they are being lectured. I want to hear their heart, their thoughts and ask questions that will lead them to truths that they discover as they process and answer. Then they'll own it.

2. When asking a question it's wise to not respond to their answers with, "You should . . . ." or "I would do this . . . ." Remember you are not having a counselling session, you are pointing them to the Counsellor. Instead, brainstorm with them, offer spiritual truths and ask more questions to draw out spiritual truths.

3. Don't make people your "righteous projects". Truly love them. I always think: how would I want to be approached? Am I acting like a salesperson? I do not want to be approached by salespeople; I always feel like they want my money or want me to join something for their advantage and not mine. Let's not make a sales pitch for our own praise and pat on the back when it comes to the gospel. Ask yourself: are you trying to get them to come to your church or to Jesus?

4. Get rid of the churchy terminology that people don't understand. Older generations may have a framework for the terms but many others don't. Is it churchy or is it understandable for someone who has never heard it? Can you explain these terms and spiritual truths without any "christianese"?
    - Redemption
    - Sin
    - Sanctification
    - Justification
    - Born again

- Grace
- Prayer
- Saved
- and many more.

5. Prepare how to give an answer for the hope that lies within you. No one wants to listen to a long winded answer that goes around in circles but never comes to a point. In response to the following questions and statements, can you explain or respond well in one minute or less:

    - Why do bad things happen to good people?
    - Why does God send people to hell?
    - How can a good God allow evil in this world?
    - Can LGBTQ people go to heaven?
    - I'm a good person so I'm good. It'll all work out in the end.
    - I believe all religions are the same.
    - I believe in science and therefore do not believe in God.
    - I believe in Love but not organized religion.
    - I believe Jesus was a good man but not God.

6. Are you ready to share your testimony? Why do you believe in God? Why have you decided to follow Jesus and have a relationship with Him? How has your life been different now that you have Jesus? Testimony is powerful and no one can argue it with you. A word of caution, don't go on and on all about yourself. Testimony is different from a life story. Share parts, share what's relevant, testify . . . serve as a witness as to why Jesus is alive, true and the only way.

7. Don't pretend - people can sniff out the difference between authenticity and depicting a shiny cover-up. We all know people who portray that everything is good, everything is joyful, nothing is ever bad in their lives because they are Christians. They come across as "holier than thou" and really turn

people off. With discernment, be honest by simply saying you have struggles.

8. Memorize Scripture! Get equipped. Know the real thing from the fake. You will hear all sorts of scripture pulled out of context, given completely different meaning than intended, and phrases told to you, claiming them as scriptures though they aren't even in the Bible. For example, "God won't give you more than you can handle" or "God helps those who help themselves". The best way to recognize falsehood is to know the truth. When you deposit the Word of God into your mind and soul, no one can take it from you and it flows out in your conversations.

9. Love. Choose to love others. They will know we are Christians by our love (John 13:35). We can do amazing good things, say wonderful words and serve others but it is meaningless if we do not love with the agape love from God (1 Cor 13:3).

As you ponder these, remember, no formulas.

Look around you. There are opportunities every day, everywhere.

"Find someone that Jesus died for and start there." – Jay Cooling

CHAPTER 34

PANDEMICS, CRISES, RESTRICTIONS . . . PERSECUTION

"He said there were two kinds of Christians: those who sincerely believe in God and those who, just as sincerely, believe that they believe. You can tell them apart by their actions in decisive moments."
— Richard Wurmbrand, In God's Underground

When do we stop evangelizing? I think if we asked those who have gone before us they would tell us the answer is never.

If we are unable to give out food, if we cannot publicly preach, if we cannot distribute Christian literature, or if we can no longer gather as a group . . . we still tell others about Jesus. All we need is the ability to communicate. Whether that is through our mouths, social media, texting, writing, or whatever form, we continue to spread the gospel. We use our feet to walk near others, our hands to serve others and our mouths to speak to them about Jesus. During a pandemic, such as Covid-19, which affected much of 2020 and beyond, or any similar event causing crisis or restrictions, we must make choices of how best to communicate to others. The more challenging the times, the more important it is to communicate the reason for the hope that lies within us. (1 Peter 3:15)

There are many ways to continue to evangelize during scenarios of pandemics, crises, restrictions, and persecution. We have to problem solve and ask the Lord what to do. Remember that saying, "If there's a will, there's a way." The need for people to hear Who Jesus truly is and what He has done for them has never changed, nor will it ever, until He returns. Think outside of the box, rather than stopping evangelism because former methods no longer work in your circumstances. Ask the Holy Spirit to provide you with opportunity.

Ask the Lord who He wants you to pray for. Pray for them and then, if possible, send them a message telling them you have prayed for them. See where the response leads. It may lead to further conversation regarding Jesus or it may seem to go nowhere. If the latter seems true, don't fret, as you are stirring up a war in the spiritual realm over their soul.

Write a handwritten letter (remember what those are?) to a senior in isolation, to a persecuted believer in prison (look up Voice of the Martyrs Canada for names and addresses), to people in your life, past or present, who have really poured into you and impacted you in some way - thank them, then tell them how they impacted you and your spiritual journey. Why handwritten? It shows effort, it's intimate, and it's intentional. Email works great as well and is also a powerful tool.

Go for a walk and when you come upon people sitting, walking, or working, stop and ask how they are doing regarding a situation that they or this world is facing. Ask the Holy Spirit what He sees about them and tell them.

Look for where people are and join them, getting into conversation naturally and deliberately. I've noticed the unleash dog parks have an unintended community that gathers while their pets play. Other places include: outside activity courts (spaces from basketball to skateboarding to tennis), grocery stores, walking paths, parks, neighbourhoods, etc. I know that construction workers, custodians, road crews, farmers in tractors, painters, gardeners, etc. love it when you bring them a hot or cold drink, perhaps a homemade or purchased snack, just to bless them, no strings attached. This shows the fruits of the Spirit and perhaps opens up opportunities for conversation as the Spirit leads. Consecrate the gift to the Lord and pray over your interaction. Be filled with the Spirit. Ask questions. Have answers.

When you are at the store paying for your items, prepare while you are standing in line to quickly share with the cashier any Holy Spirit led things you notice about them. Ask them how you can pray for them.

Speak life. Let the rivers of living water flow from your belly. (John 7:38 KJV) Some translations use the word "heart", or "inmost being". It is the Greek word *"koilia"* - the innermost part of a man, the soul, heart as the seat of thought, feeling, choice. This verse indicates that we are to be carriers of the Source of life. Let's carry the Source of life to every person, every situation, every circumstance.

I have mentioned this verse a couple times but absolutely love it. Revelation 12:11: *"They triumphed over him (the devil) by the blood of the Lamb and by the word of their testimony; they did not love their lives so much as to shrink from death"* Seriously, could you say that? Could you live that last part out?

There is another quote that has stuck in my head for years:

"A number of us decided to pay the price for the privilege of preaching, so we accepted their [the communists'] terms. It was a deal; we preached and they beat us. We were happy preaching. They were happy beating us, so everyone was happy." - Richard Wurmbrand, Tortured for Christ

It is imperative and vital to not let yourself be isolated from other believers, those who will encourage you, spur you on and brainstorm with you. Keep meeting together in whatever way that can happen. Remember, you can't give away what you do not have. If you are not free from fear, worry, anxiety or depression, anger, or whatever else, then you will not be able to show the way to freedom from those things to the world. Jesus paid a high price to enable you to be free from those things. Do whatever it takes to get free through Jesus. I did not say it was easy, and neither did Jesus.

Do not shrink back from touch. Touch is powerful. The research and science behind the importance of touch is incredible. It affects us as human beings emotionally, psychologically, physically, and spiritually. Our culture is being robbed of healthy, appropriate touch. During the Covid crisis of 2020 and beyond, touch has been deemed as a way to transfer germs and has been discouraged. Use discernment, be respectful, and where appropriate, make the physical connection.

Dr. David Jeremiah pointed out, "The Gospels use the words 'hands', 'fingers', and 'touch' nearly two hundred times, and the words often refer to Jesus: *Jesus put out His hand and touched him . . . So He touched her hand . . . He went in and took her by the hand . . . Then He touched their eyes . . . Immediately Jesus stretched out His hand . . . Jesus came and touched them . . . Then little children were brought to Him that He might put His hands on them and pray . . .*"

You may say, "I'm not a touchy person." I'd encourage you to ask Jesus why. Discover the root and get free from it. I have heard that human beings thrive when touched healthily eight to ten times a day. The world aches for appropriate, godly touch. Let's not drive them to ungodly resources.

I am, of course, not advocating for unhealthy touch or sexual touch! Be wise in how, around who and when! What I am saying is that we are losing the ability to appropriately and powerfully put our hand on a shoulder, hold someone's hand in prayer, give a good ole meaningful hug, conveying to one another, "I value you. You are my brother/sister in Christ and we are bonded by the Spirit. Or You are made in God's image. I agape you." Don't shrink back from this in the guise of morality, the fear of human criticism nor the risk of hugging a "pole" who doesn't hug back. You have no idea how I have seen over and over the importance of this. Dare I say, it's why the devil has tried to stop it, dirty it, and forbid it throughout history.

Although much more could be said, in conclusion, here are my three points: raw and real.

1. Evangelism never stops.

2. Be creative, think outside the box. Be open to trying many ways of evangelizing depending on the circumstances. Be willing to be different.

3. Honor authorities and others as much as possible in accordance with scripture. Remember that God is our final authority and the One we must obey above all.(Acts 5:29)

CHAPTER 35

JUST FOR THE ONE . . . AND FOR THE ONE . . . AND FOR THE ONE

Years ago, my young four year old son and I were going to head out. I said to him in the entryway, "Put your boots on. I'll race you to go pick up your brothers." I put my shoes on, took the garbage to the road, arranged some things in the vehicle, got into the driver's seat, pulled the car out of the garage and waited for my four year old to come to the vehicle. He didn't come. I got out of my vehicle and went back into the house. He wasn't there. I called out and thought maybe he went to play. I looked through the house, the basement, the bedrooms. I went to the backyard and he wasn't there. I was very puzzled. I had just seen him. Did he go out to the vehicle while I didn't notice? I checked and he didn't. I began walking down the sidewalk in my neighbourhood. It was a beautiful day and the windows of the neighbours were open, a couple were even out in their yards. I calmly called my son's name and walked down the street. I didn't want to panic nor overreact for all to see. I knew he couldn't be far and I didn't want to be one of those crazy, protective moms. Time was ticking though and I wondered, could my son have possibly been grabbed by a passing car? Did a neighbour I didn't know well grab him and yank him into their house? How would I ever know? I went back to the house and rechecked every room. My emotions went from confusion, to frustration, to anger, to panic. I jumped in my car wondering if he had gone into the large park behind our house. There was a creek back there - what if he fell in? I could drive around it and see better in a vehicle. I drove around it and stopped to pick up my other sons who were at the far end of the park. We drove back to the house and my sons jumped on their bikes to go scour the park area. Fifteen minutes had passed and now thoughts of kidnapping, drowning and all sorts of other horrible things went through my mind. I began running up and down my neighbourhood streets yelling my son's name. I knew I looked like a crazy fool. I no longer cared what anyone thought. Finding my son was all that mattered to me. After twenty minutes I knew I needed to act, so for the first time ever I called 911. The operator answered and as I spoke the words, "I can't find my four year old son", my voice broke and I began to cry. At that very moment, my older son came around the corner with my four year old with him. I said into the phone, "We just found him!" and I ran towards him. For a split second, I was angry at why he had gone away from me and yet my love for him was so strong, relief flooded in as I grabbed him, cried and held him. We had walked to his brother's school many times and he thought I was going to race him on foot to the school, instead of to the vehicle. Praise God that when he got to the main street, he knew he wasn't allowed to cross the road by himself and turned back. I can't explain to you the raw, intense emotions I felt having my son safe in my arms. That night when everyone was in bed, I began to talk to the Lord. This night could have been so different if he had not been found. I would have been in utter torment and sickening grief, wondering what had happened to my son. The thought made me shudder. "God, what was that!? Why did all that have to even happen?" The Lord answered immediately and clearly, "That is just a sliver of what I feel when one of my children are lost." The words were jarring. I thought about all I felt and all that happened. I responded, "If that is just a sliver of what you feel, then I repent over every time I have been worried about what others think, and every time I have not taken seriously the opportunity to speak to someone about You. I will run, yell, beg and do whatever it takes. I will act like a fool if it means one of Your children is found."

I had a dream. I was tossing and turning over people. Some were broken and hurting, others full of shame. Some poor, some sick, people in bondage, deceived, arrogant, in despair, full of evil, some struggling, and countless others who were hopeless. There were just so many and I was overwhelmed. I couldn't get to them all. Then, still in my dream, my pastor, Pastor Henry, came before my face. I knew that he was representing spiritual authority and a message from the Lord. He looked me straight in the eye and he held up one finger. He said to me, "Just for the ONE Val . . . and for the one . . . and for the one . . . and for the one."

I awoke with a start, as the dream was so vivid and evoked strong emotion in me. I knew the meaning immediately. Just look at the one in front of you, and then the next one in front of you and the next one. It was an instruction and encouragement not to get overwhelmed by all the people who needed Jesus and help, but to focus on the one person the Lord puts in front of me at each specific moment. Then when moving on to the next one person, to leave the other at Jesus' feet.

This is how I want to live my life, revealing Jesus. I don't always do it. Sometimes I turn from the one in front of me. I busy myself or am not even aware that they are in front of me. The Lord is so gracious. He knows my every weakness. He also knows how to take this jar of clay and place His treasure inside of it, to make me into a warrior for His Kingdom. I say yes and let it be done.

What about you? If you have not surrendered fully to God, through Jesus Christ, do it now. Don't waste another second of your life. It's so simple. Choose this day whom you will serve. (Joshua 24:15) If it is to be the Almighty God, who you will face when this life is over, then serve with all your heart, soul, mind and strength. (Mark 12:30) Don't be half-hearted, shallow or a pew warmer.

Leave the 99 and go after **the one** who is lost.

Stir up, build up and encourage **the one** Bride; the Church, the Body.

Passionately abandon all else to delight, fiercely love, fully live and go on adventures with **the One** King, Jesus Christ, Creator of all things, the Lord God Almighty!

For the one, and the one, and the One

About The Author

Valerie Hopman has been involved in street evangelism since 2010. She oversees and engages in evangelizing, speaking, mentoring, discipling, teaching, modelling, equipping, street preaching, developing in-depth team fellowship, and prayer ministry.

Valerie's passion is Jesus, the Church, and the lost. In her relationship with Him she wants the "real thing" and to be all that God created her for.

Valerie enjoys being with her husband and four kids; 3 boys, a daughter and daughter in law. She has grown through each member's love and adventures in her life. Running, hiking, biking, motorbiking, horse riding, rollerblading, reading, playing games, hours alone with Jesus, and being out in the country are Val's favorite things to do when she is not spending one on one time with someone she loves.